SAINT
JOSEPH'S
COLLEGE
INDIANA

Involved For Life

Presented To The
Keith and Kate Robinson
Memorial Library
by
Fr. Jeff Kirch

BELEAGUERED RULERS

BELEAGUERED RULERS

The Public Obligation
of the Professional

WILLIAM F. MAY

Westminster John Knox Press
LOUISVILLE
LONDON · LEIDEN

© 2001 William F. May

Scripture quotations from the New Revised Standard Version of the Bible are copyright © 1989 by the Division of Christian Education of the National Council of the Churches of Christ in the U.S.A. and are used by permission.

Book design by Sharon Adams
Cover design by Lisa Buckley

First edition
Published by Westminster John Knox Press
Louisville, Kentucky

This book is printed on acid-free paper that meets the American National Standards Institute Z39.48 standard. ∞

PRINTED IN THE UNITED STATES OF AMERICA

01 02 03 04 05 06 07 08 09 10 — 10 9 8 7 6 5 4 3 2 1

Library of Congress Cataloging-in-Publication Data

May, William F.
    Beleaguered rulers : the public obligation of the professional /
    William F. May.—1st ed.
        p. cm.
    Includes bibliographical references and index.
    ISBN 0-664-22339-7 (alk. paper)
        1. Professional ethics. I. Title.

    BJ1725 .M39 2001
    174—dc21   2001025857

For Ted and David May

Contents

Preface

This book on professional ethics does not examine the rules of the road in a series of guilds, nor does it treat the professions as a caste detached from the society at large. Instead, it explores the varied links between the professions and civic responsibility in America. Their specialized training hardly removes professionals from the common culture that shapes all citizens. Long before arriving at the university, young professionals-to-be have eaten Wheaties for breakfast, committed to memory the ads on cereal boxes, played video games far into the night, caught snatches of the news on television, listened to their parents complain about the government, and daydreamed about their futures in the back rows of classrooms. If the mature professional has a somewhat undeveloped sense of public responsibility, that state of affairs may but reflect, repeat, and exacerbate an attenuated sense of responsibility in the society at large.

In order to let surface the specific interplay between a profession and the wider culture, I will treat each of the eight professions in a separate chapter. Each profession responds to something deep in the American spirit. Lawyers do not simply impose adversarialism on clients; their clients often come to the lawyer adversarially disposed. Engineers do not arm the society with unwanted technologies; their inventions respond to an aggressive attitude toward nature and a readiness to deploy technologies to which the society already subscribes. Each chapter thus explores a particular profession as a point of entry for interpreting American culture: how Americans come to grips with their world and how professionals figure in their coping.

At the same time, separate treatment does not mean wholly isolated treatment. Each chapter tends to single out a problem particularly arresting for that profession, but which reverberates in others. The chapter on "Money and the Professions: Medicine and the Law" deals with marketplace pressures that not only these two highly paid groups must face, but engineers, journalists, academics, politicians, and others as well. Similarly, adversarialism looms preeminently in the practice of law, but it also defines other professionals. Doctors battle against death, engineers seek to conquer nature, and corporate managers plot to route their competitors for "market share." Politicians today stand out as members of a particularly despised and scorned professional group; however, lay suspicion and resentment shadows them all. Finally, the last three groups of professionals covered in this book—ministers, teachers, and journalists (and other media leaders)—differ from other professionals in that they wield an immense teaching authority; they cultivate the ethos in the society at large. Yet, other professionals—doctors, lawyers, business and union leaders—must also teach if they would do their work well. The book thus devotes chapters to each of the eight professions in order to develop some interior "feel" for each, and yet explores each profession with a wide-angle lens that offers some insight into neighboring professions and into the wider society from which the professions spring—even as they would lead and tutor it.

The Beleaguered Rulers

The modern professional sits on a somewhat wobbly throne. On the one hand, professionals wield an enormous power. We might number them among the members of the ruling class. Traditional societies transmitted power largely through families; their rulers inherited their power. Today we transmit power chiefly on the basis of knowledge, a knowledge largely acquired at a university. That is why ambitious parents, whether rich or poor, successful or stalled in their careers, worry about their children getting the grades that will put them into the best colleges and universities. Through education, they hope, their children will ease into the slipstream of modern power.

And power it is. Whereas the ancient Greeks celebrated the human power *for* knowledge, since the seventeenth century we have celebrated the powers acquired *through* knowledge. The Greeks recognized that reason distinguishes humans from the beasts of the field. But reason also crashes against limits—the power of fate and death from without and flaws from within. Reason offers us, at best, wisdom in the midst of suffering, not relief from its toils.

Only with the rise of the modern university did we begin to celebrate the powers which knowledge itself would generate to alter human life for the good. That extraordinary claim and prospect unfolded in two stages: first, with the rise of modern science and technology from the seventeenth century and forward; and, second, with the flocking of the professions into the universities in the twentieth century. The herald of the modern age, Sir Francis Bacon, proclaimed that science and technology would yield a mastery of nature through which benefits would shower upon the whole of humankind. Knowledge yields power; and, in the larger scheme of things, power and mastery yield a veritable cargo load of benefits to humankind. Successive revolutions—the industrial, the agricultural,

1

the biological, and, most recently, the electronics revolutions—will succeed, as the cliché now puts it, in lifting all boats. We leave aside, at this point, the dark side of this enlargement of human power and the difficulties of imparting the benefits to all. Suffice it to say that Bacon and his successors prepared the way for valuing the university as the corridor to power.

The universities played a second great role in the enlargement of human powers at the beginning of the twentieth century as the professions flocked to their doors. Traditionally, the professions relied chiefly on the apprenticeship system to train and credential their members. Only a small minority of clergy, physicians, and lawyers had a university education. But, at length, the aspiring candidates for medicine, most notably, and candidates for all the other professions, eventually, had to look to the university to secure and expand the knowledge which generated the power they exerted.

Wielding this power, professionals today have left few things in our world untouched. Modern doctors, as distinct from their predecessors, can actually cure. Scientists and engineers, in the company of industrialists, have reshaped the earth to serve the most extravagant of human wants. Geneticists will soon be able to alter the fate of generations to come. Business leaders, whether wearing the blaze of the traditional professions or stamped with the MBA, rule large corporations and, in some cases, exert a power unmatched by all but a few heads of state. Lawyers have increasingly fulfilled de Tocqueville's nineteenth-century prophecy that they would eventually emerge as the aristocrats of the new world. (The French aristocrat shrewdly anticipated that a society which eliminated the traditional privileges of class in favor of a government based on "laws not men" would inevitably rely on a newly privileged class of experts whose special knowledge of the law would enable them to control the gates that lead to power.) More recently, media professionals in an electronic age have skewed the very terms of political discourse and, through advertising, give cues for wants and behavior. And academicians, while hardly among the most highly paid of professionals, bestow great power, inasmuch as they train, accredit, and ordain most other members of the ruling class.

Professionals, it must be conceded, operate with substantial institutional constraints upon their power. They do not exclusively rule. Governments tax them and, in part, regulate them and burden them. The degree to which the government limits professionals and their guilds differs from nation to nation.[1] In France, the central government exercises substantial power in shaping the professions of medicine, law, and engineering (on the grounds that the government and large corporations represent the general interest, whereas the guilds only special interests). In totalitarian Germany of the 1930s, doctors, academicians, and lawyers submitted variously to the state, while the clergy divided into a quiescent majority and a protesting minority called the *Bekennende Kirche* (the confessing church). However, after World War II in Germany, the old aristocratic guilds recovered considerable power in a regional, corporatist setting as the government decentralized, and regional states exercised more power than their counterparts in the United States. In Great Britain, the government, although centralized in London, exercises less power over the professions, the universities, or the marketplace than the central government in France. The professions in the United States, on which this book focuses, have faced relatively little direct limitation on their power from the government and much greater pressure from the marketplace, as professionals have largely found employment in the corporations.

The large-scale organizations for which professionals increasingly work in the United States—hospitals, universities, law firms, accounting firms, corporations, and conglomerates—substantially condition professional practice. Doctors no longer enjoy total control over medicine. The hospital no longer serves, as Paul Starr once called it (in *The Social Transformation of American Medicine*) the doctor's moneymaking workshop. Increasingly, doctors find themselves salaried employees or beholden to large, third-party payers and provider organizations. Other professionals, such as engineers, accountants, lawyers, and academicians, have long since submitted to some institutional control over their practices as they massively work for large organizations and professional firms. Further, changes in inheritance laws in the United States in the 1980s permit the transmission of great wealth from generation to generation for which family, not professional, identity provides the major qualification. Established families also enjoy special access by legacy to some prestigious universities in the country, thereby compounding for at least some of their children the power of money with the power of gilt-edged professional credentials.

While not absolute, professional power is nevertheless substantial. The government and large-scale organizations condition professional practice, but professionals usually rise to the top to run them.

Doctors may complain about the encroachment of various institutions upon their domain. But this complaint only reflects their discovery that still other professionals—lawyers, accountants, professional managers—often control the large institutions with which medical practitioners must now contend. Inheritance laws permit the transfer of great economic advantage and power from generation to generation, but by no means exclusively. The overclass constantly adds to its ranks those who have made their way into it through the doors of our leading colleges and universities.[2]

Yet, while professionals exercise great power and often enjoy the vast material privileges of a ruling class, they feel beleaguered. They do not see themselves as power-wielders. They feel marginal, insufficiently appreciated, suspect, harassed, often under siege. Patients, clients, and various publics respond to them ambivalently. Society grows restless with these knowledge-bearing rulers. Lay people contest professional authority. The doctor, from one day to the next, can plummet from hero to defendant in a malpractice suit. The lawyer's client does not know what to worry about the most, his opponent's case or his lawyer's fees. Scandals such as Watergate, Union Carbide, Exxon, or the NASA "O" rings, the Savings and Loan collapses, and the clever legal defenses of scoundrels, produce what William Lee Miller once called a moral heartburn in the nation. Professional services are not distributed widely enough to reach all those who need them. Professionals only reluctantly discipline their incompetent or unethical colleagues. Society often blames professionals for the defects of the huge institutions which they serve and often control. And even the successes of the professions, their very considerable successes (for example, medical technology), have generated moral quandaries which a purely technical education does not address.

Thus the visitor to various professional groups quickly senses the contrast between the public agendas of their meetings, which resound with the self-confident tone of leadership, and the private exchanges of professional friends who often lament their plight. Doctors complain of lawyers who harass them with malpractice suits and they buck against the burden of paperwork with which a third-party payment system saddles them, even though that system has handsomely compensated them for their professional services. Lawyers complain that the society lumps them with the criminals they defend, the creditors whose harsh letters they write, and the affronted clients whose cause they advance for a fee. Engineers have found it relatively easy to obtain first- and second-level jobs in an expanding economy but recognize that their careers speedily reach a glass ceiling beyond which the engineer only rarely rises. Business leaders can hardly claim they lack power, but they often define that power as wholly private and perceive themselves as unjustly beleaguered by the government and insufficiently appreciated by the media and society at large. Michael Novak, serving as a kind of troubadour for the business community, has played up to this sense of injury, complaining, "The chief executive officers of major corporations have as much claim to high talent as do the top five hundred intellectuals and professors, the top five hundred scientists, the top five hundred musicians, painters, and sculptors of the land. . . . Yet few minorities in the U.S. are as subject to ridicule and disparagement in the public media."[3]

Other professionals who more directly shape the ethos of the society—ministers, journalists, media experts, and teachers—also feel that their fellow citizens do not value them. Religious leaders, particularly those in the so-called mainline traditions, perceive themselves as marginal, especially when they compare their power with that of ecclesiastical leaders from the fourth to the twentieth centuries. Journalists and media commentators have enjoyed a temporarily enhanced esteem during the Vietnam war, the Watergate scandal, and other crises. But they have also generated chronic resentment for their intrusive and invasive ways, their vulgar lack of respect for private grief, and their tendency to produce tachycardia in the nation over crises that will "play," while neglecting other issues that matter.

Academic professionals, despite complaints from the counterculture to the contrary, do not perceive themselves as belonging to the establishment in this country. Academics feel that they must constantly sell the importance of education. Further, specialists in the several disciplines within the academy, each for their differing reasons, perceive themselves as insufficiently loved. Professors of religious studies cope with colleagues who would relegate religion to the superstitious past. Philosophers worry that the society cloisters them in an ivory tower. Sociologists sense that their colleagues dismiss them as a Johnny- and Jeanie-come-lately among the disciplines. Historians and English professors find their fields overcrowded and underfunded. Scientists, while enjoying for several decades a golden rain of federal research money, have seen it diminish. Thus professional academics, like their colleagues in other professions, view their status as precarious.

Since professionals perceive themselves as marginal and beleaguered, they tend to overlook their duties as public servants, duties
which the community traditionally deemed to be substantial. The
professions of law, military service, civil service, education, and ministry once played out their roles in the setting of great institutions
that largely justified themselves as serving some fundamental or high
good: lawyers, the good of justice; professional soldiers, the good of
national security; civil servants, the comprehensive good of governance; educators and ministers, the high goods of knowledge and
spiritual flourishing. Even the personally oriented helping professions—medicine, and the law and ministry (viewed not institution-
ally, but in their service to particular clients and parishioners) also
served the public good. In relieving private distress, members of the
helping professions did not simply serve the private happiness of
those who received help, they served the happiness and flourishing of
citizens in their common life. Societal convictions and expectations
partly justified the decisions of legislators and benefactors who
funded professional education.

However, as want-to-be professionals hustled their way through
universities and eventually struggled through the doors into the inner
sanctums of power, their obligations to the common good tended to
fade. Their public duties seemed remote, peripheral, and occasional,
compared with the task of résumé building and career advancement
upon which income and standing depend. Although their professional decisions greatly affected the patient's plight, the client's fate,
the student's future, the city's scape, the earth's sustainability, the
worker's fair treatment, and the durability of institutions great and
small, the exigencies of competition and self-advancement took over
and a commitment to the common weal weakened. The seat of power
professionals occupied became wobbly not simply because, even as
they wielded power, they felt harassed and underappreciated, but
because the seat itself was not steadied in the fundamentals of professional identity.

The professions face an identity crisis today, which conventional
quandary ethics does not address. Case-oriented quandary ethics, as
taught in professional schools, deals chiefly with discrete dilemmas:
Should I pull the plug or not? Should I withhold the truth or not?
Should I ratchet up discovery proceedings? What balance shall I
strike between product safety and cost? Should I promise confiden-

The Intellectual Mark. Professionals draw on a *complex* and *esoteric* ...dy of knowledge, including a knowledge of first principles, that ...rs on service to some important human good. Its *complexity* means ...t it takes time and money to acquire it (an educational barrier that ...decades effectively blocked women, minorities, and most poor ...ple from becoming professionals). Inasmuch as only a few people ...of a total population can acquire this knowledge, it is esoteric. It ...vitably creates a gulf between professionals and laypeople. This ...mmetricality in knowledge creates in turn an asymmetricality in ...ver, a gap between the powerful and the relatively powerless. This ...crepancy in power intensifies the moral duties of professionals, ...ecially in the helping professions. Thus the intellectual mark bears ...he moral mark of professionals.

...urther, the professional's need to grasp first principles requires ...cation, not mere training. This knowledge differs from mere ...w-how. Trained persons know *how* to do something; educated ...sons also know *why* they do it. Trained persons can deal with ...ady perceived problems; educated persons can draw on methods ...first principles that enable them to deal with future problems. He ...he has a basis for continuing self-education.

...ince professionals require and acquire a knowledge of first princi- ..., they fittingly relate to one another collegially rather than hier- ...ically. The trainee who merely knows how to do something ...rs to the trainer who also knows why; the relationship is hierar- ...al. But educated persons who directly grasp a body of knowledge ...me masters in their own right; they should relate to other pro- ...onals as peers, not simply as subordinate employees. Thus the ...lectual mark bears on the organizational mark of professionals.

...e this knowledge base is complex, esoteric, and draws on first ...ciples, Abraham Flexner, in his Carnegie Report of 1910,[6] justi- ...educating professionals in universities, not just apprenticing and ...ing them in proprietary schools. His proposed reforms affected ...nly medical education but, eventually, the preparation and cre- ...ialling of all professionals. Further, a profession based on knowl- ...inevitably hopes for the expansion of its knowledge base; it must ...some way to support research. The need for such research sup- ...Flexner with a second reason for locating the professions in the ...rsities.

...the professional's intellectual mark consisted simply of scientific ...ledge and no more, then the student might need little more

tiality to my sources for an article? All such professio
pose the question, what shall I do?

But behind many of these dilemmas lie the deepe
professional identity. Who am I? Whom shall I be? Pro
today in the engulfing world of the marketplace and th
and they prepare for their professions in the engulfin
university. What am I? A mix of technician plus en
careerist making my way in the headwinds and crosswi
poration? Or something more?

The Marks of the Professional

Exploring the "something more" of professional id
us into the examination of eight professions in this
treatment will aid the effort to recognize the professi
tinctiveness and to site them in their particular respe
can culture. Yet we need some preliminary markers a
pursuing the identity of each. What are the marks of
What defines professional identity? And what are the
to sustain that identity, since identity for human I
partly at risk and in need of discipline and cultivatic
are no exception. They waiver in their self-interpreta
cial documents resonate with the language of a high
to the common good. However, their daily worrie
play out in the low-to-the-ground trajectory of a c
deals chiefly with the question of professional identi
ery, what Dean Anthony Kronman of Yale Law Sch
soul of a profession.[4]

The professional's covenant, in my judgment, o
directions that help distinguish professionals from c
fessional professes something (a body of knowledge
on behalf of someone (or some institution); and in t
leagues. This summary definition highlights three dist
intellectual (what one professes), *moral* (on behalf of wh
and *organizational* (with whom one professes). The
marks call for three correlative virtues—practical wi
public spiritedness. Professionals need these virtues
selves, but the virtues are hardly their exclusive pro
draw as well on some of the common traditions of

than the virtue of perseverance to acquire it. But the tasks of lawyering, healing, teaching, and counseling, as well as leading complex communities, call for the skill of an artist, not simply the knowledge of an applied scientist. Thus professionals need the correlative virtue of practical wisdom as they bring their knowledge to bear in the service of an important human good. When doctors heal, lawyers counsel, professors teach, and clergy preach and counsel, they draw on a body of knowledge, but they must also attend carefully to the persons they help and discern what will artfully serve their specific needs. A disease may illustrate a scientific generalization and a physician must surely draw on her scientific training to treat, but healing also includes securing patient compliance and, where necessary, the appropriate reconstruction of habits. Comprehensive healing requires an openness and responsiveness to the specifics of the patient's world that rise to an art.

Others of the helping professions require the same wide-angle openness to the client, student, or parishioner and his circumstance. Similarly, the business leader and the political leader may draw on the deliverances of science and the social sciences, but they must also act and lead in a world vastly more complicated and tangled than the highly artificial world that appears under the controlled conditions of a laboratory. Leaders must be open and respond artfully to the specific worlds in which they practice. Thus the intellectual mark of the professional calls for the correlative virtue of practical wisdom, what we might call "attentiveness" or "discernment," an ability to take in the specifics of a concrete case. We will need to explore further the virtue of practical wisdom in the chapters on medicine, the law, engineering, corporate management, and politics.

The Moral Mark. Professionals profess their body of knowledge and skill on behalf of someone or some institution. They should be altruistic. The word "altruistic" is linguistically bland; it means, in root, simply "the other." But the word is morally explosive. It breaks out the knowledge and power professionals wield beyond the bottled-up interests of the self into the public realm. Professionals wield knowledge not simply to exploit others or to indulge in self-display, but to serve others in their needs. Teachers who wield knowledge simply to dazzle, to show off, or to jangle the verger's keys of learning without opening the door to their students, malpractice, as surely as dentists who exploit their patients' ignorance to sell them expensive procedures.

The moral mark of the professional partly traces back to the biblical concept of a vocation or calling, directed to the service of human need. God called the prophets, the priests, and the kings of Israel to serve the needs of the people. In the New Testament, the disciples received a call to serve the sick, the imprisoned, and the needy.

This service element carries forward into our time in the modern professional requirement of *pro bono publico* service enshrined in some of the codes; but the ideal of service should control not simply the supererogatory works of the professional but the terms and constraints under which he or she daily practices. This stringent moral requirement also distinguishes the professional exchange from marketplace transactions. The disproportionate intellectual power of professionals plus the moral standard of altruism combines to demand of the professional the virtue of fidelity.

Such fidelity requires that the professional transaction be disinterested rather than self-interested, and that professionals address the deeper needs of their clients and patients and not just their marketplace wants and desires. Institutions, as well as individuals, need professionals who will give them disinterested service. (For instance, members of Congress who cast their votes with an eye to their exit into private life obsess too much on their own future good rather than on the interests and needs of the institution they currently serve.) We will need to attend extensively to the differences between the marketplace transaction and the professional exchange in the chapter on "Money and the Professions: Medicine and Law."

The Organizational Mark. Professionals organize, a characteristic that traces back to the ancient Greek crafts and to the medieval guilds. In keeping with the intellectual mark, professionals should organize collegially rather than hierarchically. Their direct access to first principles equips them for relationship to other professionals as peers rather than as subordinates. In keeping with the moral mark, the professional organization should aim at *self-improvement*, not simply at self-promotion like marketplace organizations.

The organizational mark calls for the virtue of public spiritedness, which I would define as the art of acting in concert with others for the common good: (1) in the production of services; (2) in the distribution of services; and (3) in the quality control of services, through professional education, self-regulation, and discipline. While this book deals chiefly with the question of professional identity and not with the intricacies of professional organization, that identity itself (and the virtue of public-spiritedness which it calls for) cannot be abstracted from the question of institutional embodiment. We will need therefore to deal inevitably, even if only secondarily, with organizational issues in the production, distribution, and quality control of professional services.

The Production of Professional Services. The era of the free-lance entrepreneur has come to a close. We live in the age of the large-scale organization. The philosopher Alasdair MacIntyre has observed that the ruling theoretician of the modern world is neither Adam Smith in the West nor, certainly, Karl Marx in the East, but Max Weber.[7] The German sociologist wrote about the modern bureaucracy—both governmental and corporate, profit and nonprofit. The large-scale organization dominates both the East and the West, whatever the ideological content of the several systems.

Increasingly, giant organizations mobilize the delivery of professional services. This setting creates tensions between the natural mode of organization among professionals, traditionally collegial, and the prevailing organizational form, hierarchical. While professionals should relate to other professionals as peers, increasingly they orient each other as superordinate and subordinate—in the hospital, the university, the corporation, and even in the professional firm. To what degree do the organizational pressures that young professionals feel in their formative years, while bucking for a partnership, a chief of service, a full professorship, compromise their commitment not only to collegiality, but to independence of judgment and integrity? The increasing oversupply of professionals today—lawyers, physicians, professors, and others—strains collegiality in yet another way: it tends to redefine colleagues as competitors. The social style remains one of friendliness, but an inner wariness, in a highly competitive environment, takes possession of the soul. As colleagues turn into teeth-clenching competitors, the capacity for mutual nurture and renewal diminishes, and service to the common good yields to the necessities of survival. We will attend to the issue of organizational form variously in the chapters on the doctor, the lawyer, the engineer, the corporate executive, the journalist, the professor, and the minister.

The Distribution of Professional Services. I will argue that the notion of the just and public-spirited professional entails more than a minimalist commitment to what the moral tradition has called commutative justice (that is, the fulfillment of duties between private parties based on contracts). Public-spiritedness requires a more inclusive commitment to distributive justice (that is, offering universal access to such basic goods as health care, legal protection, and education rather than restricting them solely to people who have the capacity to pay for them). The principle of universal access also springs from religious ideals (for example, the Hebraic notion of covenantal love—*Chesed*—and the Christian ideal of *Agape*). The principle of universal access derives from the spacious justice of God, who, as the prophets of Israel never ceased to proclaim, hears the cry of the voiceless—the widow, the orphan, the poor, and the stranger in the land. Distributive justice confronts us as an ideal which, in the midst of *de facto* shortages, professionals and the society should approximate.

Some would argue that the obligation to reach all in need rests on the society at large and not on the professions themselves. This argument has the virtue of addressing the problem of distributive justice at a structural level. People should not depend upon irregular charity for basic services. Still others, myself included, see the obligation to distribute professional services as both a societal and a professional responsibility. The power they wield and the goods they control have a public scale. Although the state must accept primary responsibility for ministering justice (an old term for distributive justice), professional groups, too, have a ministry, if you will, to perform. Professionals exercise power through the authority the public grants them. They are often strategically placed to know the distressful consequences suffered by the underserved and the unserved. In addition to their strategic value in achieving reform, professionals, through their *pro bono* services, also help to compensate for the shortfalls in the current system. Until reform comes, there are still human beings with needs to be met, with broken bones to be mended, and with lives hopelessly snarled in the law. And after reform comes, the new structures, no matter how cleverly devised, will not sustain the grounds for their renewal if professionals lack strong commitments to distributive justice.

Further, such *pro bono* work does not merely serve the private happiness of those individuals who receive services; it eventually redounds to the common good and fosters public happiness. Those receiving help do so not merely as individuals but as parts of a whole. And the whole, in so serving its parts, serves its own public flourishing; it rescues its citizens mired in their private distress and frees them for a more public life. In the absence of *pro bono* services, professionals signal, in effect, that they recognize only those people who can pay their way into the marketplace. To the degree that this occurs, our public life shrinks; it dwindles to those with the money to enter it. When public-spirited professionals relieve private distress, they also help preserve our common life, in a monetary culture, from a constant source of its perishing. We will need to explore these issues in distributive justice in the chapters on money and the professions and on corporate, political, and religious professionals.[8]

Professional Self-Regulation and Self-Discipline. A society entrusts professionals organizationally to pass judgment on their own, which includes the negative tasks of self-regulation and self-discipline and the positive tasks of education, research, and continuing education. Achieving self-regulation in any profession poses difficulties. Inevitably, professional colleagues exchange favors, information, and services. Compared to this collegial bond, the ties to students, clients, and patients seem transient. A sense of community develops among colleagues that becomes an end in itself and takes precedence over the population served. The peculiar source of authority for the doctor and the lawyer makes it especially difficult to achieve self-regulation in these professions. Both the legal and medical professions draw power from fear—the patient's concern about suffering and death, the client's fear of the loss of property, liberty, or life. This negative source of authority provides great prestige and financial reward for these two professions but, at the same time, renders their authority inherently unstable. Lawyers and doctors may begin as heroes, but laypeople quickly grow angry and retaliate if, for whatever reason, professionals seem to impose upon the client or patient what they were hired to resist. The chapter on adversarialism in America and the professions further explores the dynamics of a negatively derived authority in the professions.

American professionals may also be reluctant to bring charges against their colleagues because of a morally wholesome aversion to officiousness. Americans generally balk at playing politician, prosecutor, and judge when they are not directly or officially involved in an incident. However, this morally attractive *laissez faire* attitude cannot justify professional permissiveness. Professionals wield great power at the sufferance of the public. They profit from a state-created monopoly. Professionals cannot justify this state-created monopoly if they merely practice competently themselves. The individual's license to practice rests on the power to license which the state for all practical purposes grants to the professions. If the license to practice obliges individual professionals to practice well, the prior license to license obliges them to monitor their colleagues well. Not only individuals but the guild must be accountable! Professionals must be their colleagues' keepers, a principle which justifies not simply disciplining troubled colleagues, but finding positive ways to help them.

Guilds have not only a negative duty to discipline incompetent and unethical behavior but also positive duties, through research and continuing education, to pursue excellence. Too often, the exaction of minimal standards provides not simply a legal basis for ousting the grievously inadequate, but also a floor on which the mediocre comfortably rest. Thus the legal profession traditionally distinguished between disciplinary rules subject to sanction, but also "ethical considerations" which expressed the ideals that point toward distinguished performance. A profession must foster excellence through education, research, and continuing education. Too often, however, programs of research and continuing education promote an excellence too narrowly defined; they prize merely technical and procedural advances without raising foundational questions about the aims and purposes of the profession. The chapters on the engineer, the business leader, and the professor will deal with some of the difficulties in defining and maintaining quality control in the professions.

Calling and Career

Taken together, the second and third marks of a professional—moral and public—connect the concept of a professional with the ancient notion of a "calling." Roscoe Pound, the great jurist, highlighted the moral and public features of professional identity by invoking the old religious term. In an oft-quoted line, he said, "The term [profession] refers to a group . . . pursuing a learned art as a common calling in the spirit of public service—no less a public service because it may incidentally be a means of livelihood. Pursuit of the learned art in the spirit of public service is the primary purpose."[9] The terms "profession" and "calling" have a moral and public ring to them that the word "career" does not. To "profess" means to "testify on behalf of," to "stand for," or to "avow" a high good that defines one's fundamental commitment—a covenant, if you will, that shapes and constrains the practitioner, the professor. Pound associates this fundamental commitment of the professional with the word "calling" and links a calling with the pursuit of the common good.

Traditionally, the term "profession" highlights a first characteristic that not all vocations or callings share. Medicine is a "learned art." Plumbing is a skill, not a learned art. But medicine, law, and other professions cannot escape service to the common good by virtue of their being learned arts. All lines of work, but especially those callings that serve goods basic to our common life, such as law, medicine, and religion, ought to serve the common good. The religious tradition of the West reverberates in Pound's sentences. In the Scriptures of Israel, the calls to the prophets Elijah, Hosea, Amos, Isaiah, Micah, Jeremiah, Deutero-Isaiah, and Ezekiel, all emphasize the public character of their service to the people of God. Similarly the calls to discipleship in the gospels and the gifts of the Spirit, enumerated in the Pauline letters, serve not the private musings of the religiously adept but the flourishing of the community.

The late sixteenth-century theologian William Perkins, who powerfully influenced the American Puritans, explicitly defined a calling as "a certain kind of life, ordained and imposed on man by God for the common good."[10] In the language of the philosophers, God is the efficient cause of one's vocation—God does the calling; and the common good defines the final cause toward which the vocation points. Perkins did not tack on a reference to the common good casually: "he abuseth his calling, whosoever he be that against the end thereof imployes it for himselfe seeking wholly his own, and not the common good."[11] The general call to the religious life should not spiritually evanesce into a private relation to God; it must issue in concrete service in one's special calling, whatever it might be—carpenter, physician, and magistrate (or in those further services to the common good rendered in the roles of father, husband, wife, mother, and citizen).

As might be expected, the criterion of the common good permitted Perkins to criticize those jobs that do not serve it. He did not justify and sanctify all occupations. He questioned, for example, those who give useless and sycophantic service to the wealthy or those whose special role in life is idleness. Further, Perkins criticized those who instrumentalize their calling to some end other than the common good. ". . . they profane their lives & callings that imploy them to get honours, pleasures, profits, worldly commodities, &c., for thus wee live to another end than God hath appointed us, and thus wee serve our selves & consequently neither God, nor man."[12]

In the later stages of Puritanism, of course, the concept of a vocation tended to drift away from service to the common good; instead, vocational success signaled that one was saved—that is, among the "called." A vocation, therewith, deteriorated into an extended mono-logue, in and through which one attempted to prove to God, neigh-bor, and oneself that one was saved. Such a definition of vocation transmogrified into the modern notion of a career and to the psycho-logical dependency that Nietzsche once termed "the work neurosis."

Career. We should not load the word "career" with everything that is morally unsavory in the work life of a professional. A career partly solves the problem of securing what Pound referred to as a means of livelihood, an important dimension of professional identity which we will need to acknowledge in the chapter on money and the professions. A livelihood moreover entails more than earning a liv-ing for oneself. It includes supports required to sustain personal commitments to others—family and other dependents—which vary-ingly carry one beyond a merely private existence into the public arena. However, careerism today symbolizes a general shift in orien-tation toward personal success—an obsession which can distract not only from service to the common good but from the claims of inti-mates upon one's time and energies. Although the word "career" sig-nifies a venture out into a public raceway, a conspicuous public performance, the hot pursuit of a career today severs the work so pursued from the public good. The modern choice of a career often depends upon precisely those honors, pleasures, profits, and worldly commodities that the Puritan divine dismissed as unworthy voca-tional goals.

The words "car" and "career" stem from the same root; they refer to movement—to the ways in which we get off and running. A career refers to that wherein I invest myself, in response to the call of PSATs, SATs, GREs, and MCAT scores, to pursue my own private goals. Both car and career refer increasingly today to private means of transportation. The modern car appeals to us because it lets us travel alone. We prize it as an auto-mobile, a self-driven vehicle. It frees us from traveling with others; it saves us from the body contact of pub-lic transportation. Even though a car takes us out into the public streets, it wraps us in a glass-enclosed privacy as we race down public thoroughfares.

Similarly, a careerist tends to calculate privately, even in public places. At the beginning of his race, he asks, what will I be? What career will best serve my interests—provide me with the means, in both money and power, to satisfy my wants? In the course of the jour-ney he asks, what moves shall I make to get where I want to go, and most speedily? Whom shall I cultivate? Whom, avoid? And at the end of the race, he looks back on the track, the honors won, the fortune acquired, the opportunities missed, the mistakes made, and wonders whether it was all worthwhile.

In such a race, questions of public obligation and responsibility fade to the marginal and episodic. The careerist drives on public streets and largely obeys the rules of the road, but toward his or her private destination. We so accept this version of things that we do not even think of ourselves as having chosen to travel alone. Indeed, alternative modes of transportation—buses and trams—have all but vanished. The private homes in which we live, the huge debts we have incurred, depend equally on private car and career. We have not so much chosen to travel alone and calculated our competitive chances on entrance exams and job applications, as we have responded to a world that forces us on to this track. Living where we live (or hoping to live where we hope to live), how could we have chosen another means of transportation? Who could have afforded to concentrate any less single-mindedly on the furtherance of his or her professional career? Life is demanding enough, competitive enough, and dicey enough as it is.

The image of "dice" inevitably rolls into the discussion. The ambitious careerist usually has a well-developed sense of the power of fortune, the tumble of the dice, in human affairs. As he severs himself from the goal of the common good, he also adjusts his notion of efficient cause. Perkins's Providence vanishes; the careerist transfers authority and sovereignty to himself. But once he seizes control, he recognizes that he cannot fully control events. He finds himself fitfully at the mercy of family fortune, academic record, contacts made at college, professional school exams, sponsors at work, the play in the job market, and the pitch and roll of the stock market. At every turn, he perceives himself threatened by the "blind giants" of history, as Kierkegaard once called fate; and he pits his own subjective resources against the objective uncertainties of chance. The careerist lacks Perkins's faith in a Providence that "overthroweth the . . . opinion of men; which thinke that the particular condition and state of man in this life comes by chance: or by the bare will & pleasure of man himself."[13] Thus the careerist must deal with both the x of chance and the y of his own arbitrary freedom. Luck, like prevailing wind, lasts less long as tailwind than as headwind.

Under these circumstances, the modern careerist tries to reduce the margin of chance and the waywardness of his own decision making. He develops a strategy for reducing each. Wealth offers the classical route to reducing the power of fate. The word "fortune" refers both to chance, the random powers that control our lives, and to the money that secures us against them. The anxious careerist aspires to a fortune in order to protect himself or herself against Fortune. Truly giant fortunes seem to buffer their owners against all contingencies, against the vicissitudes of Fortune and against the unreliability of their fellows. Wealth supplies the means by which one can do without the will and pleasure of others, one's life safely privatized and apolitical.

Becoming a professional hardly guarantees such a fortune but professional education, until recently, has offered degree holders who lack an inherited fortune the functional equivalent, a professional fee schedule. Education provides a kind of portable security, unusually precious to an immigrant and migratory people who would sacrifice a great deal to armor their upwardly mobile young men and women against the exigencies of fate.

The careerist, of course, faces a second unknown, the uncertainties of his own irresolute will, the arbitrariness of freedom. Being a professional pulls him into the upper middle class of decision makers. But the burden of deciding generates anxieties, which one seeks to tamp down with knowledge and, if not through one's own knowledge, then by enlisting the services of those who act as though they know—modern professional consultants and counselors.

Consultants of whatever stripe have multiplied today, plying a craft as old as the Greek oracle who tamped down the anxieties of generals by examining the entrails of birds on the eve of momentous battle. By peering into the enigma of the future, the oracle calmed the uncertainty of the irresolute will. Correspondingly, an entire class of professionals has emerged today—consultants, counselors, and experts for experts—who advise the decision maker in business, politics, and the professions. The intellectually talented among lawyers, economists, engineers (and reengineers), and financial and market analysts serve latter-day generals as they cope with the winds of war in the marketplace. Still other professionals provide premium health care and education to leaders and their families. As Magali Larson observed in *The Rise of Professionalism*, modern professionals often seem engaged in serving one another rather than the society at large.[14] This self-absorption partly reflects the prior detachment of careerists from the common good and their need for (and ability to pay for and commandeer) services that minister to the psychic burdens of privacy. Meanwhile, professional services do not distribute broadly and inclusively to the whole society, and anxious careerists are loathe to push too hard within the guilds or within the huge organizations in which they work to assure the full and fair service of these institutions to the common good.

The Unfinished Agenda

The establishment of the guilds and the reforms in the twentieth century of professional education produced some positive changes: they strengthened intellectual standards by associating the preparation of professionals with the universities; they enforced an important moral standard by eliminating obvious charlatans; and they created professional organizations charged with, at least on paper, the task of enforcing intellectual and moral standards.

Critics have noted, however, a darker side to the reforms. Putting the professions into the universities and closing down proprietary schools (Abraham Flexner wanted to reduce the number of medical schools from 180 to thirty-seven) also effectively denied medical education to blacks and women, who chiefly prepared in proprietary schools. Further, closing down many medical schools imposed a kind of professional birth control, paving the way for the monopolistic price-fixing of medical services well above the rate of inflation. Thus, under the banner of self-improvement, professionals in the field of medicine (and other professions) often engaged in economic self-promotion.

These are conventional criticisms of the reforms. But the current challenge to professional identity goes deeper. First, intellectually, the professions moved into the university largely in the twentieth century, just when the universities denied moral formation as part of their responsibility. The twentieth-century positivist university felt that questions of ethics and values could not surface in the classroom. The professor could teach facts, not values, because values reflect only subjective, emotive, arbitrary preferences. Thus the university shaped the professions at approximately the same time that many faculty members began to exclude value questions from the university's domain. This objectivism in the university helped produce opportunism and privatistic careerism in its graduates. Since the university does not offer an arena in which reasoned discourse, debate, and discriminate judgment about values can occur without deteriorating into propaganda or advocacy, the knowledge the student acquires eventually goes up for grabs to the highest bidder. Since ends have no objective, public and moral heft, who can deny the claim that knowledge is itself a personal prize and possession, not a public trust, to be manipulated for private advantage alone? Thus professionals often deteriorated into careerists. They lost a sense of "calling." Further, the move into the universities tended to redefine professionals exclusively as applied scientists. The experiential features of a fully developed art, which the earlier apprenticeship system honored, weakened.

Second, the moral element of professional identity faces today the engulfing forces of the marketplace. How does one maintain the moral ingredient of altruism in a marketplace driven by the power of self-interest? How does the professional as a player in the marketplace hew to the professional transaction as disinterested rather than self-interested, as transformational rather than transactional, as addressed to clients' needs, not simply their wants? How do professionals and the society at large in a commercial culture insure that fundamental services reach all those in need?

Third, organizationally, how can professionals maintain a collegial sense of responsibility, and enforce standards, when professionals work for deferentially hierarchical organizations: hospitals, huge universities, law firms, and corporations? The title of Elliott A. Krause's book, *The Death of the Guilds*, may be too melodramatic, but the guilds have often evanesced or wilted before the power of the huge organizations in which professionals increasingly work as employees; and professionals have largely restricted their services to those who can make their way through the turnstiles of the organizational delivery system.

Under current pressures, it is tempting for thoughtful professionals to lament the adversities they face: their souls altered by the universities that educated them, their power layered in the corporations for which they work, and their services largely driven by the bottom line. But whoever said that men and women can sustain their identities, even with the best of reforms in place, without struggle? They also need the requisite virtues, the strengths of character, to sustain their identities despite adversity. Virtues are strengths of character required and acquired in adversity.[15] Surely, professionals should not expect exemption from the need for that courage which Thomas Aquinas defined as firmness of soul in the face of adversity in the pursuit of the common good.

Why do professionals owe service to the common good? Part of the answer has already surfaced. Historically, professionals assumed a public role with attendant public duties when they became lawyers, doctors, and members of the clergy. Their sense of public duty fit in with the still more comprehensive notion that a vocation calls for service to the common good. The religious origins of the notions of profession and calling have partly faded, but more than a ghost image remains in the terms and conditions under which modern professionals attain their public standing. Normally, the state licenses them. The society expects professionals to state publicly their own standards of excellence, to conform to those standards individually, and to enforce them upon colleagues within the guild. Further, modern professionals wield a public power that vastly exceeds that of their predecessors in the professions. What they do today fatefully affects human flourishing. Professionals have even less reason than their predecessors to construe their power in purely private, entrepreneurial terms.

Finally, the knowledge-based power professionals wield does not spring independently from their foreheads. It is not self-derived. No professional can go through a modern university and plausibly pretend to be a self-made man or a self-made woman. A huge company of people contributes to the shaping of professionals as they zigzag their way through college and professional schools: the janitors who clean the johns, the help in the kitchen, the secretaries who make the operation hum, the administrators who wrestle with the institution's problems, the faculty who share with students what they know, the vast research traditions of each of the disciplines which set the table for that sharing, and the patients and clients who lay their bodies and souls on the line, letting young professionals practice on them in the course of perfecting their art. And, behind all that, the public money and the gifts that support the enterprise, so that tuition fees usually pay for only a fraction of education. When professionals treat education as providing them with a private stockpile of knowledge to sell on the market to the highest bidder, they potentially distort and obscure the social origins of knowledge and therefore the social origins of the power which that knowledge places within their grasp. The recognition that professionals have hugely received can help dispose the professional to serve the common good.

(The Abrahamic religious traditions hold that one cannot fully appreciate this indebtedness of human beings by toting up the varying sacrifices and investments of others from which they benefit. The sense that one inexhaustibly receives presupposes an infinite inexhaustible source rather than a finite sum of discrete gifts received from others. Still, the secondary gifts in the human order of giving and receiving, in which professionals participate, can strengthen their sense of calling and, for some, signify, even though imperfectly, an infinite and life-defining gift.)

However, a sense of indebtedness for gifts received hardly defines the daily world in which professionals hustle for a living. Selling skills and paying bills, rather than giving and receiving, organize the day. Thus, a chapter on money and the professions ranks as the next order of business in a book on the public obligation of the professional.

Notes

1. For the material in this paragraph, see Elliott A. Krause, *Death of the Guilds: Professions, States, and the Advance of Capitalism, 1930 to the Present* (New Haven, Conn.: Yale University Press, 1996).
2. In his discussion of the overclass in America, Michael Lind distinguishes between the hereditary upper class and the institutional elite. "Members of the upper class who want to make a mark in the world tend to adopt the style of the managerial professional elite. Even though they do not have to, most members of the small hereditary upper class go to college and get executive or professional jobs. . . . Instead of serving as a model for well-to-do executives and lawyers and investment bankers, the hereditary segment of the American overclass conforms to the segment below it, the credentialled upper middle class." Michael Lind, "The Next American Nation," *The New Nationalism and the Fourth American Revolution* (New York: Simon & Schuster, 1995), 144.
3. Michael Novak, *The Spirit of Democratic Capitalism* (New York: Simon & Schuster, 1982), 175.
4. In the introduction to his book *The Lost Lawyer*, Dean Kronman has written: "This book is about a crisis in the American legal profession. Its message is that the profession now stands in danger of losing its soul." Anthony Kronman, *The Lost Lawyer: Failing Ideals of the Legal Profession* (Cambridge, Mass.: Harvard University Press, 1993), 1.
5. For an earlier sketch of these several markers and virtues applied to the medical profession, see my book *Testing the Medical Covenant* (Grand Rapids: William B. Eerdmans, 1996), ch. 3.
6. For a brief account of Abraham Flexner's definition of a professional, see "Is Social Work a Profession?" found in Proceedings of the National Conference of Charities and Correction, 42nd Annual Meeting, Baltimore, Maryland, May 12–19, 1915. For a functional, rather than a substantive, approach to the marks of a professional, see Walter P. Metzger, "What is a Profession?" found in *Seminar Reports*, Program of General and Continuing Education in the Humanities, vol. 3, no. 1 (New York: Columbia University, 1975).
7. See Alasdair MacIntyre, *After Virtue: A Study in Moral Theory* (Notre Dame, Ind.: University of Notre Dame Press, 1981), 82 and 103.
8. For earlier sketches of issues in distributive justice and the quality control of professional services in the field of medicine, see my books *The Physician's Covenant* (Philadelphia: The Westminster Press, 1983), 131–41, and *Testing the Medical Covenant: Active Euthanasia and Health Care Reform* (Grand Rapids: William B. Eerdmans, 1996), chap. 4.
9. Roscoe Pound, *The Lawyer from Antiquity to Modern Times* (St. Paul: West Publishing, 1953), 5.
10. William Perkins, "A Treatise of the Vocations or Callings of Men with Sorts and Kinds of Them, and the Right Use Thereof" in Edmund S. Morgan, ed. *Puritan Political Ideas* (Indianapolis: Bobbs-Merrill, 1965), 36.
11. Perkins, 39.
12. Perkins, 56.
13. Perkins, 37.

14. Magali Larson, *The Rise of Professionalism* (Berkeley: University of California Press, 1977).
15. Alasdair MacIntyre once defined the virtues as "those dispositions that . . . sustain practices . . . by enabling us to overcome the harms, dangers, temptations, and distractions we encounter." MacIntyre, *After Virtue*, 204.

Part I

Chapter 1

Money and the Professions

Medicine and the Law

Money is many-faced; and I don't mean the grave and graven images of the Washingtons, the Franklins, the Lincolns, and the Jacksons who gaze somberly out as we handle our bills. Rather, many-faced in that money performs variously and importantly and positively in our lives; and we had better, at the outset, acknowledge that fact. How do we need thee? How do even professionals need thee? Let me count the ways.

Money feeds. In all but the world of barter, one needs money to live. We need it to buy our daily bread. Amateurs may do it for love. But a professional, like all other workers, does it for money, and it would be a species of angelism to deny that fact. Since money feeds, it also supplies an element of stability to the relationship of professional to client. For if professional services depended entirely on love, then, of course, like love, at least at the emotional level, they would tend to rise and fall, wax and wane. But money supplies a bit of constancy to the relationship. Philanthropy is flighty. Adam Smith illustrated this when he noted that the fellow we can count on to get up at 3:00 A.M. to nurse a sick cow either owns it or is paid to take care of it. Money keeps us from being hostage to dilettantism; it steadies the attention.

Money rewards and thus motivates. Above and beyond the bread it supplies, money often marks perceived worth, especially when the good we sell is not simply a commodity but our own skills. It does not mark worth perfectly. But even those professionals whom the marketplace usually underpays, such as teachers and members of the clergy, look to salary reviews within their institutions to indicate the value placed on their performance.

Money connects us to the stranger. Families, friends, and neighbors meet in enclosed spaces, in the house, the church, and the synagogue; but the marketplace forces us into the open; it puts us among strangers. From the seventeenth century forward, professionals—the

27

doctor and the lawyer—hung out their shingles on the street. The sign signaled that one offered one's skill not simply to the enclosed world of friends, relatives, and neighbors, but to strangers. Money is ecumenical; it breaks out beyond the boundaries of the parochial. The pressures today for free trade express yet again the inherently expansive nature of the market. It transcends even national boundaries as it opens out toward the faraway, the strange.

Money also talks. Sometimes it barks out commands; sometimes it sweet-talks. Either way, it mobilizes and organizes resources and talent. Money is not inert. Since it feeds, since it motivates powerfully, and since it vaults barriers or opens doors, it is remarkably fluid; it flows easily and it carries other things along easily; it lubricates and it keeps the world moving. It is dynamic, seizing on the inventive, the novel. It also lets one adapt rapidly to change, to readjust and reconfigure the world.

Montesquieu distinguished different types of civil societies by noting that the aspiration to honor and excellence supplies the mainspring to action in an aristocratic society, whereas fear of the tyrant keeps a despotic society ticking. Clearly, the desire for money supplies the spring to action in a commercial society. Money offers us the objects of our desire and gratifies our self-interest. The pictures on the face of money may be grave and engraved—Washington and Lincoln—but money itself is dynamic and protean, so much so that when we celebrate it, we border on the blasphemous, referring to the almighty dollar.

But that thought moves us toward the dark side of money, so dark and deep that Scripture once referred to the love of money as the root of all evil. If not the root of all evil, money certainly fertilizes those roots. While money feeds, motivates, breaks down barriers, commands, and organizes, it can also vulgarize, distract, corrupt, distort, and exclude. It can vulgarize, distract and corrupt professionals as they offer their services; it can distort the services they have to offer, and it can bar the needy from their services.

The Dangers of Money

The dangers of money thrive on the complicated double relationship of money and the marketplace to the professions. Money, the market, and the professions intertwine. They are so plaited that the increased power of the professions in the modern world coincides with the emergence of the modern marketplace and with the still later emergence of the winner in the marketplace, the modern, large-scale corporation.

I see the connections as follows. Aristotle once referred to the good community, the *polis*, as a community of friends, people with shared interests and goals. Aristotle's ideal *polis* was a small community, small enough to recognize all its citizens by name and to engage everyone (well, not everyone—not women, not slaves) in civic responsibilities. The city remained relatively small until the eighteenth century. This cameo scale let people relate chiefly within the framework of family, neighbors, and friends and of accepted customs and principles. From the eighteenth century forward, the West and particularly the United States increasingly shifted from a community formed of neighbors to metropolises comprised of strangers.

In Dallas, where I live, the house with attached garage completes the process. I drive home along an alley, flick the garage door opener to avoid getting out of the car, park inside, and then flick the garage door shut and enter the kitchen. If kids are out in front yards playing, if neighbors are out mowing, I wouldn't know it. We live among strangers—sometimes friendly strangers, but still, strangers.

How do persons set among strangers connect? Mostly, not through shared interests, but through *cash* that temporarily connects people who otherwise do not share common interests. Professionals belong to that platoon of paid strangers who partly substitute for the families, neighbors, and friends who provided services in earlier societies.

Aging patients, their children in distant cities, now look to the physician and nurse as the fixed stars in their lives. Disputes, formerly resolved through the mediation of friends, relatives, and neighbors acquainted over a lifetime with the parties to the conflict, now end up in the courts. Shared customs and principles have turned into a legal system; and, since the parties to the dispute and those who will manage the proceedings do not know the principals, we have constructed strict rules of evidence and paper trails to judge a particular case. Litigation perforce metastasizes in a society of strangers; and trained experts handle the proceedings and preside fatefully over outcomes. Because the doctor/patient relationship today chiefly links strangers by money and because it points toward a desperately hoped-for favorable outcome, the relationship is increasingly less stable and, more and more often, falls into enmity. The patient resorts angrily to courts which strangers to both parties control; strangers attempt to bring closure to the disputes between strangers with money at issue at most points. Further, the corporation won the competitive battle in the modern marketplace and thus disproportionately commands the talent of lawyers, accountants, and engineers who work either directly for corporations or for those outside professional firms that serve them exclusively.[1]

While the professions and the marketplace (and therefore money) intertwine today, the professional professes and avows a commitment that transcends the marketplace. The aristocratic origin of the professional in the West offers the least satisfactory way of expressing that transcendence. "Having a profession" provided a social location for the second, third, and fourth sons of aristocrats who, in a society committed to primogeniture, could not inherit portions of the estate which went exclusively to the eldest son, and yet who, as children of the aristocracy, felt they should not have to work for a living and thus submit to the vulgarities of the marketplace. The professions—law, civil service, the church, the military, and medicine—provided the great families with an honorable social location for their surplus gentlemen.

The aristocratic ethic of *noblesse oblige* deserves some criticism. It embodied the condescension of the superior toward the inferior; it bent low with benevolence. And it welcomed into professional practice only those who would fit into the old boys' network.

But it also deserves some praise. It despised the pretensions of the more recent ethic of the self-made man or woman. It did not suffer from the illusions of those who think of themselves as self-created. Instead, it acknowledged that one mostly received what one is, a gift that generates obligations to others. While the marketplace runs on the dynamism of buying and selling, the aristocratic ethic at its best acknowledged the social lubricant of receiving and therefore giving. It inspired an ethic based on gratitude and a corresponding magnanimity.

Further, the aristocratic ethic assumed some independence from the client. An aristocratic professional did not wholly depend upon the client for a living or for a sense of worth. Such a professional belonged, prior to all contractual relations, to the moral traditions of the family and the guild. That identity placed some restraints upon what the professional would do for the client in exchange for his money.

But these very substantial positive restraints in the aristocratic ethic faded, leaving behind only a self-serving trace of the ethic in guild prohibitions—until the 1970s—against advertising. Hustling in the marketplace by advertising coarsens and demeans the professional and the profession. Thus, a ghost of the aristocratic origins of the professions showed up in the complaint that:

Money vulgarizes. However, the U.S. Supreme Court, in cases originating in Virginia (1976)[2] and Arizona (1977)[3], prohibited professional guilds and state governments from banning advertising. The Court held that advertising as a form of commercial speech cannot be prohibited. Further, critics of guild bans on advertising argued that such prohibitions violated monopolistic price fixing. The cost of professional services had been rising much faster than the rate of inflation. As the ABA itself acknowledged, "the middle 70% of our population is not being reached or served adequately by the legal profession."[4] Thus the professions, while invoking an ethic purportedly superior to the marketplace had, in effect, behaved in a fashion morally inferior to the free-trade ethic of the marketplace. The courts understandably wanted to put a stop to this hypocrisy.

Still, rampant advertising does make one wince. Money vulgarizes. Two root canals for the price of one until the end of the month. Radial keratotomy at $1,250 an eye, with $500 off for the two procedures if you decide before you leave our seminar room. If you need help on your traffic ticket, just dial 9-GOTCHA, credit cards accepted.

Recoiling from all this vulgarity, doctors daintily hand the task of collecting money from patients to their office staffs so as not to brush up against actual money. But the polite conventions of professional billing do not deceive. Professional schools increasingly require courses in business management, in which they enroll more students than they do in courses on professional ethics. Further, the recruits for the professions today hardly enter them from an aristocracy. The professions now provide the social escalator that lifts sons and daughters upward from the working and middle classes—sons and daughters who often lack clear public identities and who need to earn their entire living from their profession. Thus the modern professional sinks both feet into the marketplace. The question grows more probing. Must he or she recognize any further identity that transcends the cash nexus? Does the professional simply combine technician and entrepreneur into a mercenary who sells a skill in the law, medicine, accounting, engineering, or theology? Or does anything other than skill and cash motivate the professional? This question of double identity lies behind the topic "money and the professions."

As noted earlier, Roscoe Pound answered the question of identity by invoking, not the aristocratic, but the old religious, tradition of a "calling": ". . . the term [profession] refers to a group . . . pursuing a learned art as a common calling in the spirit of public service—no less a public service because it may incidentally be a means of livelihood."[5] When Pound referred to a profession as a common calling and linked a calling with the public service, he echoed the religious tradition of the West, which made this connection in its Scriptures. But if a profession is a calling to serve a public good and not simply a careerist vehicle for serving one's own private desire for money and fame, then we can identify a second danger and temptation of money, more serious than the first.

Money distracts, as well as vulgarizes. Philosophers have distinguished between the goods internal to a practice—such as the arts of lawyering, healing, teaching, and preaching—and the goods external to a practice—such as the fame or fortune which a practice may generate.[6] If the careerist heals, litigates, teaches, or preaches only for money or prestige, she has lost that professional single-mindedness, that purity of heart, which allows all else to burn away as the internal practice shines through. The love of money and fame distracts; it focuses attention elsewhere.

In Kingsley Amis's novel *Lucky Jim*, a college history professor answers his phone by saying, "History here." What a wonderful line! Better than "Historian here" or "Dr. Toynbee here." "History here" points to the activity, pure and simple, not to the office or to the attainment of the person. Isn't that what a distressed patient wants when he calls the doctor about a baffling symptom? "Healing here." Isn't that what the distressed client or parishioner needs, when calling the lawyer or the priest? "Sanctuary here."

Money distracts the professional from what should be his or her single-minded professional purpose, the client's welfare. Justin A. Stanley, past president of the ABA and chair of the ABA Commission on Professionalism, noted in the comprehensive report of the Commission in 1986 that

> any number of large law firms are now going into business or
> businesses which they control or manage. . . . For example, one
> firm has set up one investment advisory service, and this functions
> principally, I guess, to advise clients of the law firm.
> Another set up a lobbying entity in Washington, DC. Another
> firm has invested heavily in real estate development. . . . Why do

they do this? Well they claim to serve their legal clients better by providing ancillary services: sort of a one-stop shopping center. I suspect, however, that they could do just as well for their law clients if they introduced them to competent financial advisors, lobbyists, or investors in real estate. I think that the real reason is money.[7]

The development of "one-stop shopping centers" run by law firms has grown apace since the Stanley Report. By the year 2000 debate over the ethics of "multidisciplinary practice" had led to the charge that money may not only distract but steal the very soul of the profession, a charge that will be treated at the close of this chapter. Since the Stanley Report, law firms have further expanded their entry into the marketplace by setting up separate entities (limited partnerships or limited liability companies) to hold investments for partners in start-up clients (particularly in the technology and biotechnology fields). Law firms either pay cash, like other institutional investors, or, more controversially, accept stocks in exchange for their services. Law firms can lose time and money in such adventures, but the initial public offering (IPO) that goes into orbit can yield to the law firm a reward vastly exceeding the traditional standard of a "reasonable fee." Some firms have made fortunes overnight.[8] Critics worry that the law firm that becomes a player can expose itself variously to charges of conflicts of interest and to lawsuits. So far, lawsuits have not emerged, but, as Steve Moore, a law firm consultant with Pricewaterhouse Coopers, has observed, ". . . suits come in when times get tough, so we won't know until the economy goes bad."[9] Legal liability is not the only issue. Ethically, lawyers owe both their clients and (as officers of the court) ultimately the public, independent, and undistracted professional judgments which the glitter of IPO profits might affect. Advocates for the new practice of investing in clients have appealed to the device of contingency fees as precedent, but, to this observer, it seems easier to focus more undistractedly on legal issues, as a contingency fee lawyer than as an investor in the client's business.

Money corrupts. Eventually, a focus on the rewards external to a practice can corrupt the practice itself. The actress interested only in her Nielsen ratings and the advertising revenue it generates repeats the tricks that worked for her last week and at length her show deteriorates into a series of running gags and repeated clichés, corrupting the original theatrical performance.

Specifically, money corrupts the professional exchange by converting it into an interested rather than a disinterested transaction. A marketplace, as distinct from a professional, transaction occurs between two self-interested and relatively knowledgeable parties engaged in the act of buying and selling. Each party attempts primarily to protect his or her own self-interest. The seller does not feel particularly constrained to watch out for the buyer's interests. That's up to the buyer, who, by comparative shopping and study, learns enough to protect himself.

But a basic asymmetry shapes the relation of the professional to her client. The professional wields knowledge (and the power that knowledge generates), which the troubled client needs. The client, on the other hand, often too ignorant, powerless, and anxious, cannot protect himself from either the problem or the professional. A medical crisis, for instance, usually leaves little time for comparative shopping, even if one knew how to assess the professional's skills. Patients, students, clients, and parishioners cannot readily obey the marketplace warning, *caveat emptor*—buyer beware.

Their lack of knowledge and their neediness require that the professional exchange take place in a *fiduciary* setting of trust and confidence that transcends the marketplace assumptions about two wary bargainers. The importance of this trust should determine our view of what the professional sells. In a marketplace transaction, the salesperson does not ordinarily feel obliged to calculate my self-interest other than its value to him in clinching a sale. The salesman does his best to serve his own self-interest and sell me the car or the refrigerator. When I enter the showroom, I am a pork chop for the eating. That's part of the game.

But if I visit a physician, I must trust that he or she sells two items, not one. The physician sells not only a professional procedure but also the professional judgment that I need the procedure she offers. The surgeon does not simply sell hernia jobs, but also her cold, detached, disinterested, unclouded judgment that I need that wretched little operation. Otherwise, the physician abuses her power and poisons the professional relationship with distrust. Instead of sheltering, she fleeces the distressed. She reduces me to a mere opportunity for profit. And, if I find that out, I will resent her for taking advantage of my vulnerability.

Herein lies the ground for all the guilds' formal strictures against conflicts of interest. The professional must sufficiently distance himself from his own interests and those of other clients to serve the specific client's well-being.

Money alone does not tempt the professional to compromise the interest or welfare of his or her patient or client. The lure of fame or the interests of an institution can also undercut fidelity to the patient. In teaching and research institutions, the physician may succumb to the temptation to reduce the patient to teaching material or to recruit the patient for a research protocol not entirely in the patient's best interests. The lawyer in search of fame may find it enticing to push the client's case down a groundbreaking path in the law, a strategy which sometimes exposes the client to an increased risk. Professional codes enjoin against such breaches of fidelity in the pursuit of fame, tenure, or some institutional goal. However, money, far more than fame, creates conflicts of interest corroding professional responsibility.

The basic payment systems for professional services create different temptations for professionals (and the institutions for which they work). The fee-for-service system tempts doctors to overtreat and the prepayment system to undertreat patients. Either way, the patient's best interests can suffer.

Traditional fee-for-service medicine, coupled with laxly monitoring third-party payers, led to the overuse of prescription and medical services, especially from the 1960s through the early 1990s. The federal government through taxes and insurance companies through charges to employer plans eventually recovered their costs on whatever they paid doctors or hospitals for treating a particular patient. Doctors enjoyed economic incentives to overtreat. A primary care internist, for example, could "increase his or her net income by a factor of almost three by prescribing a wide but not unreasonable set of tests."[10] The term "not unreasonable" camouflaged the lack of cost control in fee-for-service medicine.[11] Temptations to overtest and overtreat compounded since physicians had "a financial stake in 25 to 80% of ancillary medical facilities depending on the region and the kind of facility."[12] One study revealed that doctors who handled and controlled the charges for their own radiological services "presented tests at least four times as often and charged higher fees than did doctors who referred their patients to radiologists."[13] These various financial incentives did not of themselves produce shoddy treatment or overtreatment, but they loaded the field of practice with temptations.

Money can also corrupt the medical exchange by creating incentives for insufficient treatment under prepayment systems. Under a capitation system, insurance companies and other institutional providers (and sometimes the physicians affiliated with them) profit from the difference between the annual amount received and the actual expenses incurred in the care of the patient. Money prepaid tempts providers to do, not too much, but too little. The primary-care internist, who, under fee-for-service, increased his profit by ordering dubious tests and procedures, now serves as gatekeeper and can make more money, certainly for the system and perhaps for himself, by limiting patient access to tests, procedures, medications, specialists, or hospitalizations. Money may not inevitably corrupt, but it often sorely tempts and pressures caregivers.

Managed care firms resorted to a number of devices to keep up the pressure on physicians. They informed physicians regularly of their rate of ordering prescriptions and of making referrals to specialists. They also reported on a doctor's use rate compared with that of his or her peers. They offered financial incentives for doctors to keep their costs low, established "productivity" rates to hurry up the speed with which doctors processed patients, and, until forbidden by law, imposed so-called gag rules on physicians, which prohibited them from disclosing to patients alternative treatments or additional treatments not covered by their health care plan. Usually firms also hid from patients the financial rewards physicians enjoyed for keeping down costs.

These devices eventually squeezed doctors financially. Some big health insurers, operating under a capitation reimbursement system, initially recruited doctors into contracts with them by paying doctors something close to "usual and customary fees" for services. But, in the course of time, some insurers began to pay physicians "the lowest available rates," often set by bargain rate HMOs.[14] Insurers justified these cuts by citing rising costs (new technologies and an aging population) unaccompanied by rising income (employer refusals to increase their prepayments for health care coverage). Diminishing profits led the insurers to reduce their payouts to physicians; and rapid mergers of various competing insurers have given the winners increased leverage over doctors, since they control the supply of patients.

Doctors found themselves facing other squeezes as well. Prior to congressional legislation, many contracts held doctors, not health plans, vulnerable to malpractice suits for denial of care, even though insurers had the final say as to whether a treatment was necessary. In addition, doctors could not sue the health plan for refusal of service.[15]

Irony abounds. For decades, doctors denounced Washington, D.C. as the single threat to their freedom to practice as they pleased. They celebrated the free-enterprise system as their natural ally against Washington. But the marketplace eventually spawned corporate health care institutions, which initially offered doctors a supply of patients at customary and usual rates. The birds flew into the cages but then discovered that the owners at length rationed their seed, scripted their songs, and sometimes punished them whether they sang according to script or not.

Academic medical centers, upon which we depend for medical education and research, especially suffer under a for-profit health care system. Academic centers provide care for the sickest and poorest patients (and thus usually the most costly to treat) as well as train residents and conduct medical research. Teaching and research take time, but the pressure to meet "productivity" standards pares away the time clinicians can give to their interns and residents and to their research. Arnold S. Relman, former editor-in-chief of the *New England Journal of Medicine*, dryly noted in "Why Johnny Can't Operate" that our current system of managed care, which supplies services for approximately 170 million patients, does not bode well, either for sustaining through education or improving through research the quality of medical care.[16] Without redress, the long-range interests of patients will suffer.

The legal, as well as the medical, guild has prohibited on principle actions that violate the interests of the client. It has especially enforced prohibitions against conflicts of interest that arise when lawyers and their firms serve two clients with conflicting interests. But the profession has much less determinedly protected a client's financial interests from the pecuniary interests of lawyers themselves. Monetary temptations multiply, albeit at the risk of civil and criminal liability. Lawyers may pad billable hours, string out a lawsuit to increase billable hours, engage in more expensive research than necessary, expand the list of witnesses to be interrogated, and extend discovery proceedings endlessly. Further, the normal controls of marketplace supply and demand have not succeeded in regulating fees. Increases in the per capita number of doctors and lawyers have not driven down fees; they have risen even as the supply of lawyers and doctors has swollen.

Derek Bok in *The Cost of Talent* remarked that "the most promising remedy by far . . . is more aggressive bargaining by corporations over the fees they will pay their outside lawyers."[17] That remedy, of course, does not solve the problem less powerful and efficient clients face who do not enjoy the bargaining power of corporations. Perversely, some of the strategies lawyers use to drive up their prices—for example, protracted discovery proceedings—work. These strategies may hike up the costs of legal services for the opposition so high as to price the opposing party out of the case. In that event, the client got his money's worth: he won the case. But the legal system as a whole loses. Bloated costs strain the quality of justice. Contingency fees also provide lawyers with opportunities both to abuse dependents and to diddle their clients. Defendants in medical malpractice suits complain bitterly that insurance companies will sometimes settle unjustifiable suits simply to avoid court costs even though the settlement saps the physician's morale and casts a shadow over his or her professional reputation.

Meanwhile, unsuspecting clients do not know enough about their chances of winning or about the amount of time a lawyer must give to a case to be able to protect their interests in setting the percentage for a contingency fee. As Bok wryly noted, "most plaintiffs do not know enough whether they have a strong case, and rare is the lawyer who will inform them (and agree to a lower percentage of the take)."[18] A payment system based exclusively on winning creates temptations for lawyers to exploit their clients; and, even worse, it pressures lawyers to abuse opposing parties and to tarnish the legal system as a whole. ". . . when lawyers get paid only if they win, the incentives to behave unprofessionally, if that is what it takes to succeed, are very strong."[19] When money corrupts, it leaves traces of poison throughout a system.

Money distorts, as well as corrupts, the professional relationship. The professional exchange differs from a marketplace transaction in a second way. In addition to its disinterestedness, the professional exchange should, when circumstances require, transform, not merely transact. The practitioner in the helping professions must serve not only the client's perceived wants but his deeper needs.

The patient suffering from insomnia often wants the simple quick fix of a pill. But if the physician goes after the root of the problem, she may have to help the patient transform the habits that led to the symptom of sleeplessness in the first place. The physician is slothful if she reflexively jumps to acute care but neglects preventive medicine. Similarly, the effective lawyer needs to offer not only wizardry as a litigant in the courtroom, but also the effective counseling that can keep the client out of the courtroom in the first place. Lawyers may need to edge out beyond a bare marketplace transaction, in which they simply sell the client what he or she wants, and, instead, help change a course of action or a pattern of life. No one should underestimate the difficulties of encouraging a change in habit or character. As J. Pierpoint Morgan purportedly said to Mr. Root, "I don't want a lawyer to tell me what I can't do. I want him to tell me how I can do what I want to do." The powerful client often tries through money to turn the lawyer into a simple tool of his will. In acting diligently as a professional, the conscientious lawyer may need to distinguish between what the client can get away with legally and what is wise.

The basic payment system and the flow of money can variously pressure, distort, and repress the transformational element in the professional exchange. Most of the incentives in conventional fee-for-service medicine favor acute care—at the expense of preventive, rehabilitative, long-term, and terminal care; they favor physical, rather than mental, health care. The physician who hands the patient what he wants—the sleeping pill—gets him out of the office faster. Her costs for office, secretary, and nurse run roughly the same, whether she handles more or fewer patients. This arrangement offers great temptations to become an artful people mover. To question the patient thoroughly enough to uncover his deeper problem takes time. Why does your Atlas syndrome keep you from letting go of the world for seven hours, or your perfectionist tendency make you lie in bed at night reliving the painful gaffes of the previous day or worrying about the overload of duties that fills the morrow? Transforming the patient's habits demands effective counseling and teaching; and teaching is slow boring through hard wood. Unfortunately, the fee-for-service reward system tends to undercompensate those delivering primary care and overcompensate those working at piecework medicine, thus skewing the medical goods delivered.

Most of us hoped a prepayment, as distinct from a fee-for-service, system would shift the emphasis in care away from acute to preventive medicine. Early preventions can, in some cases, save providers the huge expense of acute interventions later.[20] Accordingly, HMOs created financial incentives for patients to come in for regular physical examination and, through education, to become sophisticated about self-care. The HMOs made some progress in improving preventive medicine. However, their "productivity" standards eventually made it difficult for physicians to spend enough time with patients to counsel and teach them effectively. HMOs have also cut back on caring for the mentally ill and shortened hospital stays for acute care treatment without investing adequately in follow-up care.

Money has skewed and distorted, as well, both the deployment of legal talent and the elaboration and delivery of services. Large law firms and corporations have enjoyed first call on the graduates of prestigious law schools. The money craze has not yet denied legal talent for the bench. Judgeships still carry prestige. But federal and state agencies have suffered; they currently face increasing difficulties in recruiting lawyers, and, even more seriously, in retaining experienced professionals. Their expertise quickly converts into higher paying jobs with corporations doing business with government agencies. The money chase has also weakened traditions of collegiality within law firms and, in the era of instant fortunes, has shortened the young lawyer's frame of reference. As one senior lawyer in a large firm wryly observed, they expect to be millionaires by thirty and they don't expect to remain long in their current jobs.

Money has also affected dramatically the elaboration and moral content of legal services. Some areas of the law have developed recently and rapidly, generously fertilized by money; other fields have lain underdeveloped or have developed but tardily because their monetary rewards were few. Lawyers flocked to and developed the golden fields of commercial and corporate practice. Until recently, the money was not there for practitioners in the fields of family law, environmental law, and product liability.

Money has led to the lopsided development of the law in still further ways. As noted earlier, most professions, but especially the legal profession, gained power as our cities and the merchant class grew. This coincident growth of the legal profession and commerce in the nineteenth century affected the relative balance of power between the several players—legislators, lawyers, and judges—who shaped and applied laws. The expansion of commerce also changed the territorial boundaries (and the significance) of the various fields of legal practice themselves, and it profoundly redefined the conception of justice in which the rule of law finds its grounding.

Following a long period in which merchants chiefly viewed the law as an obstacle to the changes that the burgeoning commercial classes required, merchants between 1790 and 1820 looked to the law as an instrument of change.[21] However, merchants looked to judges, not to legislators or jurors, to bring about changes in the legal environment that would aid and abet commerce. In some respects, that alliance seems surprising. Eager for change, merchants would logically, it would seem, ally themselves with legislators, who make new law, rather than with judges who interpret and apply a huge body of received common law. However, merchants feared that legislatures, acting out of volatile, populist sentiment, might too readily throw up obstacles to commerce or enact laws too local and parochial to encourage commerce to spread beyond a region. Thus, merchants looked to the courts to provide a uniform and predictable body of enabling rules for commerce. Further, they appealed to the courts, especially to the courts located in port cities, to offer decisions hospitable to commerce across state and national boundaries.[22]

This increased confidence of merchants in decisions issuing from the courts would not have occured without a profound change in the very understanding of the common law and the role of judges as its custodians. In the hands of the judges, the common law no longer simply reflected and conserved traditional customs and practices (rooted in the natural law). Rather the common law, as creatively interpreted by judges in new settings, took on the character of legislation—something in part newly made, not wholly received. Eventually, of course, the very success of this adaptation of the legal system into a body of law hospitable to commerce contributed to a deep suspicion of an activist bench that might produce decisions interfering with business practice. Today, neither adversarial lawyers nor conservative legislators want activist judges altering a legal system friendly to commerce which activist judges originally helped create!

The interests of merchants also led to changes in the scope and importance of various fields of legal practice, particularly commercial law as opposed to family law. Before the nineteenth century, families did a large portion of work, either directly through the domestic "putting-out" system or indirectly through the apprenticeship system. The domestic putting-out system sited the home as the place and the family as the social unit for making goods. Further, the apprenticeship system expected the craftsperson filling the master/parent role in the household to accept responsibility for transforming novices into eventual masters of the craft. This quasi-parental relationship of master to apprentice chiefly defined the roles and reciprocal duties of superordinates to subordinates in the workplace. The master served *in loco parentis* to the apprentice, and the apprentice assumed quasi-filial duties to the master. Family law and convention in large part covered the workplace.

With the full emergence of the market economy and the factory system, commercial law superseded family law, such as it was, in the workplace. A purely contractual, monetary relation increasingly defined the relations of employers/employees, sellers/customers, and professionals to one another. The consent of parties alone—the contract—determines the obligations of each to the other. Parties do not take their cues from the household, where the very nature of the relationship defines the duties of parent to child, child to parent, and, by extension, master to apprentice.

Under contract law, the law functions primarily to enforce contracts; it does not serve as a substantive resource for transforming contracts morally. Standards of procedural, rather than substantive, justice largely determine the rule of law in the marketplace. A deal's a deal. Admittedly, contracts do not trump any and all other considerations. One cannot contract oneself into slavery. Courts can also refuse to enforce contracts contrary to public policy or contracts that the courts find unconscionable. However, contract law looks largely to such procedural questions as whether coercion or fraud contaminated the agreement and then requires both parties to honor the contract whatever its moral content. The law cannot go behind the contract to pose such traditional moral questions as to whether the contract specified a just wage or a fair price. A contract cannot be voided because an agreed upon price is exorbitant or because a wage agreement falls below a living wage, as long as it meets the policy standard of a minimum wage. On the contrary, such appeals to substantive justice would, in a market system, undermine the rule of law. They would surely disrupt the free flow of market exchanges under the iron law of supply and demand. Further, such traditional moral standards have long since lost their grounding in natural law; they seem merely to rationalize arbitrary, subjective, groundless interferences into contractual consent, which alone creates enforceable duties. An activist bench would have no higher ground in substantive justice on which to base interventions.

The point of this brief narrative is not to rouse nostalgia. It suggests rather that the marketplace is not simply a sea in which the legal profession is awash. Lawyers helped create the sea. The law is not simply a profession whose commitment to disinterested and transformational exchanges has weakened to the degree that lawyers, like all other professionals, must hustle in a market-driven world of interested transactions. Lawyers have distinctively contributed to the very creation of this market-driven world by the remaking of the law itself. By reducing justice largely to procedural justice alone, lawyers tossed out those traditional substantive constraints on self-interest implied by the notion of a just wage and a just price. Employers simply contract with employees, and the contract alone wholly defines the employers' responsibility. Thus lawyers, who once benefited from the transformation of their lives through an apprenticeship system that gave them their professional identity, have mightily helped both employers and the society at large shed their transformational duties.

Money excludes; it sets up new barriers, even as it breaks some old ones down. Money opens doors, but usually only to those who can wield it. Those who can't get into the marketplace, don't get the goods. That arrangement works out acceptably enough in the purchase of optional commodities—such as a walkman, a tie, or a scarf. But professionals presumably generate and offer not optional commodities, but fundamental goods—crucial to human life and growth: physicians assist healing, crucial to life; lawyers, equality before the law, crucial to justice; the military and the police, defense and protection, crucial to security; the clergy, spiritual flourishing. When such fundamental goods do not reach everyone, something has gone deeply awry. Some forty-three million people in the United States in 2000 lacked health care insurance, and another forty million were underinsured. The numbers are rising rapidly since many companies are dropping or curtailing insurance coverage for employees in response to rising insurance costs. Without access to healing, people suffer a triple deprivation: the misery of the illness, the desperation of no treatment, and the cruel proof on the part of the society that they do not really belong. The untreated ill become strangers and sojourners in their own land. So even while money leaps over and seeps under boundaries and enclaves, it also excludes.

Some defenders of current legal practice argue that we should rely on the marketplace alone to distribute legal services to the populace through the varying arrangements of fees for services, retainers fees, salaries (for in-house counsel), and contingency fees. Contingency fees extend legal services to the modestly fixed and the poor because they require no up-front money from the client. These varied arrangements obviate the need, so the argument goes, either for a societal commitment to a third-party payment system extending legal services to the poor or for a professional commitment to *pro bono publico* service.

The contingency fee system, of course, has generated criticism, especially from doctors (and corporations) who look longingly at Great Britain, which has altogether banned contingency fee arrangements and indeed requires the loser to pay lawyer's fees for the winner in a court case. Other critics of contingency fees argue that the device does not satisfactorily solve the need to distribute legal services widely and fairly. Contingency fees, as a device for providing universal access to the good of legal care, fail at several points:[23]

- Current law bans the resort to contingency fees in family law (divorce and custody), thus leaving many people too poor to secure legal services in these cases. Yet lifting the ban against contingency fees in family law would generate other problems, such as tempting lawyers to go for more money and thus exacerbate already inflamed domestic disputes. Current law also bans contingency fees in criminal cases. However, even without the ban, the results in such cases would not often or appropriately convert into a schedule of contingency payments.
- Lawyers cannot easily or accurately calibrate contingency payments to most civil suits except for personal injury cases and thus might tend to generate or pull complaints in the direction of personal injury.
- A contingency reward system tends to discourage lawyers from taking cases in which the payoff will not be large (thus denying justice to clients whose potential recovery for damages may be small in the lawyer's eyes but fateful for the client) or from taking cases in which the client's cause, from the lawyer's perspective, is not a sure thing (thus denying to citizens recourse to the law in cases that fall in the vast territory of the gray).
- A contingency fee system does not provide adequate coverage to resourceless people who do not need a full press in court, but simply a timely letter from a lawyer to persuade a bully to back off.

For these several reasons, one cannot expect the contingency fee system to meet fully the needs for distributive justice. One needs a greater societal commitment to fund public interest law, a greater professional commitment to *pro bono publico* work, and an expansion of efforts at alternative conflict resolution.

The Soul of the Professions

The rule of money imposes losses on clients and patients and the society at large when the professional exchange diminishes altogether to a commercial transaction. What of the loss to the professionals themselves? What goods internal to the practice of medicine and law do professionals forfeit to the degree that they yield to the enticements and hazards of the marketplace and increasingly work for that modern winner in the marketplace, the large organization?

The goods internal to the practice of doctoring and lawyering are the *arts* of doctoring and lawyering. We cannot adequately describe either law or medicine as an applied science. When we interpret and organize either profession simply as an applied science, we lose the soul of the activity.

We can argue the claim that medicine is an art either weakly and provisionally or strongly and intrinsically. In its weaker form, we describe medicine as an art only temporarily in the sense that we have not yet perfected it as a science. Once we have perfected medicine fully as a science, then we can straightforwardly apply the relevant general principles of the science to the particular case of the patient which falls wholly within the orbits of those principles. When practitioners claim medicine as an art only provisionally, they sound rather apologetic, as though they want simply to protect a place for themselves and their slender store of experience in turf increasingly occupied by scientists or by the managers of the huge warehouses of knowledge and equipment located in tertiary care centers.

In its stronger form, we claim healing as an art, not merely provisionally but intrinsically. It is an art and it will remain an art. A scientist traffics in universals and therefore must abstract from the particular. To achieve its generalization, a scientific hypothesis must abstract from the complexity of the universe; it selects for description a particular set of recurrent phenomena, isolated from all the variables in which they might be embedded, and seeks to arrive at a generalization that covers the phenomena under scrutiny. Science reduces water to the abstract formula of H_2O. The poet Yeats complained, I like a little seaweed in my definition of water. Artists traffic in the concrete. Poets leave in some variables. They offer not universals, but a concrete universe—Lear's universe, Antigone's world, and Michelangelo's *Pieta*.

We can define healing as an art because the individual patient whom it serves does not merely illustrate a general scientific principle into which the patient entirely disappears. Each patient is a full-bodied person with her own history and universe, seaweed and all. Her diabetes may, more or less, illustrate a generalization about the particular disease. But we cannot tidily abstract the host from the disease or the disease from the host.

Diagnosing and treating the disease and helping the ill person face her disease require knowing the patient, her habits, her world, her pressures, and strains.[24] These complex undertakings surely draw on science, but the physician must artfully marshal the generalizations of science to heal the person rather than merely treat the disease. The healer cannot prescind from the universe which accompanies the patient in order to handle a detail that fits and confirms an abstract rule. We cannot, however, lay on each and every specialized physician the complex task of knowing the patient's habits, world, pressures, and strains. Specialists operate within the boundaries of their technical competence and contribute limitedly but importantly to the total array of scientific information that assists effective treatment. But in the era of fragmented diagnostic services and often competing treatment options, directorial responsibility must be located somewhere. Otherwise the patient can find himself cut adrift, acting somewhat anxiously as his own primary care physician and making fateful choices without the steadying presence of a healer.

Institutional pressures today favor interpreting medicine as a retailable, applied science. The reduction of medicine to an applied science fits conveniently into the current corporatization of health care. If doctoring merely applies science or technical expertise, then one can diagnose, treat, and heal at a distance, the very considerable distance of an 800 number, for instance, with a case manager at the other end of the phone and with a recipe book in hand. The doctor becomes retailer and dispenser of interventions authorized elsewhere.

But, as a psychiatrist remarked to me, every thoughtful psychiatrist knows that the better you get to know a patient, the more difficult it is to classify the patient under one of the diseases listed in the DSM IV. The patient does not conveniently vanish into the scientist's law.

The doctor uses science, but healing also requires practical wisdom in bringing science artfully to bear in order to restore harmony to the patient's universe. That healing is the end purpose of doctoring.

Such doctoring takes time; whereas the name of the new art in managed care is saving time. In the name of productivity, the doctor's average contact time with patients has dropped from twenty-seven minutes to sixteen minutes and less. The technique of moving people rapidly through a system has become almost an art. Walt Disney was its twentieth-century master. Disney's theme parks enclose an expensive piece of finite space that imposes chronic, core costs. One makes money therefore by moving people through them efficiently and rapidly. (I belong to a golf club that learned its lesson from Disney. The corporation that owns and runs the club has kept trees to minimum. Why? Trees block golf shots; trees also shed leaves that make balls harder to find; thus trees slow up the game. Increase the trees, and golf scores would be higher, players less happy, the playing time longer, and the course unable to support as many members and thus yield as large a profit to the owners.) After I offered some of these remarks in the course of grand rounds at a distinguished teaching hospital, my hosts reported that the hospital had invited in as consultants just a few weeks earlier two experts from the Disney Corporation. Learning how to hustle people happily through a system surely increases profits, if it does not perhaps qualify as an art. We already talk somewhat inelegantly of the commodification and the corporatization of health care; this commodification and corporatization ends in its Disneyfication.

A parallel loss of the art occurs in the law. Dean Anthony T. Kronman argues in *The Lost Lawyer: Failing Ideals of the Legal Profession* that the traditional ideal of the lawyer statesman required "the attainment of a wisdom that lies beyond technique—a wisdom about human beings and their tangled affairs that anyone who wishes to provide real deliberative counsel must possess."[25] He holds that the *virtue* of practical wisdom, which the lawyer needs in respecting the particularities of a case, distinguishes the practitioner's art from some variety of applied social science.[26] However, scientific realism (and its dominant heirs in legal education today—the law-and-economics and critical legal studies movements) has supported ". . . an ideal of legal science that is antagonistic to the common law tradition and to the claims of practical wisdom which that tradition has always honored."[27] The ideal of legal science dominates legal scholarship today and increasingly, in Kronman's judgment, will dominate the class-room. "There are others, of course, who think that the aim of legal education is the cultivation of practical wisdom. But their numbers are declining and the authority of their position weakens year by year. The future lies with their adversaries, with those who want to make law teaching an adjunct of legal scholarship and to define its goals in similar terms."[28]

Kronman does not expect to see a reversal of these tendencies as long as the best and the brightest of the young graduates of law schools go to work in large firms or for the in-house staffs of corpo-rations. The swelling size of firms, the spread of branch offices, the concentration on minuscule skills, the dehumanizing length of the workday, and the increasingly hierarchical, rather than collegial, organization of the great firms have combined to produce an envi-ronment in the law comparable to that of corporate medicine. The generalist disappears; the large firms function like tertiary care health centers that bring highly specialized information to bear in acute cri-sis. Relations to clients become more distanced and episodic rather than continuing and holistic. Such firms offer technical, instrumental advice and orient to preset goals, sometimes at the expense of responding to the client's deeper needs. Kronman writes:

> Deliberative advice—advice about ends a client ought to choose, as opposed to the means for reaching ends already chosen—pre-supposes a familiarity with the client's past and a breadth of understanding of his or her present situation, which the move-ment toward a more transactional and specialized form of law practice has gone a long way toward destroying in the country's largest firms. As a result, lawyers in these firms are today less often called upon to give advice that requires real prudence as distinct from technical knowledge.[29]

Nor can we expect judges today to preserve a tradition of practical wisdom which the law schools and the huge firms have largely aban-doned. To mention only two major obstacles: judges face huge case loads today and they must rely increasingly on law clerks to draft their opinions in some dizzying, Disney-like effort to keep the cases moving through the system.

In varying ways, Kronman believes, the courts, law schools, and law firms today fail to encourage and sustain the art of lawyering and

the practical wisdom which its high practice requires. Nor is he optimistic about the capacity of any of these institutions, as currently
structured, to restore that ideal. However, his pessimism does not
lead him to dismiss the call to practice the ideal; and he recognizes
the possibility that in less driven, more modest, small-scale settings,
committed lawyers might bear witness to that ideal.

Two major articles in *The Business Lawyer* take opposing views of
the increasing shift from professional to commercial values in large
firms. In an article on "Multidisciplinary Practice" (MDP), Dean
Daniel R. Fischel of the University of Chicago Law School[30] sings
the praises of one-stop shopping, in which a large firm offers clients/
customers, in addition to legal services, the convenience of investment advice, insurance, consulting, and other goods and services. He
sees this commercialization of practice as the most important development in the last hundred years and quite inevitable if law firms
would seriously compete with the big-five accounting firms, already
engaged in multidisciplinary practice. Fischel abruptly dismisses the
loss of traditional professional values with a "So what?" Who needs
professional values? Buyers will eventually punish sellers when they
don't get what they want. Thus Fischel reaffirms that faith in the self-
correcting powers of the marketplace, which Milton Friedman popularized long ago. The mechanism of the marketplace dispenses with
the need for either federal regulations or guild discipline. Dean Fischel's economic libertarianism would seem to vindicate Dean Kronman's pessimism about the future of law as a distinctive profession.

However, it would appear that the profession will not go down
without a fight and its champions include some figures in the major
leagues. Three months after Dean Fischel's article, Lawrence J. Fox
(a partner, Drinker, Biddle, and Reath, LPD and former chair of the
ABA Standing Committee on Ethics and Public Responsibility)
delivered a scathing attack on Daniel Fischel's apologia called "Dan's
World: A Free Enterprise Dream; An Ethics Nightmare."[31] Fox
details the losses. Lawyers who profess the law need some measure of
independence and integrity. To stand by the law, they need to be able
to say "no" to the client even though it may mean losing the client.
But saying "no" becomes more difficult when the client is also a
major customer buying investment advice and many other lucrative
services from the MDP. Further, MDPs cannot avoid conflicts of
interest, actual or imputed. The same one-stop shopping center will
inevitably find itself offering legal services to one client and handling

other kinds of services to other customers who may compete with or end up in legal disputes with the first client. The internal flow of information within the organization (which MDPs currently advertise as an advantage under the banner of accessible expertise) compromises assurances of confidentiality. An MDP also creates an impossible cocktail of conflicting professional obligations: its auditors are obliged to attest publicly; yet its lawyers must treat information as confidential and privileged; and its business vendors must seize upon whatever information they can gather to clinch sales. Fox finds it naïve at best, cynical at worst, to hold that the purported self-correcting mechanisms of the marketplace will compensate for the dilution and dissolution of these core values.

The very existence of Fox's counterattack against Fischel suggests that Kronman's pessimism about the future of the practice of the law may insufficiently attend to the differences in moral culture that can develop from one large firm to another (and from one law school to another). Size alone need not predetermine behavior. In corporate America, the size of a business does not of itself determine its capacity for social responsibility. While the tendencies Kronman identifies and Fischel exemplifies are worrisome, they are not, in principle, irreversible or unexceptionable. Kronman also overlooks the possibility that better forms of practice, worked out in small firms, may eventually cross the border and influence the culture of the profession at large. He may also be a tad too pessimistic about the long-term capacity of law schools to turn around. As the next chapter makes clear, his voice is not alone among educators in its plea for a recovery of the lawyer's vocation. The struggle between mechanism and soul is not over. In the interim, we cannot cavalierly condemn the role of money as it feeds, motivates, energizes, and mobilizes talent, and, in part, as it distributes goods. Money is a useful but unruly servant and a vicious master. Whatever the setting, we ought not let its unruliness distract us from our commitment to what patients and clients have reason in our common tradition to hope for: healing here; sanctuary here.

Notes

1. For the details on this flocking of the professions to the corporations, see Derek Bok, the former dean of Harvard Law School and president of Harvard University, in *The Cost of Talent: How Executives and Professionals Are Paid and How It Affects America* (New York: Maxwell Macmillan International, 1993).
2. The U.S. Supreme Court, in *Virginia Pharmacy Bd. v Virginia Consumer Council*, 425 US 748, 96 S. Ct. 1817, 48 L. Ed. 2d 346 (1976), held that a state statute prohibiting the advertising of prescription drug prices violated the protection of the First Amendment.
3. The U.S. Supreme Court, in *Bates v State Bar of Arizona*, 433 US 350, 97 S. Ct. 2691, 53 L. Ed. 2 d 810 (1977), upheld the right of two Arizona attorneys, operating a legal clinic for persons of modest resources, to advertise the prices of their services.
4. Thomas D. Morgan and Ronald D. Rotunda's report on the survey conducted by the ABA Special Committee to Survey Legal Needs in *Professional Responsibility, Problems and Materials*, 4th ed. (The Foundation Press, 1987), 304–5 and 305 fn. 33.
5. Roscoe Pound, "The Lawyer from Antiquity to Modern Times" (St. Paul: West, 1953), 5.
6. Alasdair MacIntyre offers the following definition: *"A virtue is an acquired human quality the possession and exercise of which tends to enable us to achieve those goods which are internal to practices and the lack of which effectively prevents us from achieving any such goods." After Virtue: A Study of Moral Theory* (Notre Dame, Indiana: University of Notre Dame Press, 1981), 178 (emphasis in original).
7. Justin A. Stanley, "Professionalism and Commercialism," *Montana Law Review*, vol. 50 (1989): 9.
8. See Debra Baker, "Who Wants to Be a Millionaire?" *American Bar Association Journal* (February 2000): 37–43.
9. Quoted by Vanessa Blum in the *Legal Times*, April 3, 2000, 20.
10. Marc Rodwin, *Medicine, Money, and Morals: Physicians' Conflicts of Interest* (Oxford: Oxford University Press, 1995), 55.
11. Harold S. Tuft called the use of such tests "so common as to be almost standard practice; yet some clinicians would argue that few of the tests . . . [were] actually necessary." Rodwin, *Medicine, Money, and Morals*, 55. Under fee-for-service practice, related financial incentives to physicians could either slant decisions about the treatment of patients or increase worrisomely the number of tests and procedures ordered. Physicians could:

   - receive kickbacks for referrals to hospitals, specialists, clinical laboratories, and medical suppliers;
   - earn income by referring patients to medical facilities in which physicians themselves have invested, a practice which, in effect, constitutes self-referral;
   - dispense drugs and sell medical products;
   - sell medical practices to hospitals and, more recently, to HMOs;
   - receive payments from hospitals in the course of being recruited to a particular practice;
   - receive gifts from medical suppliers.

12. Rodwin, *Medicine, Money, and Morals*, 17.
13. *New York Times*, October 26, 1993.
14. The California Blue Cross, for example, cut payments to doctors from 1994 to 1998 by as much as 40 to 50 percent for some procedures. *New York Times*, June 28, 1998, B6.
15. See the *New York Times*, June 28, 1998, 1.
16. Arnold S. Relman, "Why Johnny Can't Operate; The Crisis of Medical Training in America," *The New Republic*, October 2, 2000, 37–43.
17. Bok, *The Cost of Talent*, 153.
18. Bok, 140.
19. Bok, 142.
20. Alvan R. Feinstein of the Yale University School of Medicine, in the unpublished paper "Is a Pound of Prevention Worth an Ounce of Cure?", challenges the claim that preventive medicine in the form of screening large populations generally saves money, as compared with the proper diagnosis and treatment of symptomatic disease. Specialist physicians profit from the widespread use of screening procedures, but it is doubtful whether such screening (for prostate cancer, for example) can be justified by a cost/benefit analysis.
21. For what follows in these paragraphs on the law, see Morton J. Horwitz, *The Transformation of American Law, 1780–1960* (Cambridge Mass.: Harvard University Press, 1977).
22. In the nineteenth century, the power of trial judges also expanded at the expense of juries. The expansion of judicial power included: (1) the designation of special cases reserved to judges alone; (2) the setting aside of jury verdicts harmful to commerce or the awarding of new trials for verdicts contrary to the weight of evidence; and (3) the restriction of juries to questions of fact, reserving questions of the law exclusively to judges. Horwitz, *The Transformation of American Law*, 142.
23. Bok, *The Cost of Talent*, 138–43.
24. In *The Healer's Art: A New Approach to the Doctor-Patient Relationship* (Philadelphia: Lippincott, 1976), 48, Eric Cassell writes: "Disease . . . is something an organ has; illness is something a man has."
25. Anthony T. Kronman, *The Lost Lawyer: Failing Ideals of the Legal Profession* (Cambridge, Mass.: Harvard University Press, 1993), 2.
26. Kronman, 165–270.
27. Kronman, 267.
28. Kronman, 269.
29. Kronman, 290.
30. Daniel R. Fischel, "Multidisciplinary Practice," *The Business Lawyer*, May 2000, vol. 55, no. 3.
31. Lawrence J. Fox, "Dan's World: A Free Enterprise Dream; An Ethics Nightmare," *The Business Lawyer*, August, 2000, vol. 55, no. 4.

Chapter 2

Adversarialism in America and the Professions

The Law

Lawyers, journalists, and other professionals do not simply impose adversarialism on their citizens. Adversarialism as a professional ideal reflects an adversarial *animus* already at work in the society at large. Combativeness does not distinguish lawyers or journalists from their fellow citizens. It answers to something deep in the American spirit.

Not that adversarialism is purely destructive. The modern conviction that journalists must challenge the high and mighty or that lawyers should speak for the resourceless derives from the earliest religious and cultural traditions of the West. The Hebrew prophets upbraided the powerful and took up the cause of the widow, the orphan, and the stranger as God's own. Sophocles' Antigone, surely the most impressive lawyer in all literature, defied Creon the king and demanded the right, the duty, to bury her brother even though a traitor, a mortal enemy of the State. Thereby she insisted that a state cannot wholly reduce a person to the political terrain, to the purposes of the state, subject to its will alone. She invoked what Jacques Maritain has called the extraterritoriality of the person.[1] Behind the metaphor lies the laconic sentence of Thomas Aquinas: "Man is not formed for political fellowship in his entirety or in all that he has." A person is not wholly exhausted by his association with the state. A vast territory of the soul escapes its power. Modern democracy reflects this conviction when it construes a professional's loyalty to the client as a public duty. A democracy thus extends its protection and services to those at odds with the society or whose experience of distress has pitched them out beyond the habits of civil life. In effect, through the adversary system some dignity attaches even to being wrong.[2]

To the degree that the professional protects the lawbreaker, the deviant, the defiant, and the distressed, she also serves the society. The principle of extraterritoriality implies that the professional, for the sake of the common good, cannot act simply as an agent of the state. Her loyalty to her client protects society against the totalitarian tendencies of the government. The principle of confidentiality, the prohibition against conflicts of interest, the distinction between the prosecutorial, defense, and judicial functions of the law all serve to protect liberty in which the public itself has a stake. Hence the lawyer serves as an "officer of the court" even when she defends a client against the state's prosecution.

A second, very different justification for the adversary system cites its value, not simply in protecting the powerless in criminal cases, but in advancing in civil disputes the causes of emergent, dynamic parties in the society, from whose plans and projects the society may eventually stand to benefit. Insofar as it orients a society to precedent, the common law tradition is inherently conservative. However, the adversary system injects some flexibility into law. It lets a variety of dynamic individuals and institutional leaders (inventors, entrepreneurs, reformers, developers, corporate executives, and visionaries) push the law (and their opponents) to the limit, while still operating within a legal framework. In effect, the adversary system is an enabler, particularly on the frontier of nongovernmental innovation and development. It gives creative forces within the community some wiggle room under the law; it lets the society be law-abiding yet dynamic.

Although this second justification for the adversary system figures less prominently in the rhetoric of democracy, it variously drives both lawyers and the powerful clients for whom lawyers largely work today in the private sector. The client, today, has become (increasingly) the powerful organization, and only resembles minimally the solitary, resourceless individual in whose name and for whose protection professional duties to the client assumed such proportions in the early codes of the profession and in the rhetoric of democracy. More often than not, the talented lawyer today works either directly for a major corporation, or for a firm largely devoted to its service.

These large organizations, meanwhile, turn toward competitors a self-interested, adversarial face. Self-interest drives corporations as they compete with one another for survival and supremacy; and self-interest guides them as they bargain with other groups organized according to different interests—labor, the media, consumers, farmers, and the like—all pawing the ground and swinging their horns at shifting allies and enemies as opportunity presents. Such subgroups within the society only marginally interpret themselves—and often for PR reasons—as having an obligation to the common good. They operate as factions within the society rather than as publics within the public at large.

Finally, this adversarial vision of interest group pitted against interest group sees the government itself as the product of a deal between all self-interested parties. This social contract legitimates the government as the protective framework within which all parties can pursue their own interests with the least inconvenience to themselves. The political vision of John Locke, especially his *Second Treatise of Government*, helps clarify the eventual development of interest group politics in the United States; and it illuminates the connections between adversarialism in the law and adversarialism in the society at large. The Lockean myth helped shape both civic consciousness and the perceptions and tasks of the professional class. (Influential historians, such as Carl Becker and Louis Hartz, saw the spirit of Lockean individualism as pervasive in America.[3] Other commentators have recognized that a wide variety of causes contribute to the power of adversarialism in America: religious pluralism, ethnic diversity, an open frontier, social mobility, the harshness of its climate, and the even harsher intellectual climate of Social Darwinism. Still, Locke's *Second Treatise* offers a convenient way of exploring important features of the American civic consciousness—both as it shapes the professional and as it defines the professional task adversarially.)

The first section of this chapter contains two parts: first, it offers an exploded diagram of the Lockean political myth; then, it applies this political myth to the prevailing interpretation of the professional relationship. A story acquires mythic proportions precisely because it offers an important way of ordering the experience of a people. John Locke, in effect, tells a story of political origins that accounts for the relative place of the state and civic order in human life. His story of origins has nothing to do with the deeds of a founding hero, a Romulus or a Remus, a Mazzini, a Garibaldi, a Washington, or a Ho Chi Minh. Rather his account of the origins and aims of government focuses on a primal political deal.

The political theory that justifies cutting that deal rests on at least five elements. First, it describes the original condition of humankind, prior to the social contract, as marked by individual autonomy but marred by threats to that autonomy. Second, it assumes that any subsequent civil society must work to satisfy interests and wants rather than attain moral ideals. Third, it traces the origin of the state to the threat of a supreme evil rather than to the inspiration of a supreme good. Fourth, it encourages a passive rather than an active understanding of citizenship. And, finally, it authorizes leaders to manage transactions rather than guide transformations.

These five Lockean elements, in turn, shape a dominant way of interpreting the professional relationship. The professional, like the state, derives original power from the threat of evil. This threat defines the role of the professional as adversarial. The client correspondingly thinks of himself as the relatively passive beneficiary of the power which the professional wields on his behalf. Further, the professional, like the political, contract basically satisfies wants rather than pursues ideals; thus it encourages a transactional rather than a transformational understanding of the professional relationship. This Lockean vision, in summary, offers what I have in the preceding chapter on money and the professions called a contractualist (or transactional) rather than a covenantal (or transformational) understanding of both political and professional relationships. In my judgment, this contractarian and adversarial outlook dominates, though it does not exhaustively and fatefully define, the American character.

The Political Myth

The very notion of a social contract—the central idea in Locke's political philosophy—assumes that we can properly assess current social arrangements only if we measure them against a time when the social contract was not. Locke called this pre-political time the state of nature. The "state of nature" partly describes for Locke an actual, original state of affairs, but also posits a natural, undistorted ideal condition, in which each enjoys autonomy, a kind of executive and legislative power over his or her own life. Each is born "absolute lord of his own person and possessions; equal to the greatest and subject to nobody."[4] This definition of autonomy associates freedom with a kind of negative liberty—that is, a freedom from interference at the hands of others, a right to do, not absolutely, but largely as one pleases, as long as one's actions do not interfere with the similar autonomy and authority of others, or undercut, as in the act of suicide, the very possibility of the self's own further action.

Second, free and autonomous individuals would leave this state of nature and enter into a social contract only if and as it serves their self-interest. The very concept of a social contract implies that self-interest, rather than moral ideals, supplies the *Arche*, the basic energy, the ruling principle, that establishes and preserves civil society. Like any marketplace transaction between merchants, the contract justifies itself by serving the interests of all parties to the agreement. All share the rational desire for a government that maximally protects the wants and interests of each. Locke does not envisage a state which heroes found and sustain through their sacrifices. No Washington or Lincoln figures in Locke's story line.

Since such a society cannot rely on heroic self-sacrifice or various interior moral transformations of its citizens to hold it together, it needs a series of mechanisms that will keep the power of self-interest within bounds and yet mobilize its energies to serve the aggregate interests of most citizens. In the perspective of interest group politics, the United States has depended upon four basic mechanisms to accomplish these purposes. The Constitution of the United States heads the list.

The framers of the Constitution recognized the need for a government that would restrain, without eliminating, self-interest in human life, because eliminating self-interest and factionalism would also eradicate the liberty at their root. Thus they devised a mechanism which, far from curtailing self-interest, would actually use its omnipresent power to limit its negative effects. The devices they adopted are familiar: they separated powers into legislative, executive, and judicial, and they divided powers between local, state, and national centers. These devices would not eliminate the drive of self-interest in human affairs, but would pit ambition against ambition so they would limit each other. No person, faction, or majority can dominate all others. Through this device of countervailing powers, the framers sought to solve the problem of governance that human nature posed (what James Madison called the "defect of better motives").[5]

Second, Americans rely on the mechanism of the free marketplace. Adam Smith assumed that people act out of self-interest. A society need not exhort the butcher to act according to public virtue; he need simply be a good butcher, which serves his self-interest. His rigorous pursuit of his own interests will eventually add, through the mechanism of complex market exchanges, to the common wealth of a nation. The marketplace assumes technical and personal virtue in those who participate in its exchanges, not public virtue. Workers and shopkeepers can pursue their own interests without a wandering eye on the common good. The latter will result invisibly and eventually from the self-interested pursuits of each.

The free market eventually produced a third mechanism: the large-scale organization. It contributes to social life by mobilizing professional skills. This organization of technical skills gives the corporation the advantages of superior productivity and efficiency over "ma and pa" stores. The large organization depends, to be sure, upon semi-public virtues in its personnel—cooperativeness, orderliness, and the personal discipline required to develop specialized skills; but, on the whole, it places no extraordinary demands upon its workers. It offers people the opportunity to do great things without themselves being great. Rather than heroism, it requires only a self-interested careerism that will enable employees to perform assigned tasks within a larger whole. The large organization encourages managers to develop the art of politics—the ability to act in concert with others—but the art of politics shorn of its traditional object—the *common* good. Managers need only serve the primary mission of the organization from which the private advantage of its members can be mediately derived.

Finally, the mechanism of the modern, positivist university does not pretend, in the fashion of the ancient academy, to prepare people for citizenship or to cultivate virtue in its citizens, but rather to develop skills. The marketplace, and especially the large-scale organization that flourishes within it, needs trained people. Both look to the university to supply them. Meanwhile, the university aims to produce and transmit objective knowledge, an aim which by definition excludes subjective moral questions from the classroom. By implication, graduates can do largely what they please with their acquired knowledge and skills for their own private and intellectually unassailable reasons. Consequently, careerists have graduated from professional schools and promptly flocked to the large corporations which the universities of thirty thousand to forty thousand students increasingly came to resemble.

These four mechanisms have reinforced one another in American life. The universities train people to serve corporations that compete in the marketplace within a constitutional framework; and none of these mechanisms demands more than prudent self-interest from individual citizens. So goes the theory in each of its contributing parts.

Lockean theory of the social contract offers a third baseline: its account of the state's origin. In classical Greek and several other strands of thought, the state originates in a *Summum Bonum*; it derives variously from the beneficent work of the gods, the sacrifice of heroes, the natural sociality of humankind, the philosopher's approximation of eternal ideas, or the supervening activity of providence. The state derived from a supreme good undertakes a positive mission above and beyond the protection of citizens from the evils of theft, murder, invasions, and strife; it must enhance the common good and enable its citizens to achieve levels of personal excellence unattainable apart from communal life. (The biblical tradition in I Samuel more complexly derived the state both from the positive intentions of God and from God's somewhat reluctant accommodation to a negative, the sinfulness of humankind. But the biblical tradition never so completely derived the state from sin as to place it utterly beyond God's purposes.)

Social contract theory, unlike biblical and classical theory, traced the origin of the state not to a supreme good, but to a supreme evil. Thomas Hobbes heads this tradition, characterizing the original state of nature as one of relentless war. In their natural condition, humans (imagined apart from the existence of the state) endure "continual fear and danger of violent death." This miserable condition results less from human helplessness before a harsh and inclement natural environment than from the predatory assaults of human nature itself. Innately, a boundless lust for goods and glory motivates humans and creates enmity between them. Thus they enter into the social contract to protect themselves from themselves. They create and hand over to the state a monopoly over the power of death (the power to enforce contracts, to jail, to execute, and to make war) in order to shield themselves from the violent death that they would surely meet without the protection of the state. Thus, the state rests on a negative—what Gerald Strauss in his studies of Hobbes called a *Summum Malum*. The fear of death crowds us together according to the Hobbesian account of origins.[6]

Although Locke paints in somewhat lighter colors, he hardly works in pastels.[7] Like Hobbes, he founds the state in the provocation of a negative. Men compact together not because they want a common good, but because a common evil threatens them. What, after all, could prompt a self-interested man in the state of nature to "give up his empire" as "absolute lord of his own person and possessions" except that he experiences a severe threat to the enjoyment of his goods and stands to gain some protection through the exchange? While the original condition of man is lordly and autonomous, unfortunately the security of his status is "very uncertain and constantly exposed to the invasion of others." The enjoyment of property is equally "unsafe and very insecure," and freedom is "full of fears and continual dangers." Thus man surrenders a portion of his powers, legislative and executive, to escape the "inconveniences of nature."

Clearly, for Locke, the state derives its powers, not from a positive aspiration, either divine or human, but from negative threats. Indeed, the state would overstep its negative functions if it appropriated to itself more positive goals. The state must chiefly aim to protect persons and property against the threat of enemies without and thieves and murderers within and not to undertake any further tasks to enhance the common good or to assist its citizens to attain personal excellence. Since, moreover, self-interest establishes the social contract, citizens have the right to dissolve the contract or withdraw from it, if and as the sovereign should fail to keep his side of the bargain either by failing to provide basic protection or by exercising additional, arbitrary powers.

Apologists for this Lockean liberal understanding of the state believe that a merely negative justification for the state keeps it limited. But ironically the emphasis on negative threats can encourage the state to enlarge its powers. The fear of the negative so dominates the modern psyche that it tends to justify any and all efforts to fight the evil *du jour*. The defense department in a government usually finds it easier than other units to expand its budget, even in times of financial stringency. Advocates for other items in the budget usually like to cast their arguments in the negative rhetoric of battle: the war against disease or the war on poverty. Most dictators have usually enlarged their power not through the good that they would promote, but through the evils from which they would protect their nations. Hitler needed his Jews, Stalin, his *kulaks*, and Senator McCarthy, his communists, to inflate themselves in the eyes of their followers.

Further, the negative myth about origins contributes to and reflects the power of the otherwise private emotion of resentment in modern politics. In a sense, humiliation and resentment give birth to the Lockean state. In its original condition, humanity enjoys, at least ideally, freedom, autonomy, property, and equality. But the individual cannot protect his own life, liberty, and property; this weakness forces him, in Locke's terms, to "give up," "part with" a portion of his sovereignty and necessitates a humiliating surrender.[8] In our first act as a citizen, we capitulate (consentingly, in a sense, but also compelled by threat).

Moreover, the protection we acquire through the exchange—protection for our persons and property—chiefly secures our private life.

Therefore, we view the social contract with all the natural suspicion that we bring to other commercial transactions. We look at politics and politicians as we look at any other item bought to see whether the purchase gives fair value or whether we have been had. The social contract makes governing, not what we do, but what we consent to and continue to buy with taxes. We quickly resent it should it fail to support our pursuit of private goals.

The liberal myth treats the citizen as a passive beneficiary rather than an active participant in politics. Michael Walzer has observed that the Lockean citizen acts fully at only two points: at a pre-political moment to create the state, and at a post-political moment to dissolve it through revolution.[9] In between inception and revolution, Lockean theory assumes that the state will protect the citizen, who thus may pursue private wants, interests, and happiness. Politics concerns the Lockean citizen only temporarily when the state intrudes on private happiness. We lose the sense of public and communal happiness, found in working actively together with others for a common good.

Finally, to borrow terms from James MacGregor Burns,[10] the Lockean vision encourages a transactional, rather than a transformational, understanding of political leadership. Transactional leaders take at face value the preferences and interests of people and strike off the best bargain they can in gratifying wants. They do not move beyond wants to deeper needs. They dare not address, much less seek to transform, the citizen's character. Transactional leadership denies the validity of criticism or transformation.

This vision of the political order in its most stringent libertarian form allows for no concept of the common good other than a fortuitous aggregate of the overlapping private interests of individuals or groups of individuals who are members of the society. The politician acts as broker, negotiator, bargainer, and compromiser—pure and simple. The politician who appeals to the public interest, except in matters of security, uses empty rhetoric; and the leader who advocates action or education on behalf of his or her own notion of the common good risks displaying a dangerous pride.

The Political Myth As It Shapes
the Professional Transaction

Structurally, the professional's relationship to the client resembles the relationship of the Lockean state to the citizen. Both the state and the professional owe their original authority to a threat. Both the citizen and the client benefit relatively passively from powers others exercise. Both the citizen and the client are basically active at only two moments: the points of entry and exit when they establish and dissolve ties. These structural similarities frame the other resemblances between the Lockean social contract and the contract that usually obtains between client and professional. The client-professional relationship orients to negative liberty, satisfies wants rather than pursues ideals, and encourages a transactional, rather than a transformational, understanding of the professional exchange.

Just as the state derives its authority from its capacity to protect the citizen from a negative, so professionals draw authority from their power to protect clients from lawsuits, plagues, and other threats to their well-being. Men and women would be better off if they could survive in a state of nature without the interventions of the professional. Unimpaired sovereignty is the ideal state of being. However, the client needs the professional to handle problems that exceed his competence and power. We hear the advice "You need a doctor," or "get a good lawyer," when we need someone to battle for us against sickness, disease, death, theft, or jail.

These negative roots of professional authority lead to an adversarial understanding of the professional task. The modern physician largely defines himself or herself as a fighter in the war against disease, suffering, and death. Medicine generalized from the germ theory of disease and interpreted all disease, along with the underlying professional task, in military terms. Correspondingly, the patient fears the attack of an alien, destructive power, so he resorts to the fighter-physician whose tactical skill and weapons will kill the enemy.

Other professions also perceive their tasks adversarially. The press behaves as though it has not done its job well until it draws blood from those interviewed. Why rest content with watching for a conflict if a sly photograph or an intrusive question can help create the fight? The professional corporate manager presses relentlessly for advantage against competitors, unions, markets, and the government in an environment he or she sees as menacing. The laconic engineer, equipped with his computer and slide rule, slips into an adversarial mode as he designs the technology to conquer space, time, and a hostile nature. And the mild-mannered certified public accountant, whose very title emphasizes the importance of *public* accountability, has nevertheless increasingly interpreted her primary task adversarially, serving the client in battles against enemies such as competitors and tax collectors. Even the academic profession in this country has depended mostly on a negative justification for its authority. It sells education not as the pathway to truth, but as the ticket to an escape route from poverty and insecurity. It dangles before all takers an expansion of power, control, and opportunity. Selling themselves on these terms, educational institutions often dwindle into vocational training camps, equipping recruits for combat in a hazardous market.

However, no profession, save the military, defines its task as adversarially as the legal profession. Adversarialism so dominates the practice of law in the United States and Great Britain that it names the system itself. In 1820, Lord Brougham gave the famously flamboyant statement of the lawyer's duty to his client in the course of defending Queen Caroline on trial before the House of Lords:

> An advocate, in the discharge of his duty, knows but one person in all the world, and that person is his client. To save that client by all means and expedients, and at all hazards and costs to other persons, and amongst them, to himself, is his first and only duty; and in performing this duty, he must not regard the alarm, the torments, the destruction, which he may bring to others.[11]

Almost 150 years later, Monroe H. Freedman, Dean of Hofstra Law School, almost matched the monotheistic ferocity of Lord Brougham in his unflinching defense of the adversarial criminal lawyer.[12] In his programmatic article on the subject, Freedman argued that the conscientious criminal advocate must be willing to: (1) cross-examine for the purpose of undermining the reliability or credibility of an adverse witness whom he knows to be telling the truth; (2) put a witness on the stand whom he knows will commit perjury; and (3) give his client legal advice even when he has reason to believe the knowledge he gives him (about the legal consequences of alternative scenarios) will tempt the client to commit perjury.

Freedman's controversial "three hard cases" pushed adversarialism to the limit in litigating criminal cases. However, an adversarial spirit can dominate the practice of civil as well as criminal law; and, in civil proceedings, it often animates, in addition to litigating in the courtroom, the additional lawyerly tasks of counseling and negotiating.[13] The balancing mechanisms of the adversary system itself seem to require that in all activities the lawyer perceive herself to work only as the client's agent, nonaccountable in all else.

Apologists for the system, including Freedman, usually invoke the picture of the powerless, resourceless individual pitted against the majesty of the state. But, given the distributions of money and talent in the marketplace, the gifted lawyer today, more often than not, works for a large corporation. The poor and the middle classes often cannot afford to pursue their grievances in court. Inequities in the distribution of legal talent and delaying tactics in the courtroom often stack the deck in favor of the powerful.

The adversarial game, moreover, can encourage antinomianism in the client. The lawyer lets the client know how much he can maximally get away with. The lawyer treats the law not as a minimal statement of obligations to the neighbor that points beyond itself to a higher righteousness, but rather, as a bright line that aids and abets the client's attempt to crowd the border of unrighteousness.

The negative derivation of professional authority generates three adverse consequences that should provoke in us some readiness for shifts in balance and emphasis. Professional authority derived from fear can be limited only with difficulty; it costs too much, and it eventually provokes a backlash.

Authority derived from the reflexive struggle against evil is difficult to limit. I have already tried to press this point with respect to the state's power. A professional authority based on a negativity alone seldom can stay within limits because patients and clients do not keep their fears under control. "Whatever you say, doctor" may be the prudent compliance of a man or woman who has experienced a brush with death. But the patient soon translates it into "whatever tests you order," and "whatever paces you put me through in the hospital because I obviously need your help in fighting this battle." Similarly, the lawyer who fights for a client against a threatened loss of liberty and property tends to feed upon the seriousness of the crisis. The right of appeal, the rules of evidence, the threat of equally or more adept lawyers on the other side of the case—all serve to generate a momentum in which the necessities of battle override other considerations. Litigation soon turns into a way of life for the driven client, and the lawyer expands his power, control, and fees accordingly. Such litigation has pervasively infected American life. At a time when Japan, a country with half the population of the United States, supported a total of under 15,000 lawyers, the U.S. had over 700,000 licensed lawyers and graduated some 35,000 additional lawyers from law school every year.[14] This oversupply, Derek Bok noted in the *Cost of Talent*, has not worked to reduce lawyer's fees. Thus litigation has inflated the cost of doing business in America.

Further, even the effort to combat the negative effects of professional action contributes to the growth of professional power and increases the cost of services. One needs, in the first instance, experts to fight against threats to life, limb, and property, but then, additional professionals to protect laypeople from those dangerous powers mobilized to wage the fight. The professional must both devise the technology to battle disease or conquer a hostile environment, and then devise further technologies to lessen the collateral damage the technology itself inflicted. One needs a surgeon to perform an operation, but also an anesthesiologist to make it safe and the opinion of a second surgeon to determine its necessity. If it was not necessary, the doctor may need a lawyer to defend him in court, and accountants to monitor costs. The negative derivation of authority imposes high costs even in the effort to contain costs.

The negative derivation of professional authority can lead clients, eventually, to resent the professional. The professional wields great but precarious authority and prestige. Physicians and lawyers can arouse great anger. They face the danger of retaliation if, through incompetence, greed, or bad luck, they impose on clients what clients hired them to resist. Since the stakes are so high and since institutions can suffer from the revealed incompetence of a single practitioner, professionals quickly draw around the endangered colleague like a herd around a wounded elephant.

The interim passivity of the client in the contractual model reinforces resentment of the professional. The client/patient tends to act at two points—in hiring and in firing the professional. He often resents a relationship he feels diminishes his autonomy. The patient obeys his doctor and squirms against his obedience. To the degree, moreover, that the patient is passive—triply subject to the ravages of disease, the manipulations of the professional, and the technologies which he employs—the patient seems to make no contribution to the ends pursued. The professional offers a product, gratefully received at the outset, but this gratitude slides only too easily into disappointment and resentment. So the patient regains autonomy by dissolving the professional tie or retaliating with the malpractice suit.

The client in legal proceedings falls into a somewhat more

complicated passivity. The lawyer does not impose adversarialism on a wholly passive client. Most clients come to lawyers under the steam of their own wants and fears. They want a lawyer who will speak, act, and negotiate on their behalf, just as surely as citizens under the social contract want a government that will defend and protect their interests. Although the client actively desires the ends which he has hired the lawyer to pursue, he is passive in two important ways. First, the client yields to the lawyer the technical task of pressing to the limit his advantages under the law. The root of the word "client" reflects this passivity. A client literally listens; as an auditor, he needs another, an advocate, to speak for him and his cause. Second and more important, the client does not usually feel morally responsible for what the lawyer says or does in that zealous pursuit. The client will readily fire the lawyer who fails to advance and protect to the hilt his interests, but he feels little responsibility for any harm to others that results from the lawyer's zeal. In effect, the adversary system itself erects an encompassing mechanism that produces a kind of moral passivity or what David Luban has called the principle of nonaccountability in both the client and the lawyer. Principals appear before the court adversarially, in both criminal and civil cases, and they resort to lawyers as agents who will act with adversarial zeal. The mechanism itself seems to accommodate only the play of force pitted against counterforce. Everyone, client as well as professional, feels driven into an adversarial mode.

I doubt whether we can wholly excise adversarialism from American life and professional practice. One cannot expect self-surgery on the American character. Further, one cannot altogether dispense with an adversarial element in political and professional life. All positive derivations of authority contain a negative aspect. The state that derives from a Supreme Good cannot do without some military or police power that notices mundane evil. The physician who aims to enhance the health of his or her patient must also, ordinarily, relieve suffering and prevent death. The teaching profession aspires to the truth, but requires, as well, the negatives of discipline and censorship; no educational system gets along without them.

However, a society differs mightily in spirit and atmosphere, depending upon whether it emphasizes the positive or negative aim. The schoolroom varies immensely depending on whether discipline serves education or itself becomes the secret purpose of the facility. The medical task changes substantially when relieving suffering and preventing death, rather than pursuing health, dominate the enterprise. The agenda looks different when serving a good rather than repelling an evil shapes the state or the professional relationship.

Inevitably, a more positive definition of the professional's task requires a more active understanding of the relationship of professionals to their patients and clients. In a sense, both the doctor and the patient must become more directly engaged with one another, if physicians would aim not merely to fight death, but to increase and enhance health. Doctors must seek the more active collaboration of their patients in health maintenance. This redefined medical transaction entails cooperating to transform habits, not just buying strategic services.

Similarly, the lawyer, less adversarially defined, must counsel and negotiate, not just litigate, on behalf of clients; and such counseling and negotiating must become more than the pursuit of courtroom tactics by other means. Thus the Kutak Commission, which drew up the Model Rules of Professional Conduct, held that the lawyer as counselor and negotiator owes his client moral advice as well as technical, legal skill. Similarly, our engineers will not find a long-range solution to the energy needs of the country simply through ever more intense technical efforts to plunder nature, but through technologies that serve a collective effort to transform national habits.

The term "transformation," of course, awakens fears of paternalism. The call for physicians, lawyers, managers, and political leaders who will transform habits (rather than merely gratify wants) recalls the overbearing authority figures who haunt the American past: the moral officiousness and cramping paternalism of the Puritans; the pomposities of professionals who adopted the tone of "father knows best." Further, our efforts to transform usually founder on the reef of pluralism. A society with diverse constituencies cannot afford too many efforts to transform. A pluralistic society finds attractive a libertarianism that would restrict institutions and professional groups largely to instrumental goals. Why not assume that all community among us is merely useful rather than moral and works to gratify our appetites rather than to foster our aspiration to excellence? Why not rely on mechanisms rather than insight to cope with conflicting interests?

Professionals who would direct others to positive goals would fall prey to paternalism in a pluralistic society unless we accept teaching and persuasion as essential ingredients. No physician can engage in preventive, rehabilitative, and chronic care medicine without teaching his or her patients. Words are to a prescription what a preamble is to a constitution: they illuminate and help support the process of healing. Teaching helps to heal the patient, to "make whole" the distressed and distracted subject. Other professions must also teach. The constitutional powers of the President of the United States founder if the President fails in that job which the Constitution never specifies: teaching the nation. Jimmy Carter's presidency demonstrated the difficulties we face without a leader who knows how to use the persuasive powers of the presidency. Lawyers offer technical services in drawing up contracts and litigating in the courtroom, but through counseling they must also teach their clients. Lawyers must teach if they would uphold justice and not merely burrow for holes in contracts.

Justifying the Adversary System

The foregoing sketch of adversarialism in America and the professions has highlighted those evils from which clients might seek rescue through the services of a professional. However, we have not yet turned to the question of justifying the adversary system as a whole. The law especially requires a systemic justification since the adversarial lawyer and client in the particular case battle humans rather than a cosmic adversary as in medicine. What justifies pressing the client's claim to the hilt, come what may to others? We need to explore the overriding ends the adversary system serves, which might either vindicate the existing system (despite the havoc it wreaks in particular cases) or justify its replacement, or, if not its replacement, its moderation and reform.

At one extreme, unyielding apologists for the system associate it indissolubly with the democratic form of government. Put negatively, they argue that moderating adversarialism would set us on the path toward the evil of totalitarianism. They freely concede that lawyers, marching to the sound of Lord Broughham's war cry, must turn a deaf ear to all else. The system requires a kind of moral heedlessness when defending the client. Further, these apologists hold that a democracy requires the clear-cut separation of the defense, prosecutorial, and judicial roles which an adversary system supplies. Any blurring of the roles would begin to fuse the three functions, a fusion brought to its completion in totalitarian countries.

This unqualified defense of extreme adversarialism by raising the specter of totalitarianism resembles the defense that Friedrich Hayek offered for libertarianism. Hayek defended the minimalist state on the grounds that governments that venture beyond the negative functions of protecting life, liberty, and property push a country firmly down *The Road to Serfdom*. The libertarian state offers the only alternative to totalitarian communism. Hayek denied the possibility of mixed economies which hold to a third way—neither libertarian nor totalitarian.

Just so, Monroe Freedman insufficiently appreciates the existence of a third way in the law: neither adversarial fission nor totalitarian fusion. Specifically, the civil legal traditions of European democracies offer an alternative to both an adversarialism fiercely protective of the individual and a totalitarian dissolution of the individual into the power of the state. The continental civil law tradition, with its more inquisitorial method of investigating cases and resolving controversies, has proved compatible with European democracy—contrary to the specter of totalitarianism raised by Freedman. Adversarialism cannot be placed beyond reform as the indispensable legal accompaniment to democracy.

I doubt, however, whether adversarialism can be wholly excised from American life. It is deeply embedded in the American character. Nor would the result, even if achieved, be altogether desirable. The adversary system is not without its strengths. Its method of getting at the truth, while abrasive and sometimes evasive and abusive, has nevertheless often worked. As a practical matter, it is dumb to perjure or to destroy a credible witness. A lawyer can put his or her client on the stand and let him lie, but the lawyer cannot use the testimony in argument. The system, as earlier noted, has scored important successes, in protecting the rights of the powerless and in accommodating and facilitating emergent powers. Its weaknesses, moreover, may be no greater than those of the civil law tradition in Europe; and, at least, its weaknesses have the advantage of being recognizably our own. Finally, the social, economic, and cultural costs of supplanting the adversary with another system in the United States would be immense.

While radical self-surgery on the American character may be undesirable and almost impossible, leaning against the weaknesses of one's specific character, to recall Aristotle's advice, is imperative. One needs moderation and reform in this case to counter the downside of adversarialism in American life. David Luban opens the way toward such discriminate reform by arguing that the adversary system enjoys only a limited "pragmatic justification." A common law country, such as the United States,

> (1) needs some procedural system; (2) the available alternatives are not demonstrably better; and (3) the adversary system is the system in place."[15] This cautious, pragmatic justification leads Luban to urge that the adversary system should be "reformed not abolished; however, the adversarial ethics of non-account-able partisanship should be abolished, not reformed.[16]

Justification for reforming, rather than indiscriminately defending or replacing, the system requires us to revisit the question of its overriding ends.

The Ends of Truth and Justice
and the End of Order

Some apologists for the adversary system see it as the best mechanism for getting at the truth and reaching a just judgment, the more so in those cases where the heat of the conflict obscures both truth and justice or where the majesty of one of the parties—the state—desperately requires a balancing voice in the courtroom if the full truth would have a hearing and even-handed justice would prevail. Advocates claim that the adversary system (the system in general, rather than its inevitable, incidental miscarriages) allows, be it ever so tortuously through contentious proceedings, for the best outworking of truth and justice. Each party to a dispute needs a loyal advocate stating its case vigorously. The system stumbles if the legal profession fails to maintain a strict division of labor between prosecutor, defense attorney, and judge. Thus, if the attorney is to make her specific contribution to truth and justice, the system demands, and demands morally, that the defense attorney give loyalty to the client, unmuddied by private scruple or by a confusion of roles with the prosecutor or the judge.

David Luban in *Lawyers and Justice* has taken apart the claim that the adversary system provides the only way in legal controversy to gain access to the truth. This claim, he notes, is implausible, misleading, and abstract: implausible in that other legal cultures offer ways of gaining access to the truth; misleading in that it rests on a false analogy to scientific inquiry; and abstract in that the analogy to science shows just how far removed the adversary proceeding strays in detail from a disciplined quest for the truth.

> Science does not, or at least should not, try to exclude probative evidence, discredit opposing testimony known to be truthful, fight efforts at discovery, use procedural devices to delay trial in hopes that opponents will run out of money or witnesses die or disappear, exploit the incompetence of opposing counsel, shield material facts from a tribunal based on privilege, or indulge in sophistry and rhetorical manipulation—all, arguably, tactics required by the principle of partisanship.[17]

On the face of it, if the ends of truth and justice justify a legal system, then, Luban would argue, the adversary system needs reform.

Other apologists for the system have observed—some approvingly, others, critically—that the positive, justifying aim of the law is not truth and justice but the great social good of order. The law chiefly provides a mechanism for the regulation of controversies. To put it negatively: anarchy more than injustice is the great social evil from which our legal system protects us. Preeminently, it keeps peace rather than seeks truth or makes right. It substitutes a contest in the courts for a brawl in the streets.

Further, the adversary system, while preserving order and peace, maximizes liberty. It does not directly enforce order by fusing the processes of investigation, prosecution, defense, and judgment at the expense of the liberty of the accused or the contested in criminal and civil disputes. It resolves controversy by the indirect route. It provides for a game played out through representatives—a gladiatorial combat, a tennis match—once removed from the parties to a dispute.[18] It empowers both parties to seek counsel, to pour out to counsel the full turbulence of facts and resentments built up in a controversy without fear that this information will be looped back into the system and used against the client. The system then provides a ritual occasion on which counsel can deploy all its resources and skills to combat the adversary according to rules; determines the winner; and provides for successive appeals to be sure that the game has been properly played, duly refereed, and concluded.

Thus lawyers plead not to ascertain truth, but to win. Judges judge, not to achieve justice, but to see that contestants abide by the rules. It would be as inappropriate for a judge to intervene in a trial in which counselors were unevenly matched for the sake of justice, as it would be for a referee to line up with the Chicago Bears because the more talented Green Bay Packers threatened to outscore them in a football game. This appeal to the metaphor of a game figures in the overstated observation of the Honorable Simon H. Rifkind, former judge of the United States District Court for the Southern District of New York: ". . . the object of a trial is not the ascertainment of truth but the resolution of a controversy by the principled application of the rules of the game."[19]

A more balanced way of justifying any legal system would be to insist on the societal importance of the values of both truth/justice and order. These values are more than arbitrary and subjective; they are fundamental goods. Just laws justly enforced spare a society the evil of tyranny. Social order legally enforced spares a society the evil of anarchy. Both goods are fundamental; both evils, lethal. Each pole, in some degree, contends with its opposite. Fierce campaigns against injustice can unnerve the established order and threaten to plunge a society into anarchy. Fierce defendants of law and order can ignore injustice and threaten a society with the oppression of tyranny. The wise reformer, while prizing justice, does not neglect altogether the claims of order; the wise conservative, while prizing order, does not overlook the claims of justice.

At their deepest levels, the philosophical and religious traditions of the West tend, in my judgment, to place truth and justice at the foundation of all else in our common life. Truth and justice are ultimate; order, while fundamental, ultimately derives from them. The Greeks expressed this view philosophically when they asserted that *nomos* (the law, the source of order) does not stand higher than *nous* and *logos* (that is, reason and the word). The law should not impose from the top down laws which are opaque and arbitrary, incapable of rational explication and defense. The Jews and Christians expressed this outlook religiously when they proclaimed that the God of order and peace is, first and foremost, righteous and just. In the name of a just and righteous God, the prophets inveighed against injustice and tyranny. (They differed strikingly in spirit from the keepers of conscience in ancient Babylonian civilization. In the setting of the Babylonian Creation myth, the foundational struggle pitted, not justice against injustice, but Order vs. Chaos—Marduk vs. Tiamat—the political term for which is anarchy.)

Foundational myths aside, one can argue pragmatically and psychologically that, while both justice and order are basic, justice is preeminent as the final standard by which one must measure the law. In the end, justice legitimates the legal contest—the game—and renders its verdicts acceptable as a resolution of controversy. The forensic contest has fateful consequences for the life, liberty, and property of contestants. Its verdict is not acceptable merely because the decision has been reached according to Hoyle, but because those rules themselves, in the aggregate, seem most likely to reach the truth and deliver just judgments.[20] A society rightly prizes order, and that prizing is acceptable (and not itself the cause of disorder) only as it cumulatively provides just resolution to grievances. Otherwise, the law itself compounds grievance. In civil cases, its unjust resolutions add a grievance against the state to the original grievance against a private party. The law rests on its enduring and sustaining foundation when it rests on justice. For these reasons, one needs to be open to strategies that will render more just and therefore more acceptably ordered the deliverances of the adversary system.

Reforming the System

The several strategies for reforms include: (1) changing the rules in the professional code of responsibility for lawyers; (2) changing the laws of the nation which set the basic ground rules under the adversary system; and (3) redefining more directly the ideals that shape professional character and virtue.

Changing the Rules in the Professional Code. The Kutak Commission of the American Bar Association drew up new rules for professional conduct to redress the adversarial tilt in the older ABA Code of Professional Responsibility. Whereas Canon 7 of the ABA Code stated, "A lawyer should represent a client zealously within the bounds of the law," the Model Rules of Professional Conduct (adopted now by the Bar Associations of more than forty states) substituted, in Rule 1.3, "reasonable diligence" for the earlier, more aggressive term "zeal." While the term "zeal" still appears in comments on Rule 1.3 ("a lawyer . . . should act . . . with zeal in advocacy on the client's behalf"), there are limits. A "lawyer is not bound to press for every advantage that might be realized for a client"; and a lawyer "has professional discretion in determining the means by which a matter should be pursued."[21]

The Model Rules made some headway, at least theoretically, on another matter. They no longer assumed (in the fashion of the older code) that the lawyer chiefly litigates. They place the lawyer's responsibilities as advisor and counselor ahead of her duties as courtroom advocate; and they expand the list of the lawyer's roles to include counselor, advocate, negotiator, evaluator, and arbitrator. (Symbolically, at least, this shift in focus away from litigation corresponds roughly to the effort in medicine to shift the emphasis from acute interventions to preventive, rehabilitative, and long-term care.) However, insofar as the adversarial spirit already dominates the tasks of advising, counseling, and negotiating, the expansion in roles may offer less than meets the eye.

Changing the Law. A second strategy for reform would seek changes, not in the professional code per se, but in the law of the land. It would press for changes, for example, in the rules of evidence, in discovery proceedings, and in sanctions against lawyers for procedural abuse; and it would provide for alternative dispute resolution. More ambitiously, Judge Marvin Frankel proposed in his Cardozo Lecture of 1974 that the adversary system be modified (not abandoned) to increase the importance of the quest for truth in the resolution of cases. To this end, he proposed that judges be vested, like their European counterparts, with some investigatory powers so that judges are not wholly restricted to competing counsel for their access to relevant evidence. (An analogous reform in corporate organization would provide members of a board of directors with some staff support so as not to depend entirely upon top management for the board's information.) In support of this substantial increase in the investigatory powers of the court, Frankel also proposed changing the Code of Professional Responsibility to specify for lawyers on both sides of a dispute what it means to be officers of the court with more positive obligations to disclose material facts and forbid material omissions (and not just a negative obligation to refrain from committing perjury).

While Frankel did not want to replace the adversary with the continental inquisitorial system, he clearly borrowed from the latter in order to lean against the weaknesses of the former. He believed that the U.S. legal system would improve if the courtroom were the scene of an inquiry and not just a contest; lawyers, independent agents in that inquiry and not just hired guns; and judges, charged with responsibilities to the truth and a just verdict, not simply with assuring that a contest has been fought according to mutually agreed upon rules. The late-twentieth-century hostility to "activist judges" makes Frankel's proposals for the expansion of the judge's investigatory powers politically unlikely.

It should be noted, however, that the charge of judicial activism today largely targets appellate judges driven by ideology, not trial judges who enforce the rules. Thus some opponents of aggressive reform argue that the basic rules and laws required to make the adversary system work are already, for the most part, in place. Discovery abuse, for example, is possible, but it violates the rules. If the trial judge is good, a lawyer cannot get away with such abuse. In this view, the chief problems emerge when judges, for reasons of excessive case load and other causes, resort to bureaucratic processing and abdicate their supervisory function. They give lawyers too much leeway. Stand pat rule-enforcers surely have a point. However, the existence of rules and monitoring judges who enforce them does not fully secure justice any more than a code of honor and a posse of proctors monitoring exams assures the intellectual rigor of a university. The deeper cultural problem still remains: the basic character and probity of those who practice the law, however strictly or laxly rules circumscribe them or judges monitor them.

Reshaping Professional Character and Virtue. A third strategy would address the question of the lawyer's character and call for a reconsideration of the virtues which should mark the good lawyer. Clearly some advocates of reforms in the nation's laws governing adversary proceedings oppose this strategy. For example, A. Kenneth Pye, former dean of Duke University Law School, would change some of the rules of evidence and procedures for determining members of a jury and the venue for a trial; however, he stoutly opposes tempering the adversary system by changes in the character and habits of lawyers.[22] Pye insists that lawyers, whatever the rules, remedied or not, must play (almost) to the hilt their roles as zealous advocates. He thus separates structural reform from the character of the professionals who operate under the system. Modest structural reform? Yes. Changes in the adversarial character of lawyers? No.

Pye, however, justifies the lawyer's zeal on grounds very different from those marked out by Monroe Freedman. Freedman argued that anything short of zealous support of the client will cause a social slide toward totalitarianism (that is, the social evil of injustice or tyranny). Pye assumes that anything short of zealous advocacy would cause a legal slide toward the social evil of disorder and anarchy. Why? The law is positive, objective, and concrete; whereas ethics is private, subjective, and abstract. If the lawyer does not push to the limit the objectively permissible, the fate of the client will depend upon the happenstance of the lawyer's ethic, his own subjective moral formation, his particular take on the abstraction of justice. Thus Pye fears the chanceful, the arbitrary, the anarchic, in a pluralistic culture such as ours. While we should change the rules of evidence and other procedures, lawyers should push their client's case to the limit under the rules governing the system, whatever their personal ethics may be.

Pye's position is vulnerable on two points. First, his dismissal of the entire arena of ethics as too subjective, arbitrary, and abstract, undercuts the possibility of his arguing ethically for the reform of current procedures in the adversary system. Particular reforms (which he advocates) will require some sort of appeal to standards of truth and fairness that justify them. If, however, ethics is arbitrary and subjective, it lacks weight to press for changes. If the principle of justice is dismissed as abstract, how can it be invoked to change procedures that produce so-called unjust outcomes?

Second, if lawyers play to the hilt their roles as zealous advocates, whatever the rules, the new rules themselves will hardly succeed in remedying the flaws that led to their adoption. Clearly lawyers have found ways to exploit rules of discovery, originally designed to facilitate the quest for the truth. They have manipulated those rules to delay trials, to exhaust the resources of the opposition, and to frustrate equitable judgments. If the spirit of the players within a system is mean, it can turn almost all reforms against their original intent. David Luban has noted, ". . . the law is inherently double-edged: any rule imposed to limit zealous advocacy (or any other form of conduct, for that matter) may be used by an adversary as an offensive weapon."[23] For example, "one might respond to an interrogation by delivering to the discoverer tons of miscellaneous documents to run up their legal bills or to conceal a needle in a haystack . . . Similarly, rules barring lawyers from representations involving conflicts of interest are now regularly used by adversaries to drive up the other side's costs by having their counsel disqualified."[24] In the law, as well as in ethics, character and the ethos that shapes character count.

I do not mean to dismiss the importance of structural reform. The right rules can help form character. They also help to create a level playing field so that the self-restrained lawyer, up against a ruthless attorney, does not have to martyr his client to be moral. However, structural reforms alone—unaccompanied by changes in character— quickly twist and yield to an unreformed spirit still animating the system if a profession pays no attention to its soul. Historically, at its best, the lawyer's vocation amounted to something more than tutoring clients in the ways of using the law against other parties and the state.

A range of authors has recognized that better procedures, whether enshrined in the law or in professional codes, will not of themselves redress the needful balance. Character and virtue matter. Anthony Kronman of Yale Law School urges the retrieval of the ideal of the lawyer-statesman.[25] Mary Ann Glendon of Harvard Law School invokes the image of the wise counselor.[26] Thomas S. Shaffer of Notre Dame relies in part on the same professional ideals in the portrait of Atticus Finch in *To Kill a Mockingbird* and Gavin Stevens in Faulkner's *Intruder in the Dust*.[27] The names of Henry Stimson, Dean Acheson, John McCloy, Robert Jackson, and Carla Hills surface at the very beginning of Kronman's effort to recover the lost, or barely surviving, ideal. And, lest the image of the lawyer-statesman gather dust in a gallery of privileged Ivy Leaguers or trivialize into the sentimental legal equivalent of a Marcus Welby, M.D., one should add to the image such persons as Thurgood Marshall, and the urban Italian lawyer in Shaffer's *American Lawyers and Their Communities*.[28]

Inevitably, however, at the head of such lists of exemplary practitioners is Abraham Lincoln—a principled man acquainted with the muddy complexity of things, a no-nonsense counselor who went to the heart of the matter. Lincoln once concluded a session with a client, saying:

> Yes, we can doubtless gain your case for you; we can set a whole neighborhood at loggerheads; we can distress a widowed mother and her six fatherless children and thereby get you six hundred dollars to which you seem to have a legal claim, but which rightfully belongs, it appears to me, as much to the woman and her children as it does to you. You must remember that some things legally right are not morally right. We shall not take your case, but will give you a little advice for which we charge you nothing. You seem to be a sprightly, energetic man; we would advise you to try your hand at making six hundred dollars some other way.[29]

Dealing with the larger client of the nation, Lincoln continued to evince the ideal of the lawyer-statesman:

> As he struggled to find a way to save the Union and democracy too, Lincoln had no formula to guide him. He possessed no technical knowledge that could tell him where the solution to America's dilemma lay. He had only his wisdom to rely on—his prudent sense of where the balance between principle and expediency must be struck.[30]

Often, of course, the balance Lincoln needed to strike was not between principle and expediency, but between two contending principles: the sometimes conflicting goods of union and of emancipation from slavery; that is, order and justice.

In recovering the ideal of the wise counselor, the legal profession will need to revisit the question of character and virtue. It goes without saying that the first and most troubling of the virtues in the practice of the law is *fidelity*. The lawyer cannot treat her client merely as a profit opportunity. Everything said in the chapter on money and the professions applies here in force. The lawyer/client relation must be disinterested rather than interested. The client's interests come before the lawyer's interest in achieving fortune and fame. She should not opt for a more costly defense of a client for the sake of her own enrichment or seek to enhance her fame by breaking new ground in the law that places her client at greater risk. Loyalty to the client is itself a public responsibility inasmuch as it lifts the lawyer beyond the private maneuvers of a careerist. The lawyer does not enter the public arena only when she adds *pro bono publico* service to her other duties. In a democratic society, service to the client itself serves the public.

Fidelity to the client is the lawyer's first virtue, but troubling if it is the only virtue. Charles Fried emphasized fidelity to the client as the overriding, well-nigh exclusive responsibility of the lawyer by appealing to the phrase, "the lawyer as friend." In the sardonic judgment of Edward A. Dauer and Arthur Allen Leff, this phrase overlooks the factual circumstance of much legal practice in which the lawyer performs as free-lance bureaucrat more than friend.[31] In addition to the question of its accuracy, the metaphoric ideal of the lawyer as zealous friend marginalizes too much else important to the lawyer as statesman and wise counselor. Mary Ann Glendon unmasks Fried's statement of the ideal as follows:

The friend-of-the-client ideal is easy to espouse under current conditions, a real crowd pleaser . . . A lawyer who regularly gives priority to client loyalty . . . can generally look good while following the course of least resistance. His or her other aspirations—to be an artisan of order, a peacemaker, a public-spirited court officer, or a lawyer of a situation—don't have to be completely abandoned, just subordinated. . . . The lawyer is relieved from the agonizing struggle to give each of his loyalties its due and becomes a virtuoso of simple-mindedness—like a professional soldier, or the surgeon who drapes all but the affected part of the patient under a sheet.[32]

Where does loyalty to the client reach its territorial limits in the courtroom? When and how does it give way to other loyalties? When does loyalty require the lawyer to push beyond the client's expressed wants and respond to his deeper needs?[33] Not even friends need prove their friendship by pandering to their friends' wants at their worst. These issues of fidelity partly require treatment in the law of the land and in professional codes. But not even the weightiest of documents can anticipate and resolve all the questions which loyalty itself poses. Manuals can assist but not substitute for the virtue of wisdom in the concrete case.

The very ideal of the wise counselor highlights the importance of the ancient cardinal virtues in which the virtue of *practical wisdom* heads the list. Wisdom requires a spacious openness to often competing ends or goods which the lawyer must balance and proportionately honor in a particular case. Wisdom also requires a prudent choice of means in negotiating ends. The lawyer surely professes a body of knowledge, including a set of laws and guild regulations governing professional conduct, but neither a limitless elaboration of that knowledge nor a mastery of the cognate social sciences will of itself produce a wise counselor. Scientists—even applied scientists—traffic in generalizations; wise counselors may draw on such generalizations but they must also artfully take in the scene and counsel, in the light of the complex of players and particulars that congregate in a given case, whether it be a divorce proceeding, a contract, or a criminal trial.

William H. Simon recognizes the importance of "ethical discretion," that is, practical wisdom, in lawyering, which a system of formalized rules alone will not produce. He argues that lawyers should exercise judgment and discretion in choosing what clients to represent and how they represent them. "Lawyers should have ethical discretion to refuse to assist in the pursuit of legally permissible courses of action and in the assertion of potentially enforceable legal claims. This discretion involves not a personal privilege of arbitrary decision, but a duty of reflective judgment. . . . the basic consideration should be whether assisting the client would further justice."[34] Such ethical discretion need not push legal practice into a sea of normlessness and unpredictability. Rather, it demands that lawyers take seriously the contextual norms that the law itself supplies; such standards as "reasonableness, good faith, usage of trade, customary practice, and public convenience and necessity."[35] Such norms help stabilize decision making even as they call for discretionary judgment and practical wisdom in the particular case.

Today, the ancient virtues of wisdom and prudence tend to dwindle into a low-to-the-ground cunning. A blinkered attention to the law, with a view to discerning what the client can maximally get away with, replaces wisdom with cleverness. A grasp of the law per se does not of itself take in all the nonlegal, often moral, issues hard-packed in a case. Lincoln swiftly cites a few of them in the quarrel over six hundred dollars: his client's legal claim to the money, to be sure; but also the straitened circumstance of the widow and her children, and the turmoil which pressing the case has created in the town. These further issues of justice and peace cannot be dismissed as abstractions.

The wise, discerning lawyer must also be just or *public spirited*. The exercise of the virtue of justice cannot be restricted to judges alone, as some apologists for the adversary system would have it. The lawyer's public-spiritedness begins, to be sure, with her duties to the client. Client advocacy surely is a public duty. But even her duties to the client often require something other than an aggressive, full-court press up to the limits of the law. Lincoln put it succinctly. In pushing to the limit of the law, the nominal winner may well be the real loser. In addition to serving as advocate *for* the client, the lawyer may also need to be advocate *to* his client. Otherwise, he treats the client as merely a bundle of declared interests, which he is hired to serve, not as a moral being susceptible to the just claims of others.

The public's interest bears in three ways on Lincoln's too-easy case; first, the peace of the community is an issue; the mean-spirited client would place a neighborhood at loggerheads; thus, extreme adversarialism weakens the link between law and order. Second, even if one could keep the court's disposition of the case quiet and avoid scandalizing the community, the dispute would not subside into a squabble between two private parties. When either of two parties goes to court and asks for the resolution of the case with the full majesty of the legal system and its enforcement powers behind the decision, it is no longer a private matter, but of public record. Through the instrumentalities of the court and its enforcement powers, the public itself becomes a player. Third, even if the case never goes to trial (because the very threat of a trial extends the widow beyond her resources to cope with the dispute), both the lawyer directly and his profession and the public indirectly become implicated in an unjust outcome. The virtue of justice cannot be reserved to the judge alone, as though it were the judge's specialty in the panoply of virtues, while the lawyer contributes only zeal and cleverness to the whirring of the legal system.

The lawyer must be just not only in her dealings with clients and adversaries but also by providing *pro bono publico* services. Through *pro bono* work, the lawyer helps the profession and the society honor the claims of distributive justice. The earlier tradition of the West distinguished between three dimensions of justice. Commutative justice referred to just dealings *between* various parties within the society; legal justice, to the discharge of duties by parts *to* the society as a whole; and distributive justice, to the fair distribution of goods by the whole to its several parts. We have chiefly discussed in this chapter the task of tempering the adversary system to achieve just dealings between contending parties within the whole and to achieve justice in a proceeding between a part and the whole. But we have taken only marginal note of the problems of distributive justice—the degree to which the whole delivers or fails to deliver a fundamental good to its several parts, in this case the good of legal aid to all its citizens. A maldistribution of legal services in a society adversarially organized severely exacerbates the problem of achieving justice in the other two dimensions. Citizens denied adequate legal services cannot expect to compete credibly in proceedings either against other parties or against the state. Injustice in the distribution of legal services, in a highly adversarial system, geometrically compounds commutative and legal injustice. Just lawyers therefore must think through their responsibilities not only as lawyers in civil and criminal suits, but also as players in a system that does not yet distribute services adequately to produce just outcomes.

Solutions to the inequalities of access that the current system produces include: (1) the device which the marketplace itself has developed: a contingency fee system; (2) the donation by lawyers (or their firms) of *pro bono publico* services to the needy; (3) resorting to alternative conflict resolution; and (4) the provision of third-party support for legal aid through the tax system.

For various reasons detailed in the chapter on money and the professions, a contingency fee system will not of itself achieve universal or adequate coverage for the poor and the less powerful. (To cite only one problem here: A large number of meritorious malpractice cases fall below the "big case" definition that will attract talented lawyers, or their firms, to take on the cost of legal research, expert testimony, and professional time required to pursue a case.) The second strategy of donated *pro bono* service has the moral advantage of reminding the profession that it wields its power by privilege and license from the state, that the justice which the law serves includes distributive, as well as commutative and legal, justice, and that public-spiritedness includes giving and not just selling services. Clearly, public-spirited philanthropy can supplement the limited world of selling with the more extended reach of giving to the needy. But donated time alone bestows services too marginally, too episodically, too limitedly, sometimes too impatiently and condescendingly to solve the problem of universal access to legal protection. Even if the society further develops the possibilities for alternative conflict resolution, it will still need to distribute better legal services to the needy through taxes.

A third-party payment system, funded through taxes, has the advantage of recognizing the importance of delivering the fundamental good of legal aid to all citizens in need. It spares the distraught from relying utterly on the kindness of strangers. In the judgment of some lawyers, it locates the basic responsibility for universal access where it ought to lie—with the society at large through the agency of government, rather than with a minority of public-spirited professionals who irregularly respond to a broad social need.

However, in my judgment, we would make a mistake to locate the responsibility either exclusively in the profession or in the society at large. The good of legal protection is too basic to depend exclusively on either the marketplace or philanthropy to deliver it. The society at large, through its agent, the government, bears a responsibility for extending adequate coverage to all. At the same time, lawyers also bear some responsibility for delivering services to those in need.

This book has pressed for a broader understanding of those who wield, and therefore who bear responsibility for wielding, public power in a society like ours. Not only government workers but independent professionals are public servants. Professionals, and preeminently lawyers, in a society that lives by the law, bear responsibility for distributive justice. Further, the *pro bono* efforts of professionals and the support of the society at large through taxes can reinforce one another synergistically. The *pro bono publico* work of doctors in the slums of London not only offered modest, discrete relief from misery, it also provided the testimony helpful in eventually producing legislative relief—through child labor laws, sanitation codes, and poor laws that helped address health problems more structurally. The virtue of public spiritedness evinced by professionals can serve the cause of distributive justice.

Finally, a lawyer, however wise and public spirited, cannot fully discharge her duties without some measure of independence in her dealings with the powerful. Thus the virtue of independence or integrity—that *sine qua non* of professional performance—calls for the classical virtues of *temperance* and *courage*. Without curbing one's appetites for money and fame (temperance) and mastering one's fears and worries (courage), a professional fails of that integrity of judgment and tenacity in execution that should mark the professional. The engineer and the accountant compromise their core identity if they shave the data to please the boss. The journalist turns into a flack, if the political leader or the business executive, through charm, perks, whatever, compromises the independence of the journalist's column. In the contemporary practice of the law, the dependence of the lawyer for his money and prestige on rich and powerful clients chiefly undercuts the traditional virtue of independence. "The main pressures on the ethics of large-firm lawyers always came from powerful clients who were not interested in being lectured on the public interest or the good of the legal system."[36] Fiercely competing in the marketplace today, law firms have normalized and encouraged runaway desire, as they extravagantly compensate their rainmakers and distribute monies on the principle of "eat what you kill." Moreover, runaway desire quickly generates runaway worries and fear. The avaricious lawyer serves the client with a slippery cunning; the fearful lawyer holds his tongue before abusive displays of power. In hanging on to their clients, lawyers fear words and deeds that might offend. They need the virtue of courage.

Lawyers earn their money and acquire their power by means of their tongues. They draft the legal instruments that transform our great cities, reconfigure our corporations, and carve up the country-side; they run state legislatures and populate the halls of Congress; and, as lobbyists, they often whisper in the ears of those who draft the legislation that becomes the law of the land. Yet, standing before the powerful, they too often perceive themselves to be mute and power-less; they lack the courage of the women servants in Moliere's come-dies who stand up to the lord of the house. Elihu Root believed that "about half the practice of a decent lawyer consists in telling would-be clients they are damned fools and should stop."[37] But, as Archibald Cox noted in a speech before the ABA, few lawyers today are "willing to say to clients, 'Yes. The law lets you do that, but don't do it. It is a rotten thing to do.'"[38]

The kinds of encounters that Lincoln, Root, and Cox have in mind pose clear contrasts between right and wrong. They call for courage on the part of the advocate as he speaks to his client directly and bluntly. But most moral encounters pose questions more complex. They raise questions, not of right and wrong, but of competing goods, no one of which can be fully realized, or competing evils, no one of which can be fully avoided. Moral decisions of this order fall into the class, not of temptations, but of quandaries. In working with such complex issues, lawyers need more than the courage to say no to misbehaving clients. They need the virtue of wisdom conjoined with the skill of a teacher if they would wend their way through to just agreements and settlements in complex cases.[39]

Serious efforts at transforming the client's take on his own case requires that the lawyer teach well.[40] The lawyer and her client need to engage in the give-and-take of discovery as they work through the quandary and reach in the circumstance the best possible approxima-tion of justice. Only a naive mysticism of the adversary system can assume that just outcomes result only if and as the players in the sys-tem reserve all responsibility for wisdom and justice to judges and juries alone.

Notes

1. See Jacques Maritain, *True Humanism*, 5th ed. (London: Geoffrey Bles, 1950), 171.
2. David Luban attributes this "human dignity argument" in recent philosophy to Alan Donegan: "The core notion underlying the adversary system is the human dignity of the client. A society respects our human dignity by provisionally testing the positions we maintain in legal disputes (civil or criminal) as good faith positions even when they are not. . . . That is why we have an adversary system in which parties present their own cases, rather than, say, an official inquiry into the matter conducted by the state." David Luban, *Lawyers and Justice: An Ethical Inquiry* (Princeton, N.J.: Princeton University Press, 1988), 85.
3. Louis Hartz, *The Liberal Tradition in America* (New York: Harcourt, Brace Jovanovich, 1955). Other commentators have emphasized older communitarian, less adversarial layers in American life, both religious and civic republican. See, for example, Gordon S. Wood, *The Creation of the American Public* (New York: W. W. Norton & Co. Inc., 1972); Robert N. Bellah, *The Broken Covenant* (New York: Seabury Press, 1975), and Robert N. Bellah et al., in *Habits of the Heart: Individualism and Commitment in American Life* (Berkeley: University of California Press, 1985).
4. John Locke, *The Second Treatise of Government*, ed. Thomas P. Peardon (Indianapolis: Bobbs-Merrill, 1952), chap. IX, par. 123, p. 70.
5. In this interpretation of the framers and apologists for the Constitution, I follow Gordon S. Wood (*Creation of the American Republic 1776–1787*) rather than Gary Will or the authors of *Habits of the Heart*. Bellah and his colleagues attempt to hyphenate the revolutionary thinkers and the apologists for the Constitution. To air brush the stark picture of human nature found in the *Federalist Papers*, they cite Madison's comment of 1788: "To suppose that any form of government will secure liberty without any virtue in the people, is a chimerical idea." But this sentiment does not figure prominently in the *Federalist Papers* themselves, an omission which, in those essays relentlessly oriented to persuasion, reflects better the tenor and mood of the times.
6. Thomas Hobbes, *Leviathan* (Cleveland: Meridian Books, the World Publishing Company, 1963), chap. 23, p. 143. Modern terrorism might be read as an assault on the Hobbesian state. The terrorist proclaims to magistrates: You do not have a monopoly over the powers of death, nor are you able to protect people from the threat of death. At an intense moment in London life, when bombs exploded in the pubs, a public official proclaimed: "From now on, everyone is his own magistrate!" He said, in effect, that London was returning to a Hobbesian state of nature.
7. For the following, see crucial discussion of the "Ends of Political Society and Government" in Locke, *The Second Treatise of Government*, chap. IX, par. 123.
8. Ibid.
9. Michael Walzer, *Obligations: Essays on Disobedience, War and Citizenship* (Cambridge: Harvard University Press, 1970), chap. 10.
10. James MacGregor Burns, *Leadership* (New York: Harper & Row, 1978). For a discussion of transactional leadership in business and politics, see chapter 5.

11. J. Nightingale, ed., *Trial of Queen Caroline* (vol. 2, London: J. Robins & Co. Albion Press, 1820–21), 8.

12. Monroe Freedman, "Public Responsibility of the Criminal Defense Lawyer: The Three Hardest Questions," *Michigan Law Review* 64 (1966):1469–84, later expanded in his volume, *Lawyers' Ethics in an Adversary System* (Indianapolis: Bobbs-Merrill, 1975).

13. See David Luban, *Lawyers and Justice: an Ethical Study* (Princeton, N.J.: Princeton University Press, 1988) chap. 4; Mary Ann Glendon, *A Nation Under Lawyers: How the Crisis in the Legal Profession Is Transforming American Society* (Farrar, Straus & Giroux, 1994), chap. 4; and Anthony Kronman, *The Lost Lawyer: Failing Ideals of the Legal Profession* (Cambridge, Mass.: Belknap Press of Harvard University Press, 1995).

14. Thomas D. Morgan and Donald D. Rotunda, *Problems and Materials on Professional Responsibility* (Mineola, N.Y.: Foundation Press, 1987), 419.

15. David Luban, "Truth, Contracts, and Adversarial Ethics," a paper delivered at the Maguire Center for Ethics Conference on "The Ethics of Contract and Other Promises," and a portion of which will appear in *Beyond the Adversary System*, ed. Michael Lavaorch and Helen Stacy (Canberra, Australia: Federation Press, forthcoming).

16. Ibid. Luban sees nonaccountable partisanship as combining two principles: "(1) the principle of partisanship . . . requires advocates to advance their clients' partisan interests with the maximum zeal permitted by law; and (2) the principle of nonaccountability . . . insists that an advocate is morally responsible for neither the ends pursued by the client nor the means of pursuing those ends, provided that both means and ends are lawful."

17. The quotation comes from an as-yet-unpublished paper on "Truth, Contracts, and Adversarial Ethics" delivered at a conference on " The Ethics of Contract and Other Promises" at Southern Methodist University, February 25, 1998, a portion of which will be published in *Beyond the Adversary System*, ed. Michael LaVaorch and Helen Stacy (Canberra, Australia: Federation Press, forthcoming). Professor Luban offered a longer reflection on this point in his earlier volume, *Lawyers and Justice: an Ethical Study*, 68-74.

18. See Johan Huizinga, *Homo Ludens, A Study of the Play Element in Culture*, for a spacious historical account of the element of "play" in a legal system (Boston: Beacon Press, 1955), chap. 4.

19. The Honorable Simon H. Rifkind, "The Lawyer's Role and Responsibility in Modern Society," *The Record*, vol. 30, no. 8: 534–47.

20. While I have linked truth and justice, in a sense, they also must be distinguished. As Charles P. Curtis observed, "Justice is something larger and more intimate than truth. Truth is only one of the ingredients in justice. Its whole is the satisfaction of those concerned. . . . It [the law] must give the losing party, and his friends and his sympathizers, as much satisfaction as any loser can expect. . . . The whole has been shaken out into the sun, and everyone concerned is given a feeling akin to the security which you get when you have told yourself the worst before you make a decision (Charles P. Curtis, "The Ethics of Advocacy," 4 Stanford Law Review [1951] 12). However, Curtis garbles the distinction between truth and justice when he concludes that such satisfaction demands that

a lawyer, if pushed to it, ". . . is required to be disingenuous. He is required to make statements as well as arguments which he does not believe in" (Ibid., 9). At that point, Curtis pushes beyond the claim that truth is but an ingredient in justice; he also claims that untruth is an ingredient in justice. By this further claim, justice is not well served.

21. Professional discretion is somewhat limited in that resignation is the only recourse available to the lawyer who disagrees with his client about objectives and means; and, as a practical matter, the lawyer's financial dependence on the client means that resignation is an option seldom exercised.

22. A. Kenneth Pye, "The Role of Counsel in the Suppression of Truth," *Duke Law Journal* 4 (October 1978).

23. Luban, *Lawyers and Justice*, 51.

24. Ibid., 51.

25. Kronman, *The Lost Lawyer*, 3.

26. Glendon, *A Nation Under Lawyers*.

27. Thomas L. Shaffer, *American Lawyers and Their Communities* (Notre Dame, Ind.: University of Notre Dame Press, 1991).

28. Ibid., chaps. 6 and 7.

29. William H. Herndon and Jesse W. Weik, *Herndon's Lincoln*, vol. 2 (Chicago: Belford, Clearke & Co., 1989), 345.

30. Kronman, *The Lost Lawyer*, 3.

31. "Most lawyers are free-lance bureaucrats, not tied to any major established bureaucracy, who can be hired to use, typically in a bureaucratic setting, bureaucratic skills—delay, threat, wheedling, needling, aggression, manipulation, paper passing, complexity, negotiation, selective surrender, almost-genuine passion—on behalf of someone unable or unwilling to do all that for himself." Edward A. Dauer and Arthur Allen Leff, Correspondence, 86 *Yale L. J.* 573 (1977), 581.

32. Glendon, *A Nation Under Lawyers*, 273–74.

33. The father of American legal ethics David Hoffman (1784–1854) states: "Should my client be disposed to insist on captious requisitions or frivolous and vexatious defenses, they shall be neither enforced nor countenanced by me. And if still adhered by him from a hope of pressing the other party into an unjust compromise, . . . he shall have the option to select other counsel." Thomas L. Shaffer cites Hoffman's "Resolutions in Regard to Professional Deportment" in *American Legal Ethics: Texts, Readings, and Discussion Topics* (New York: Bender, 1985), 63.

34. William H. Simon, 101 *Harvard Law Review* 1083 (1988).

35. William H. Simon, *The Practice of Justice* (Cambridge, Mass.: Harvard University Press, 1998), 71.

36. Glendon, *A Nation Under Lawyers*, 271.

37. Quoted by Gerald W. Gawalt in the introduction to the volume *The New High Priests*, 4; cited in Glendon, *A Nation Under Lawyers*, 273.

38. Reported in Gary Hengstler, "News," American Bar Association Journal (April 1989), 36, as cited by Glendon, *A Nation Under Lawyers*, 271.

39. Sometimes transforming the client's take on his own case leads in the direction of what we have come to call today "alternative conflict resolution." Lincoln points the way toward the lawyer's role in reaching such extralegal accommo-

dations to justice. In *Lawyer Lincoln* (New York: Carroll & Grof, 1936), 156, Albert Q. Woldman tells the story:

"On another occasion, when Lincoln was riding to Lewiston to try a case in the circuit court, a farmer whom the lawyer had known as Uncle Tom hailed him and sought to retain him to 'git the law' on Jim Adams, a neighbor, concerning a land line dispute.

"Uncle Tommy, you haven't had any fight with Jim, have you?"

"No."

"He's a fair to middling neighbor, isn't he?"

"Only tollable, Abe."

"He's been a neighbor of yours for a long time, hasn't he?"

"Nigh onto fifteen years."

"Part of the time you get along all right, don't you?"

"I reckon we do, Abe."

"Well, now, Uncle Tommy, you see this horse of mine? [and he pointed to his plodding, weather-beaten nag.] He isn't as good a horse as I could straddle and I sometimes get out of patience with him, but I know his faults. He does fairly well as horses go, and it might take me a long time to get used to some other horse's faults. You and Uncle Jimmy must put up with each other, as I and my horse do with one another."

And another lawsuit was averted and another friendship saved.

40. See the closing chapter on the professor in this book, which emphasizes the teaching responsibility of all the professions.

Chapter 3

The Engineer

From Nature's Adversary to Nature's Advocate?

Flannery O'Connor once said, "You know a people by the stories they tell." She had in mind, of course, myths, by which she meant, not fictions, but rather stories that coincide with and reinforce common human experiences. Myths are so deeply true of the human condition that people repeatedly act them out or relive them in their dreams. Myths order human expectations and mold sensibility. They shape us both cognitively and morally. Cognitively, they give us a vision of the world and ourselves. Morally, they cue us in, telling us how to behave in the light of these perceptions; they assign us duties toward ourselves and others. For example, the Horatio Alger myth of the self-made man tells us that we create ourselves; thus it charges us morally to charge ahead—undistracted by collateral responsibilities to others, who, in the last analysis, must also create themselves. A much older story, the myth of Icarus, which fascinated F. Scott Fitzgerald, warns the Horatios of the world not to overreach their station lest their wings melt in the sun and they crash to the ground.

This chapter on the engineer turns on a couple of myths. The first myth emerges from the disaster of the manned (and womanned) space vehicle the *Challenger*, a prime-time catastrophe that scored the national consciousness. NASA's launching of the spaceship reenacted the ambitious project of Icarus (if not to reach the sun, at least to slip "the surly bonds of earth"), and then ended disastrously before the eyes of millions of viewers, including impressionable young students amassed before TV sets in every schoolroom across the country. As a subsequent inquiry into the catastrophe made clear, the event painfully tested the professional identity of engineers and exposed the strains which engineers face in playing out their identity under the control of their modern paymasters—the government and the corporation.

The second myth figures in the last half of this chapter. The story, echoing the Beowulf myth, is even more ambitious cognitively. It poses the still larger, indeed cosmic, question of our relationship to nature. The story defines nature as a hostile power which we need to subdue in order to survive and flourish. By implication, it assigns an heroic, adversarial role to the engineer, and not only to the engineer but also to the technologies which engineers create and to the industries (and the nations) which employ them. In reflecting on this second story, we will need to ask whether it is the task of technology, as the poet put it, to break "the surly bonds of earth." Or should a different, less antagonistic, story line shape our perceptions of nature and consequently our sense of the engineer's task?

Take Off Your Engineering Hat

Shortly after its launching, hot gases leaked through the *Challenger's* booster seal, ignited, and blew up the ship in full view of a daytime television audience of millions. As the Rogers Commission subsequently reported, "There was nothing either the crew or the ground controllers could have done to avert the catastrophe." The Commission, "pointedly fixed the blame elsewhere."[1] Investigators identified that "elsewhere" as the failure of engineers and nonengineering managers to heed earlier warnings that rubber O-ring gaskets in the rocket booster seal lost their resiliency in low temperatures and thus failed to maintain the seal. (Tests after the catastrophe showed "sealing is poor to non-existent below 40 degrees"; records showed the "ambient temperature at the time of launching was only 36 degrees."[2] The gap in the seal allowed hot rocket gases to escape during any launching that occurred under anything less than optimal conditions. Morton Thiakol, Inc., the booster's manufacturer, and NASA ignored these warnings and refused to delay the launching and conduct further tests.

At a harried and hurried moment before the launching, a Morton Thiakol boss spoke to his balky subordinate, Robert Lund, the vice president of engineering and an engineer himself, urging him "take off [your] engineering hat and put on [your] management hat" and sign off approval for the flight. When Lund wore the engineer's "hat," of course, he valued all that troubling information about the rubber O-ring gaskets above profit.[3] However, wearing his manager's hat, he knew that still further information about many other parts of the vehicle tested out well. In addition, managers up and down the line knew that NASA wanted an early triumph. Meeting deadlines would save a great deal of money; a successful launch would generate favorable publicity and grease the passage of still further funding bills through Congress, which in turn would benefit NASA and its contractors. NASA put even further pressure on itself by asking President Reagan to mention the teacher, Christy McAuliffe, in his State of the Union message and by drafting for him the following melodramatic but, in the event, undelivered line: "Tonight, while I am speaking to you, a young elementary school teacher from Concord, NH, is taking us all on the ultimate field trip as she orbits the earth as the first citizen passenger on the Space Shuttle. . . . Mrs. McAuliffe's week in space is just one of the achievements in space we have planned for the coming year."[4] Considering all these factors, the managers, instead of delaying the launch, fiddled with the standards, lowered the threshold of the "acceptable," and treated the seals as a "redundant," rather than a "nonredundant," critical item. Robert Lund took off his engineering hat and put on the proffered manager's hat; he reversed his decision on the O-rings and agreed to the launch: The results etched themselves in the memories of most schoolchildren in America on that unseasonably wintry day for Florida, January 28, 1986.

The catastrophe backlit a number of professional issues that deserve attention, but the question of the engineer's identity heads the list. The image of doffing and donning a hat makes that professional identity transient and dispensable, not indelible. It resembles a tan more than a tattoo. As a person rises in a corporation, he or she may sometimes need to shed the firmly defined identity as a professional engineer and assume the broader responsibilities of a manager. The engineer, as a technician, serves and reports on a very limited aspect of an undertaking; the manager must cope with additional knowledge pouring in from every side and with additional pressures from the media, the government, budgets before Congress, and the like. The engineer *qua* engineer sees only part of the picture. He or she is not in a position to survey and judge many other items that affect the success of an enterprise.

I listened to an extensive discussion of this case at a conference on professional ethics, in which the seminar leader pressed vigorously and sympathetically the manager's point of view, but her part/whole analysis seemed faulty. I tried to test out the case against a morally comparable scenario facing the coach of a college basketball team. Imagine Coach Dribble, who, unfortunately, in the rush of championship playoffs, learns from the team doctor that the star of the team has a leaky heart valve that back-floods and strains the boy's heart. The coach and the president of the college try to persuade the doctor to certify the boy for play. The president, sensing some reluctance, argues: "But you don't see the whole picture. The boy's dentist says his teeth are fine; his hearing is excellent; he has all his hair; and you yourself have testified that, unlike other basketball players, he has no problem with his knees. Besides that, we have sold a lot of tickets for this game; the team's advance in the tournament is at stake; and the enthusiasm generated by a championship will surely cinch the funding for a new stadium. So take off your cardiologist's hat, put on the coach's hat, or my hat, and go with it."

The moral implausibility of that conversation compounds in the case of Morton Thiakol and the *Challenger*. Neither engineers nor managers working for an engineering firm can afford to take off their engineering hats. The quality of the firm's engineering *is* the larger picture. The firm in its essence depends upon the integrity of its product, which in turn rests upon the competence of its engineers' skills and the probity of their judgments. Both the firm and its managers—whether engineers or not—must remain rooted in the engineer's identity.

But what is the engineer's professional identity? We will need to revisit the three marks of the professional—intellectual, moral, and organizational—sketched out in the introduction. The ancient Greeks identified the intellectual and moral marks under the rubrics: *philotechnia*—the love of technique; and *philanthropia*—the love of humankind. The Greeks associated these marks with the physician,[5] but the West eventually assigned them as well to the engineer. What the Greek god Asklepios is to medicine, Hephaistos is to engineering, the god of the forge, the hearth, the smithy, the master of technique.[6]

Philotechnia prizes, in the first instance, resourcefulness and inventiveness. But the lover of technique is not absolutely inventive. Hephaistos creates, but not something out of nothing; rather, he wreaks something out of something else. Thus, Hephaistos, and all those who follow him, must be precise, observant, and accurate. Like the wordsmith, the engineer must not be tempted to say too much or too little, either exaggerating or belittling; he must stay on the money, on target. The engineer's integrity depends upon precision, an unwavering devotion to accuracy, a respect for "what is," even as he (and now she) creates what is "not yet." As the distinguished physicist Richard P. Feynman, a member of the Rogers Commission, wryly put it: In developing a successful technology, reality must take precedence over public relations, for "Nature cannot be fooled."[7] If, moreover, the engineer skims over the facts, or misinterprets the results, he strays not simply from nature but from himself. The gods laughed when the crippled Hephaistos foolishly disported himself as though he were the beautiful, perfectly formed Ganymede.[8]

In later Greece, *philotechnia*, or the love of the art, requires not just training, but education. A fully developed love of the art leads to the love of knowledge. The merely trained person knows selectively *how* to do something, but the educated person knows more deeply and widely *why* he does it; he knows first principles. Therewith, the ideal of observant, accurate knowledge broadens out to require a more systematic, comprehensive, and inclusive reading of the universe of which we are a part. *Philotechnia* ultimately leads in the direction of the modern university contemplating the universe.

However, not immediately. The Greek lovers of *techne* did not anticipate the university in its modern form, replete with technical institutes and schools of engineering. They celebrated the human power *for* knowledge, but not yet the powers acquired *through* knowledge. It took the work of Giordona Bruno and Francis Bacon in the late sixteenth and early seventeenth centuries to inflate *philotechnia* by linking knowledge with dominion and power and thus show the way to the modern feats of engineering. Human beings image forth the divine not simply by virtue of their possession of contemplative reason but creativity. Bruno thus linked intelligence with the hands, that is, an intelligence not simply to the contemplation of what is, but to manipulations that would bring into being what has not heretofore existed.

> The gods have given man intelligence and hands, and have made him in their image, endowing him with a capacity superior to other animals. This capacity consists not only in the power to work in *accordance with* nature and the usual course of things . . . but beyond that . . . to the end that by fashioning, or [having] the power to fashion, other natures, other courses, other orders by means of his intelligence [and] with that freedom without which

his resemblance to the deity would not exist, he might in the end make himself god of the earth.[9]

Bacon, from this point forward (about 1583–1585), felt that "a new order of events was at hand, the specific quality of which would consist no longer in a mere *imitation* of nature but in her *domination* by man."[10] Inasmuch as knowledge is power, the virtue of curiosity leads to virtuosity—the capacity to work great changes in nature—to produce *magnalia naturae* to match *magnalia dei.*

In Bacon's view, the power that flowed from knowledge should redound to the benefit of humanity. The intellectual mark of the professional should link with the moral mark; *philotechnia* should yield *philanthropia.* In linking knowledge, power, and universal benefit, Bacon thus broke with the magicians and alchemists before him, to whom, nonetheless, he owed a great deal. The wizards and magicians linked knowledge with power, but they were tempted to think in proprietary terms about that knowledge. Bacon complained that they transformed nature, but simply to arouse wonder rather than to serve some larger human purpose: they were vain-glorious and self-seeking; they believed themselves to belong to a privileged class of *illuminati*, hermetically sealed off from the rest of the human race. Thus Bacon insisted on adding the virtue of philanthropy to those of curiosity and virtuosity. Benjamin Farrington has written that the new knowledge gained thereby was to be

> fed back into the industrial life of the nation. This was no small task, as Bacon well knew. It was King's business. It should not be left to the monk in the cloister, the alchemist's furnace, the rich nobleman's curiosity or the workshop of the artisan. It required to be taken under the wing of the government. . . . For it was not simply an addition to knowledge but the inauguration of a new way of life, the great installation of man's dominion over the universe.[11]

Bacon, take note, spoke of *man's* dominion over the universe, not the dominion of *some* men over the universe, or the dominion of some men over other men, or one generation over future generations. For Bacon, this universalism distinguished the scientist from the parochial magician, the wayward wizard, and the hermetical alchemist. Bacon believed that the enlargement of powers through science should not be construed as the limited triumph of some, but the enhancement of the many. To this very day, we invoke this sense of universal participation in knowledge and power—"One small step for man, one giant step for mankind." And to this day, when we hear talk about enlarging human powers through science we neglect the questions of whose power over what, over whom, for whose benefit, and at what price. We pass over these pointed questions and assume that the power acquired through knowledge eventually runs off into a kind of reservoir at the general disposition of the human race. Indeed, the several links between knowledge, power, and philanthropy interlocked and eventually justified and produced the land-grant universities in the United States and their equivalents in technical institutes the world over, which have remade the face of the earth under the banner of benefit to humankind.

Professionals traditionally organized: the Greeks, into crafts; the medieval crafts, into guilds; and modern professionals, into their societies. These professional societies, at least according to the traditional ideal, should reflect in their organizational structure the intellectual mark of *philotechnia* and the moral mark of *philanthropia*. The intellectual mark demands organizationally that professionals should congregate in a company of peers. They should organize themselves collegially rather than hierarchically. The ideal of collegiality follows from the professional's knowledge of first principles. The merely trained person, lacking a knowledge of first principles, remains subordinate to his trainer; however, the educated professional, understanding first principles, eventually attains equal footing with other professionals, including even his teachers. Professionals should naturally associate as colleagues unfettered by the obsequies of hierarchy.

Similarly, the moral mark of philanthropy or altruism makes a demand on the organization. The guild should orient to self-improvement rather than to self-promotion. It must develop ways to discipline the unethical or incompetent professional, and, through continuing education and other devices, to improve the performance of all members. So at least goes the organizational ideal.

One can, of course, ring the changes on the ways in which traditional professional guilds have fallen short of both organizational ideals. Informal hierarchies develop in guilds; and guilds have only too often pursued self-promotion rather than self-improvement. But these lapses in the performance of the guilds hardly compare with the systemic pressures engineers face as they respond to a further all-encompassing development in the modern world: the emergence of the modern state and the modern corporation.

We live in the age of the organization. Most of the approximately 1.6 million engineers in the United States in the 1980s worked for large institutions, either corporations in the private sector (approximately 77 percent) or the government (approximately 15 percent).[12] Elliott A. Krause estimates that in the 1990s 85 percent of U. S. engineering graduates worked for corporations and about 10 to 15 percent, for the government or in the academy.[13] Working for a business or doing "the King's business" inevitably and powerfully strains the organizational marks of the professional. Altruism tends to narrow. The more spacious horizon of philanthropy shrinks into an exclusive loyalty to the organization which pays one's salary and defines one's place in the corporate hierarchy.

Further, the naturally collegial structure of professional relationships tends to yield to the relatively hierarchical ordering of the corporation and the state. The large-scale organization tends to force the horizontal lines of collegiality (and candor) into the verticals of deference (and data doctoring). Subordinates quickly learn to tip their hats (or take off their hats) to superordinates. The employee can tend to dwindle to a pure instrument, forfeiting the egalitarian status and citizen's voice in a *polis*.

What can the *Challenger* disaster teach us? Clearly, more than the importance of the engineer's commitment to accuracy. Professionals in this case misinterpreted the results more than they fudged the facts; doctoring the data occurred less than spin-doctoring. They changed the meaning of results by raising the levels of the tolerable, once it became clear that the test results would not fall within the previously established limits of the acceptable. If only one third of an O-ring on a previous flight eroded, "it was asserted there was a safety factor of three," a phrase that misleads.[14] Beforehand and throughout the tests, officials had classified the seals as "non-redundant" (that is, critical). This classification prompted officials to put in a second O-ring as a backup, but one of bad design. Thus the discovery and remedy did not protect NASA from the ensuing catastrophes.

The *Challenger* disaster also exposed systemic, organizational problems in the flow of technical information in bureaucracies, public and private. The information system at one and the same time committed the sins of excess and defect. The Rogers Commission reported, on the one hand, that "the existing internal communication system is disseminating too much information, often with little or no discrimination in its importance."[15] This excess of information, all of which needs to be processed, quickly turns the discriminating mind into pulp. Ironically, commissions of inquiry can similarly render themselves insensate by requesting reports from any and all parts of a far-flung enterprise, and thus generating an avalanche of data which they must then submissively process. The free-spirited member of the commission, Dr. Richard P. Feynman, struck out on his own to talk with scientists and engineers (without their bosses around) as much, he said, to block out irrelevant data as to target on the crucial lapses that led to the disaster.[16]

At the same time, a hierarchical organization suffers from a defect of information and thus forestalls the engineer's humility in the face of fact. Relevant information, particularly bad news, does not readily flow upward. Long before the *Challenger* disaster, Charles Peters and Russell Baker wrote:

> In any reasonably large government organization, there exists an elaborate system of information cutoffs, comparable to that by which city water systems shut off large water-main breaks, closing down, first small feeder pipes, then larger and larger valves. The object is to prevent information, particularly of an unpleasant character, from rising to the top of the agency, where it may produce results unpleasant to those in the lower ranks. . . . Thus the executive at or near the top lives in constant danger of not knowing, until he reads it on Page One some morning, that his department is hip-deep in disaster."[17]

Peters and Baker's comment needs adjustment in only three particulars. First, the managers and engineers of the *Challenger* were hip-deep in disaster not simply on Page One but on Live Television. Second, bad news resists rising to the top not only in the government but also in business corporations. Christopher Stone demonstrates that sludgy resistance to an upward flow of information in his book on corporate responsibility, *Where the Law Ends*. Third, the "lower ranks" do not bear exclusive responsibility for the failure of bad news to rise to the top. The authorities send myriad signals through their rhetoric and incentives that they do not want to hear bad news. Such signals and pressures set up a rhythm and tempo that cycle through an enterprise. People tend to tap their feet to an optimistic beat.

They may begin to justify decisions which, free of that can-do spirit and rhythm, they would not condone. The upbeat that pulses through the enterprise can encourage recklessness and carelessness; and it can create a resentment toward anyone who would disrupt that beat by "blowing the whistle."

Remedies

Blowing the whistle breaks the rhythm in a sporting match; it can also temporarily halt spouse-battering or bureaucratic malfeasance. When the organization violates the professional's sense of integrity, the professional can, of course, appeal to the boss, go over the boss's head, or go outside the organization to the newspapers or to the courts. As a last resort, the professional can resign. British politicians have been much more inclined than their American counterparts to use the moral power of resignation. But, generally it is easier for fully established persons with independent resources and reputations, than for professionals at middle-level jobs, to blow the whistle and resign. Major leaders do not need letters of reference from their offended bosses to secure their next jobs, but middle managers do. Further, lacking independent resources and/or a portable or vested pension, the professional who resigns faces not only the loss of a job but the forfeit of retirement monies. Ordinarily, the whistle blower needs some protection. It is a bad system that demands that one be a martyr to be moral.

Thus organizations need structural remedies to encourage the free flow of information, good or bad, and to tolerate indispensable self-criticism. Such remedies may include adequate protections for the whistle blower through the assurance of anonymity (balanced against fairness to the accused); the provision of adequate, portable, or promptly vested pensions; and the installation of independent reviews after the whistle has been blown.

The old Catholic "principle of subsidiarity" argues that one should try to handle a problem at a point closest to its origin before appealing to more distant, higher, or external authorities. But, when such direct efforts at remedy have been exhausted, the professional may need, as a last resort, to go public, by appealing either to the courts or to the press. It would be still better if one could resolve disputes by appeal to the professional guild. But, the engineering guilds have failed to develop the means to discipline corporations.

Engineers in the United States have never wielded effective guild powers. "Unlike American medicine or American law, there never has been much question about the status of American engineering: engineers were and are . . . middle-level employees."[18] Engineers have never enjoyed the rank and status in the American corporation that some graduates of the Ecole Polytechnique and other elite engineering schools in France have held, where, until 1920, the head engineer "worked at the right hand of the patron or owner-manager."[19] Although engineers in the U. S. corporations are partly in control of their workplace as they circulate among colleagues in a firm, upper-level management sets the parameters of their work and decides on projects.[20] Engineers have no independent community of guild members to which they might appeal, as Perucci and Gerstl conceded in the very title of their book, *Profession Without Community*.[21] Engineers need not join their respective engineering societies or even register with the state registration boards as engineers. If membership were required, the professional societies might actually establish legally enforceable standards; and engineers might appeal to those standards if pressured by companies to engage in unprofessional conduct. As it is, the guilds can only promote, they cannot enforce, professional standards.[22] Under these circumstances, the possibility of organized guild action against corporations does not exist.

Engineering guilds lack, for example, the disciplinary powers, which the American Association of University Professors (AAUP) can bring to bear on behalf of aggrieved faculty members against misbehaving colleges and universities. While the AAUP does not directly control the accreditation of universities, the culture of the academic guild has shaped accreditation procedures and thereby exercises a substantial review power over the conduct of universities. Further, the AAUP can and does provide some legal funds to support professors in court cases of merit. While their codes urge engineers to stick to their professional conscience when the companies for which they work pressure them to violate an article of the code, the guilds offer the beleaguered engineer only a pat on the head, not the required financial back-up or legal funds. When I asked a professor of engineering ethics why the guilds lack the grit to enforce their codes, he wryly observed that they depend heavily on corporate contributions to finance their activities and often choose engineers who have shifted into top management positions to lead them. Many firms even pay the guild dues of their employees. Edward Layton, a historian of engineering, observes that corporations ". . . might join with others in withdrawing support from the professional societies if they thought the societies acted contrary to their interests. . . . Actions [such as forbidding employees to attend meetings or serve as officers or withdrawing advertising and financial support] might deal a severe blow to the continued viability of the societies themselves."[23] In effect, the fox has bought the chicken house, designed its polity, and set its agenda to suit his own convenience. First steps in the advance of professional integrity require recapturing the guilds and setting agendas that help sustain and empower their members who must live out their calling in the modern corporation.

Environmental Ethics

This chapter, so far, has focused only on obvious lapses in professional conduct, such as falsifying, misinterpreting, and suppressing data, and with the difficulties of enforcing professional identity and standards in the organization. But engineering ethics must attend to a further, even more important, issue. It must deal not simply with obvious lapses in technical performance but with the secondary and tertiary effects of that performance. Smoothly accurate technical performance may serve environmentally destructive ends. We cannot fool nature, but we can despoil it. Ordinarily, engineers do not ignore phenomena or falsify, misinterpret, or suppress data but they are daily and fatefully engaged in changing the face of the earth. We need therefore to turn to the issues that cluster today around the term "environmental ethics."[24]

The burgeoning field of environmental ethics may be distinguished but not separated from engineering ethics. A total separation would falsely detach the discipline of professional technique from the awesome gift of nature and the discipline which nature places upon professionals in the exercise of technique. Engineering ethics should deal not only with technical correctness and decorum within the corporation and the marketplace, but with the cumulative, spreading impacts on nature of the processes and products which technique makes possible. Responsibility for the deleterious impacts of technology falls on professionals, not simply on the society at large. At the same time, maintaining a distinction between environmental and engineering ethics reminds us that the profession hardly bears exclusive responsibility for despoiling the environment. The habits, appetites, and wants of the American people help push the bureaucracies of the marketplace and the government, which, in turn, deploy professionals. Thus the following review of six contending American nature myths will explore their implications, not only for the role of professionals, but for the organizational deployment of professional technique, and for the habits of a society that help shape our perceptions, uses, and abuses of nature.

Contending American Nature Myths

Like many other teachers of ethics, I answered the call to make a speech on the first "Earth Day" celebration in the early 1970s. The only memorable part of the invitation was its location—Gary, Indiana. I raced north from Bloomington (in the rural part of the state) to make my pitch for Mother Earth. No representatives from U.S. Steel or Bethlehem Steel joined me on that occasion to tell audiences about company initiatives to sweeten the air, freshen the rivers, and relieve the grass and trees of the industrial grunge that coated them daily. Rather, it fell to one of my hosts to explain, with a shy trace of local patriotism, that Gary, contrary to popular opinion, was not the most polluted city in the state. That distinction belonged to Terre Haute, whose cement factories produced a fine, airborne dust that matched the ubiquity of God and settled on everything. Popular opinion notwithstanding, Terre Haute, not Gary, was the Gary of Indiana.

What could anyone say on Earth Day in the industrial underbelly of Chicago? I thought back to W. H. Auden's comment, on a cold winter evening in New England, 1953, about the American attitude toward nature. In his offhand, epigrammatic way, he said, "In Europe, nature is an animal to be trained; in America, a dragon to be slain."

Auden's two compressed stories anticipated what we later came to call the ecological crisis. By ecological crisis, I mean several developments chiefly associated with the industrial, agricultural, and, increasingly, the biological revolutions. The pollution of the nonhuman environment on a scale so massive as to affect the life chain to which human beings belong and therefore to threaten human existence itself—if not in this generation, then within a biblical three or four. The exhaustion of nonrenewable energy sources at a pace sufficiently rapid to provoke the nations eventually to turn to other energy sources troublesome in their own right, by virtue of their being exhaustible (coal), and/or polluting (coal and nuclear fission), or expensive in energy to produce (fuel from coal shale). The gradual encroachment upon and destruction of the wilderness and various species of nonhuman life, an encroachment of consequence, whether or not it negatively affects human survival. The threats to the health and safety of both workers and neighbors of manufacturing plants, as well as to the consumers of their industrial goods and biochemical artifacts, including, in some cases, risks to their children. Threats to the ecology of the human body, which result less from an adversarial relation to nature at large than from an antagonistic attitude toward the body itself, an attitude that affects our view of disease and the healing arts. Finally, the chilling recognition that only a few nations have undergone development and that the problems which have confronted us so far will worsen geometrically if development in Latin America, Africa, India, and Southeast Asia proceeds as recklessly and destructively as it has in the West and the Eastern Rim.

Slaying the Dragon. Auden's phrase invokes a myth, the Western version of which appears in *Beowulf*. Briefly, it tells the story of a land in the grip of hostile power and of a hero who lifts a curse from the land by killing the dragon (Grendel), the dragon's mother, and finally an airborne monster. The people prosper through his victory, but in the course of the final battle, Beowulf, abandoned by his fellows, is himself slain.

The myth (except for the Christian element—Beowulf's abandonment and death) usually includes the following ingredients: a battle with a hostile and destructive power that exceeds the ordinary measure of humankind; the emergence of a hero with special resources for combating the enemy (Beowulf wears a special coat of mail and wields an exceptionally powerful, indeed magical, sword, fashioned by giants, with which he kills Grendel's dam); the slaying of the dragon and the extraction of riches from its slashed belly; and (by implication) the ugly residue of a vanquished carcass.

I do not want to suggest that the Beowulf myth has "influenced" the American perception of nature through the retelling of this particular story. (The biblical stories from Genesis and Deuteronomy about "subduing the earth" figure much more prominently in the ritual life of the American people as they settled a continent.) However, the Beowulf myth roughly corresponds to the lived experience of the American struggle to survive in a harsh environment and exposes the direction in which Americans took the early biblical injunctions.

Briefly applied, America was a land of great distances, harsh extremes in climate, and a relatively small population, but a land that also promised extraordinary riches to those who conquered it. The country thus needed heroes: first, pioneers, then second, engineers and industrialists, who could subdue the environment. It needed central heating to fight the cold; air conditioning to fight the humidity; drugs to fight disease; trains, cars, and planes to conquer space; bulldozers to carve up the terrain; shafts and tunnels to mine it; test tubes to manipulate materials into prodigal new forms; and reactors to unleash their even more prodigal energies.

The story promises that after engineers and others subdue the hostile environment, great riches will pour out of the dragon's slashed belly. These riches will create personal fortunes for those who funded the war on nature, and add to the gross product of the nation from which others will more remotely prosper. The battle, to be sure, may leave a slashed carcass and scarred earth in its path. But the plunder is worth the fighting; and who is to say otherwise? The fruits of victory belong to the victor.

This adversarial view of nature does not appear to jibe with the picture-postcard portrayal of nature, the storied peace and quiet of the country which Americans prize. But, in fact, the pioneers endured a harsher, more inclement environment than the Europe they left behind, tempered as Europe is by the Gulf Stream. Americans so accept today the technologically enforced world-within-a-world which central heating and air conditioning create, that they often forget the severity of their climate. But others notice it. Several decades ago, the Russian basketball team made a tour of the United States. Its schedule was rigorous; members of the team were homesick. But when they landed at the airport in Iowa, to play the University of Iowa team, a member of the Russian squad descended the icy aluminum steps, felt the Canadian winds howling, surveyed the banks of snow whipping about him, and suddenly broke into a broad smile of recognition, saying, "Siberia."

The heat can be equally extreme. A visitor in Houston asked a distinguished lawyer to what he would attribute the rapid growth of that city. Ship channel and cotton port? Oil and petrochemical industry? Space technology and its electronic spinoffs? "All these developments were important," the lawyer replied, "but you left off your list the most important factor of all, without which this uninhabitable area would not have become a world class city—central air-conditioning."

Consider how differently U.S. history would have unfolded if the coasts were reversed and the Puritans had landed, not in New England, but in San Diego. What would San Diego weather and avocados have done to soften up the Puritan spirit? Jonathan Edwards in a hot tub? Sinners in the hands of a laid-back God? A landing in San Diego would have removed the sinews from the Beowulf story and the early desert command to subdue the earth.

The immensity of its space as well as the extremes of its climate provoked an adversarial response to the natural environment in America. The huge American land mass, sparsely inhabited (in most areas the American Indians counted for less than the Canaanites), created in settlers the conviction that they had to conquer space.

The Americans, to be sure, related to space ambivalently. For those weary of social inequality, poverty, and class differences in Great Britain and Europe, the great empty spaces of the North American continent offered sanctuary and opportunity. A latent hostility to humankind partly provoked the trek to the West. To have a neighbor was to have an enemy. The romance of the wilderness expressed a yearning for a manless and womanless nature, a desire to recover a pre-political, imperial self, a self without competition and limits.[25] The struggle with nature offered partial relief from the social struggle. At the same time, however, a harsh climate and huge distances punished pioneers with loneliness. Limitless space offered them relief from the tensions of community, but it also deprived them of its solace and it severely limited commerce.

Thus, ambivalence notwithstanding, Americans needed technologies with which to conquer space. They even managed to engineer a political system that would span the continent's distances. In the Constitution of the United States, they created a device that ingeniously utilized both the vast distances of the continent and the fierce conflicts within nature itself to solve the political problem which human nature presented. Factional self-interest threatened to tear the country to pieces after the Americans won the Revolutionary War. The Constitution incorporated two devices to counter both the tyrannical and the anarchical effects of factionalism. First, a federal system of checks and balances set faction against faction, and thus limited the power of any one faction; second, the device of *representative* government insulated the federal government from the fierce heat of local passion. In both cases, the founders of the nation contrived devices that slyly exploited nature itself. The device of pitting "ambition against ambition" through checks and balances mimicked the natural phenomenon of force and counterforce. Second, the device of representative government converted continental scale itself into an ally as it permitted leaders to function at some distance from local passions. The founders did not see this constitutional system as growing organically out of the American's experience of the natural environment. They deliberately engineered the political system; they conceived it as an invention, a mechanism, to overcome the problems that nature and human nature presented. This devised political machinery foreshadowed later American uses of technology; it was a harbinger in politics of the technology to come.

The American experience of an outsize nature derives not only from the huge expanse of the continent but also from its outsize particulars: its coastal plains, mountains, rivers, prairies, skies, deserts, and the great oceans that separate this country from the rest of the world. These boundless particulars do not easily masquerade as a tamable animal, trained to fit into the system of human purposes. Quite the contrary, nature in America appears to exceed in grandeur, might, and destructive fury the petty calculations of men and women. The best of our novelists sensed this power keenly. Melville devotes a chapter in *Moby Dick* to the size of the white whale, but, after attempting to convey its magnitude, he concedes that the malevolent beast exceeds all efforts to describe it. In a similar vein, Faulkner tells a story about a convict assigned to rescue a woman trapped on a flooded Mississippi River. The river sweeps them both out into the flood and the man finds himself "in a state in which he was a toy and pawn on a vicious and flammable geography."[26]

Not even the original river bed is discernible. He does not know "whether the river had become lost in a drowned world or if the world had become drowned in one limitless river."[27] At one time, the flood appears to be a brief interlude in otherwise peaceful natural rhythms, but it also ominously recalls the geologic catastrophe from which the country itself derives: "He was now in the channel of a slough, a bayou, in which until today no current had run probably since the old subterranean outrage which had created the country."[28] The jail to which the convict eventually returns seems like a refuge and sanctuary after his ordeal in the dangerous expanse of the flood.

The Americans, confronting the continents, thought of themselves as "pioneers," a word that should leave no doubt that they perceived their environment to be strenuous. Like the Brazilian *bandeirantes* (who faced an even more ungovernable natural environment),[29] *pioneer* is a military term in origin: it refers to foot soldiers in advance of a main body of troops; volunteer soldiers at that, because they assume special risks in going beyond the normal reach of human knowledge and safety. Some of the heroic qualities attached to the pioneer gathered later around the American myth of the free-lance entrepreneur and capitalist, who ventured out into the unknown, or, still later, around the scientist, inventor, and engineer who discovered the unknown, invented the wondrous, and applied it with ingenuity. Together, these figures provide the heroic virtues and the magic sword with which to subdue nature and wrest a prodigal life from a new land. They deserved the land by dint of their labors; John Locke taught them that; and Adam Smith reassured them that the people at large would prosper through their own private flourishing. Eventually, engineering schools would justify the disciplines as the intellectual foundries that would fashion the mastering swords that would yield the fortunes ensuing.

Befriending the Wolf. A second story, growing out of the Franciscan legends, has shaped the modern romantic, environmentalist reaction to the dragon slayer. St. Francis, like Beowulf, contends with a beast— the wolf of Gubbia—who ravaged the countryside but whom St. Francis, instead of killing, befriends. No Beowulf, he. The historian Lynn White seized upon this story to counter the dominant Christian tradition, which, he believes, helped produce the current ruthless exploitation of nature.[30] The Jewish and Christian scriptures, according to White, assigned man dominion over every creeping thing and commanded him to fill the earth and subdue it. White sees a straight causal line from this scriptural authorization (abstracted from the biblical notion of stewardship) through the arts and crafts of the Catholic Middle Ages to the high technological arrogance of modern times, and the arrogation of engineering by economic incentive.

White recommends instead that we substitute for this dominant myth of exploitation the Franciscan attitude toward Nature (albeit culturally "recessive" in the West) that hails "Brother Son and Sister Moon, Brother Wind and Sister Water, Brother Fire and Sister Earth, and Sister Bodily Death," in a kind of holy democracy, or intimate family, of all living things. He recommends St. Francis as the patron saint of ecologists, a designation which Pope John Paul II eventually made official.

This myth has chiefly shaped the romantics in the environmentalist movement who demanded the renunciation of technology and the slowdown of engineering. Specifically, these romantics worried more about the destructive powers which industrial societies mobilize to conquer nature than the destructiveness of nature itself. They worry about air and water pollution, the vanishing of the wilderness and treasured species within it, the depletion of nonrenewable resources, and the potential impacts of powerful new processes and products on workers and consumers. In effect, technology replaces nature as the mythic monster that plunders riches from their rightful owners. (Giants, after all, forged the sword that Beowulf used to kill Grendel's mother; he owes his equipment to huge, rebellious, dragonish powers.) Thus one looks for ways to call back the dragons unloosed to fight the dragon. Environmentalists looked particularly to the regulatory interventions of the federal government as the only agent powerful enough to halt the onslaught against nature.

The Reagan-Bush years, in turn, produced a powerful reaction against any such federal intervention. The myth of slaying the dragon took yet another twist. The Reaganites viewed the government as the destructive power that separated the bounty of nature from its rightful owners, the developers. They took it as their task to get "the government off the backs of the American people." The phrase evoked the image of an incubus, an evil spirit or power, that descends upon and burdens its victim. Free market apologists argued that we face no energy shortage, no shortfall of goods and jobs that private enterprise cannot overcome if unleashed from government shackles. President Reagan appointed as his secretary for the Department of Energy a South Carolina dentist and protégé of Senator Strom Thurmond who, before liquidating the department altogether, hoped to develop nuclear energy as the cheapest source of energy. Secretary Edwards proclaimed, "We need to unleash it, to free the private sector." To that end, he said, "It would be my pleasure to try and cut down DOE's size, to dismantle it, to redistribute it."[31] Meanwhile, the Secretary of the Interior at the time, James Gaius Watts, whose Department would take over the dismembered remains of the DOE, believed that the Government had stolen from the people their own holdings. Hence the populist ring to his statements: "'I'm people oriented . . . If you knock down a hill, because there was coal underneath it, you ought to take the result and use it for people.' Useless land can be improved with a flat area for a hospital or a school or a playground or whatever, a housing development or the like. 'If I err, I'm going to err on the people side.'"[32] This latter-day Beowulf would tear an arm off Grendel—the United States government—lift a curse from the land, and let the people prosper. Subsequently, President Bush sought to subvert the power of federal regulatory agencies with his Council on Business Competitiveness, headed by Vice-President Quayle, which passed on any and all regulations with a view to their impact on business and jobs. Once again, the Council struck a populist note. "Environmental extremists" would severely impair Americans in the marketplace by burdening American business with costly regulations which, in turn, would cost people their jobs.

Nature as Stage Scenery and Prop for the Human. The Renaissance humanist Pico della Mirandola, offered a third portrayal of the relation of humans to the natural environment. Less aggressive than the Beowulf myth, it nevertheless prepares the way for the human mastery of nature. In his "Oration on the Dignity of Man," Pico recounts that God, the Father, the supreme Architect, faced a problem in creating humankind. He had already produced a full range of beings from highest to lowest; he had used up, as it were, his treasure house of various natures. All was discouragingly complete. However, God ingeniously solved the problem of bestowing something distinctive on humankind by giving to Adam no fixed form or abode. Adam could be the maker and molder of his own nature, free to ordain the limits of his nature in accordance with his own free will. In creativity, human beings would resemble divinity itself. The gods were amazed. Adam could have whatever he chooses and be whatever he wills. "Who would not admire this our chameleon?"[33]

Another Renaissance figure, Juan Luis Vives, shifted the image from chameleon to actor. Man, the archmime, performs in the great amphitheater of nature and plays whatever roles he chooses. His resourcefulness and creativity remind the gods of Jupiter himself.[34] In effect, this image of man, the actor, loosens the ties between humans and all other creatures, bolted down as they are to specific natures. While renaissance artists duly savored the natural world, nature, ultimately, retires into the background as scenery and prop for the consummate actor who performs in the foreground of creation on center stage.

Conjoined later with Francis Bacon's account of the power of science and technology, the great actor engages in constantly refashioning not only himself but the set on which he performs. In the unfolding of Western history, the reengineering of the external scenery, by means of the industrial revolution, comes first; and the remolding of the human reality, through the biological revolution and genetic engineering, comes later. In any event, at length, nature and even human nature recede into raw material upon which the protean power of the human works. In a libertarian marketplace setting, raw nature acquires its significance and value through human labor and imagination. Value does not inhere in things; it depends upon human projects and investments and transformations; value becomes value added. This basic story-line offers a different "take" on nature from the Beowulf myth, but, like the Beowulf narrative, it encourages an aggressive surmounting of nature and its limitations.

Taming the Animal. A fourth story—Auden's image of an animal to be tamed—lies behind traditional European sacramentalism. It differs from the story-line that would interpret nature as a hostile power and from the libertarian tradition that would dismiss nature to incidental prop and raw material. But it also breaks with the Romantics among the environmentalists who would deny the necessity of taming nature. The Romantics tended to repudiate technology altogether and blame the biblical tradition for legitimating technological imperialism in the Genesis passage about subduing the earth. However, biblical scholars took Lynn White to task for lifting the Genesis passage out of its wider context in Scripture. The biblical command to subdue the earth hardly justifies the modern airport advocates of nuclear energy or the hotel room pitchmen planning to dry up the Everglades and sell real estate plots in former Florida wetlands. In fact, the Hebrew word which we translate "subdue" more accurately refers to tilling the ground and growing crops—nature cultivated rather than vanquished. We need to get the biblical story straight and not simply interpret it through the lens of modern industrial civilization.

In addition to his exegetical distortions, Lynn White wholly ignored the sacramental traditions of East and West. Sacramentalism provides a further great option in response to nature. It emphasizes the goodness of the nonhuman creation. Far from disdaining natural elements, it takes them up into the orbit of human purposes—bread, wine, water, and oil—and honors them as the bearer of sacral power. Sacramentalism rejects that enmity toward the material realm that characterized dualistic religion in the ancient Near East. It also rejects the libertarian marketplace outlook that relegates nature to raw material. Further, it links the reception of these sacred natural elements with the great turning points in human life—birth, growth, marriage, sickness, and death—and the prosaic bodily actions of washing, eating, and reproducing. Thus sacramentalism presupposes and celebrates the ties of humankind to the great biological rhythms of the nonhuman world.

At the same time, sacramentalism, unlike romanticism, does not indulge in a mystical view of nature that elevates the nonhuman into the divine. It pronounces the nonhuman world good (not absolute good) and draws nature up into the orbit of human purposes. Significantly, the central Christian sacrament takes precisely those natural elements—bread and wine—that have been compounded with human labor and tending, and makes these elements the bearers of sacred power.

This sacramentalism teases out theologically the alternative story which W. H. Auden associated with traditional Europe. Nature resembles an animal to be trained. Nature is a largely living, creaturely good, not itself directly divine, but a fit bearer of the divine. Further, nature is susceptible to, and even better for, the respectful interventions of humankind—like a domestic animal, to be trained and reared in the household of human purposes. The Benedictines and Cistercians symbolized this view of nature. They deliberately settled in swamps which they needed to drain to eliminate mosquitoes carrying malaria; and thereby they learned something about farming. Accordingly, René Dubos proposed St. Benedict, rather than St. Francis, as the patron saint of ecologists.[35]

While the Franciscan Romantics wished to dismember the beast—dismantle the technology—and repair to a nature, worshipful and adoring, W. H. Auden, E. F. Schumacher (*Small Is Beautiful*), and René Dubos ("A Theology of the Earth") urged that we neither fear nor worship nature. We should reckon with nature on a more comfortable, still disciplined, domestic scale. We should also scale down the instruments with which we discipline nature. We need "intermediate technologies," in Schumacher's words, a "technology with a human face," technologies more oriented to process than to product.

What does it profit a man to double the Gross Domestic Product if the processes by which he attains the goal grossly deform the habitable earth and waste his children's legacy? Politically, we must housebreak humankind, in order to preserve the wilderness, regulate pollution, limit the depletion of nonrenewable resources, and protect producers and users from harmful products.

The Tragic Myth. The tragic law of ethics and politics may be stated as follows: the perception of a problem and the readiness to do something about it rarely surface before the solution is beyond reach. Ethics breeds a series of "musts." Politically, we must preserve the wilderness, regulate pollution, limit the depletion of nonrenewable resources, and protect producers and users from harmful products. But the efforts to remedy and repair stir up reactions driven by all sorts of interests, habits, addictions, myopias, and legitimate concerns that make it all but impossible to undo what has been done. The tragic myth highlights the irreversibility of evil. What technique has done cannot be easily undone.

No writer has compressed the tragic intertwining of the human and the natural better than Cormac McCarthy in *The Crossing*, the second volume of his *The Border Trilogy*. McCarthy tells there the story of yet another marauding wolf of mythic proportions.[36] McCarthy's she-wolf has traveled across the border from Mexico into the boot heel of New Mexico, where it has killed calves and heifers in the winter snows. In this case, no St. Francis appears to befriend and tame the animal. Rather, a sixteen-year-old son of a rancher, at the urging of his father, sets out a series of traps to snare the predator. But the clever wolf springs the traps without getting caught; and the boy, increasingly challenged, obsesses on his opponent. To catch her, he must, like any good hunter, "see the world the wolf saw," a discipline, however, which gradually bonds him to the predator. At length he succeeds in snaring the wolf, her forefoot caught in the jaws of a trap. But the boy has now so powerfully bonded to the animal—carrying a litter of pups—that he cannot kill her. Neither, however, can he set her free to resume killing his father's herd. So he determines to take her back to her habitat in the mountains of Mexico, to set things right again. Ingeniously, with the help of ropes, some leather, an improvised muzzle, and a long pole, he manages to spring the wolf from the trap without himself being torn to pieces; and he and the wolf start out together for Mexico.

After crossing the border, however, soldiers capture him and his high-strung companion and sell the wolf to a carnival, the owners of which cage, exhibit, and hype the wolf as a man-eating beast. The boy rescues the wolf from this commercial degradation, and, once again, they set off for the mountains—only to be captured again by the soldiers. This time the soldiers sell the wolf to dog handlers running an arena for gamblers, where the wolf must face a series of killer dogs, sometimes singly and then, hopelessly, in twos and threes. At length, the wolf weakens and will be torn to pieces. This time the soldiers stand guard; the boy cannot rescue her. Appalled, he leaves, then changes his mind, returns to the arena, takes out his gun, and kills the wolf before the dogs can shred her alive.

McCarthy's story tracks out a tragic attempt at restoration; it counters the optimism that has driven so far the project to conquer nature. The romantic calls for the renunciation of offending technologies. The European sacramentalist looks to small-scale substitutes. Adversarialists, even when they recognize that they have defiled and wasted nature, argue, in effect, not to worry. What technology has done, technology can undo. Evil is reversible. The dragon's despoiled carcass, if it bothers enough people willing to pay for its removal, will become a profit opportunity for yet another inventor/entrepreneur. If high-rises have encroached too much on the coastlines, then sea walls will protect them. If cars have converted small trolley towns into great sprawling metropolises with clogged highways, then a mass transit system will clear the roads again. If the energy appetites of new technologies have produced a troublesome greenhouse effect, still newer technologies will right the wrong.

However, technology cannot so conveniently reverse harms. Sea walls have often speeded the very erosion they were supposed to impede. The automobile has created a huge urban sprawl without enough congregate living to enable a mass transit system to serve a city successfully. The MTBE additive to gasoline, which we mandated to make gasoline burn cleaner and lower air pollution has began to enter the underground water system and compromise drinking water. And the greenhouse effect, allied with other global changes in temperature, may irradiate in every direction, affecting crops, wildlife, skin cancer, ice caps, water levels, and the shorelines of continents, which petty sea walls will not begin to contain.

The Covenantal Myth. Yet another story and its implied ethic of nature, which I would associate with the word "covenantal," demands attention, especially on the American scene. In many respects, the covenantal narrative overlaps the sacramental, but it differs in two particulars that capture the distinctively adversarial features of the American experience of nature and community. First, nature does not confront Americans as a pussycat to be trained. The country that *Lonesome Dove* portrays, with its violent winds, its snows, its ice storms, its sudden lightening bolts on the prairies, and its deep frost lines, suggests an outsize, powerful nature, not readily tamed, a nature obeying its own imperatives which do not necessarily serve human comfort or convenience.[37]

Further, any nature myth and environmental ethic in America (or anywhere) must take into account the experience of conflict between humans, including conflicts between humans in their attitudes toward nature. A philosophy or a theology that treats nature as a pet and neglects the social covenant will intensify antagonism in the human community and ultimately sharpen antagonism to nature. Such environmentalism deteriorates into the political sport of the well-to-do, who respect nature but ignore the need of the poor for jobs. It feeds the populist resentments which opponents of the environmentalist movement have sought to enflame.

The covenantal myth also differs from the tragic myth. While the covenantal myth (and the rituals by means of which it is appropriated) fully acknowledges the terrible misadventures, the disfiguring, the waste, the cruelties and betrayals that mark human life and the human stewardship of nature, it places the sorry human scene within a mythic setting that makes even what cannot be undone bearable, even while it inspires efforts to acknowledge, repair, and amend.

A covenantal ethic originates in Scripture, but the novelist William Faulkner offers, in my judgment, a helpful contemporary restatement of that ethic for ecologists on the American scene—a covenantal ethic that highlights one's responsibility both to the land and to the community. Significantly, Faulkner develops that ethic in a story about an essentially adversarial activity—the hunt—an activity for which I have no personal talent or enthusiasm. But, symbolically, the hunter's target—the wild animal—contrasts with the metaphors for nature as depicted in both halves of Auden's epigram. Nature does not resemble a domestic animal that submits to a human voice and face, nor a dragon that demonically confounds the human. The specific images in Faulkner of wild animals—the deer and the bear—symbolize an outsize, untamed nature that environs us and yet does not crush us; indeed, a nature that can and does feed us and discipline us. The hunt entails the shedding of blood—not dragon's blood (the blood of the tyrant oppressor), but the blood of a worthy adversary in the wilderness to whom the hunter in killing becomes bound: ". . . perhaps only a countrybred one could comprehend loving the life he spills."[38] Faulkner's short story "Delta Autumn" will serve conveniently to define his understanding of a covenantal ethic.

The very title of the story marks the time and place of a man's ritual return to the decisive moment in his life when, as a boy, he learned to hunt, killing his first stag in the Delta Wilderness. Just as the marked Jew, the errant, harassed, and estranged Jew recovers the covenant of Exodus and Mount Sinai through ritual renewal, Isaac McCaslin returns to the Delta every autumn to renew the hunt and to suffer his own renewal there despite the alienation and pain and compromise and defeat which he (and the wilderness) has subsequently endured across his lifetime. That annual trek into the wilderness helps renew for Isaac that event which occurred almost seven decades earlier, what Faulkner calls elsewhere "the binding instant." The original defining event includes the elements of promise and gift.

The Promise. On that initiatory occasion, the boy came of age as a hunter, acquiring his life-long commitments and identity. Old Sam Fathers, an Indian of mixed blood—part Indian, part black, and part white, his own blood through his mother a virtual battleground—tutored the boy in the technique of hunting. They tracked after the deer until the buck loomed before them, and the old man urged the boy to:

> "Shoot quick and shoot slow": and the gun leveled rapidly without haste and cracked and he walked to the buck lying still intact and still in the shape of that magnificent speed and bled it with Sam's knife and Sam dipped his hands into the hot blood and marked his face forever.[39]

The boy then binds the whole of his future in the instant—not saying then, but, if he could have said, he would have said: "*I slew you; my bearing must not shame your quitting life. My conduct forever onward must become your death*."[40] The language recalls the covenant into which the Israelites entered at Mount Sinai, their foreheads marked there forever.

The Gift. While a covenantal ethic centers in a promise, it does not begin with a promise. It begins preveniently with what has been received and assumed, "gladly, humbly," as a gift. In the logic of scripture, the gift of deliverance—Exodus—precedes the binding promise of Mount Sinai. The gift settles into the being and bowels, the imagination and will of the Israelites, changing their identity. The promise ratifies rather than creates out of nothing this alteration in identity. The following passage from Faulkner's story gets it just right.

> He seemed to see the two of them— himself and the wilderness as coevals, his own span as a hunter, a woodsman not contemporary with his first breath but transmitted to him, assumed by him

gladly, humbly, with joy and pride, from that old major de Spain and that old Sam Fathers who had taught him to hunt.[41]

The gift is double: it includes the technique of hunting which the boy has received from his mentors; but it also includes the gift of the natural world which the activity of hunting opens up. These two gifts are not externally related to each other. The first gift of technique carries with it a discipline that lets the boy perceive, receive, and savor the second, encompassing gift of the wilderness, the natural world.

The Double Discipline. The hunter's specific technical discipline includes learning how to use a rifle to bring down game and a knife to kill quickly and without pain. But it includes much more. In pursuing the deer, the hunter must also learn to scan his world: the patterns of feeding, the weather, the direction of the winds, smell and sounds, the condition of his equipment, the vagaries of the woods and terrain. The activity of hunting, in effect, brings into view a concrete universe that the hunter sees fully only with disciplined eyes and body. He must also bring into the wilderness his tents, which place him closer and more vulnerable to a nature from which the sheltering techniques of a civilization have distanced him; and he must refrain from bringing in his own supply of meat; he must live entirely off the animals he kills. His technique, far from supplying him with the means to slip the surly bonds of earth, reminds him of his fragile dependency; it reconnects him and bonds him to the nourishing earth. To hunt the deer, he must see the wilderness with its eyes. The logic of the hunt also requires of him the broader discipline to protect the species upon which the hunt depends. He must not incoherently learn the technique of killing efficiently only to do so wantonly. He must learn self-restraint. The hunter must protect both the doe and the wilderness so crucial to its flourishing. The covenant broadens out still further to enjoin fitting ways to use land and to respect the human community that uses it.

It is no accident of the story that the man who initiates the young boy into the hunt is an Indian. Sam Fathers comes out of a people who use technique, and, indeed, must collaborate with nature to survive. But the world which they fabricate through technique participates in and reflects, rather than displaces, an unfabricated nature. I visited once a modest American Indian museum in the Acoma village (an hour west of Albuquerque, New Mexico), before ascending to see the pueblo on the Mesa above. A showcase in the museum displayed a piece of pottery, a bowl, abstractly decorated with a series of clouds and black rain lines descending from the clouds. The design on the pottery expresses the villagers' sense that, even though they refashion nature into a product, the product never leaves behind the natural world of which it is a part. But more than that, many of the Acoma people think of the bowl itself as a cloud holding water; for, when a bowl breaks, an Acoma woman will say, "Let it rain." Instead of resenting the loss of a valuable object through which she transcends nature, she consents to an event that locates her in the cosmic scheme of things. After the visit to the museum, I returned to my car and worried whether I had enough gas to get me back to another civilization, more inclined to vent its frustration over the breakdown of its machines than to return thanks for its participation, through technique, in the deeper rhythms of nature.

The culture of the Acoma villagers reminds us that something has gone awry for a technology which we vindicate solely on the grounds that it lets us defeat or transcend nature by setting artifacts, such as levees, against, rather than within, natural systems. Faulkner warns us toward the end of his story that a technique out of control which despoils the game and the wilderness eventually cancels itself. On the last night of his return visit to the wilderness as an old man, Isaac McCaslin, lying awake in the tent, muses:

> The Delta, he thought: This Delta. This land which man has deswamped and denuded and derivered in two generations. . . . No wonder the ruined woods I used to know don't cry for retribution! he thought: the people who have destroyed it will accomplish its revenge.[42]

Clear-cutters destroy forests, rivers, and their own communities and companies. Nature can be despoiled, but only fools persist in mocking it.

The Covenantal Myth and the Engineer

The Faulkner story and its biblical antecedent illuminate the moral issue of identity that surfaced in the *Challenger* disaster. When the boss urged the Vice President of Engineering to take off his engineer's and put on his manager's hat, he assumes that the professional has no binding instant, no abiding identity to profess. He speaks out of a general social milieu today in which "50 percent and 75 percent . . . of individuals who started their careers in engineering positions . . . ultimately moved into management positions of one sort or another."[43] Baum observes, "It is not only unclear as to when a person enters into the profession of engineering; it is even more vague as to when a person *leaves* the profession."[44] Becoming an engineer hardly matches the irreversible alteration of identity that occurred at Mount Sinai, but it ought to mean more than a straw boater, lightly donned and doffed. A professional vow or promise goes to one's core identity. Professionals profess something, a discipline, which their bearing must not shame, their conduct thereafter must embody.

The Gift. The engineer's gift is double. It includes, first, the gift of a discipline and technique. At first glance, the acquisition of technique through a lengthy, disciplined, and demanding education hardly seems a gift. The engineer works especially hard to acquire knowledge. Indolent undergraduate students of the humanities regularly dismiss engineers as quintessential "grinds." But without the gift of natural aptitude and the subsequent gifts of nurture, the aspiring engineer labors in vain. A huge social investment, public and private, funds the laboratories and equipment and the cumulative research traditions upon which young engineers depend for success in their grinding, disciplined labor which embodies humility before fact.

Further, the engineer's gift of technique ought to help retrieve a sense of nature as gift. In one view, the practice of engineering does not entail receiving nature as a gift; indeed, engineering cognitively depends upon a method which engages in abstracting from nature. The scientist, so the argument goes, needs to filter out the world in its heterogeneity and deal with purified experience in order to form generalizations about a targeted phenomenon. Hence the scientist needs a laboratory that controls variables. Only by abstracting from the concrete world can one know and measure the behavior of the entity in question and anticipate its behavior under similar conditions. Second, instrumentally, the scientist/technologist creates a product out of raw material which succeeds in transcending, improving upon, substituting for, defeating, or banishing some feature of the world as received. A Gnostic contempt for, or dispatch of, the world as it is, seems to drive the aspiration to create an artificial world. Technologists offer impermeable, nonbiodegradable plastic receptacles as a substitute for the cloud bowl of the Acoma Indians.

However, this view of engineering fails to illuminate fully both the theoretical enterprise of science and the practical vindications of technology. In their theoretical inquiry, engineers enjoy a privileged access to nature of the kind that physicians are permitted to have to the human body. Physicians profess not simply a distanced and abstract knowledge of health and disease but a knowledge acquired as they scan, handle, probe, and question the human body (and the patient) with the most intimate of queries. They become privy to its secrets. This probing, this unveiling and disclosing, generates a special responsibility for attentive care. Physicians cannot, they must not, be simply voyeurs. They are called to attend and to heal as best they can, irrespective of the complex factors that may have contributed to the patient's plight; and, indeed, their privileged position calls for their forthright public advocacy, their readiness to testify on questions of sanitation, air quality, and other factors, fateful for bodily well-being but not fully within their control.

By the same token, the engineer and the bench scientist acquire a body of knowledge, not distantly, but through a probing of nature, through an agenda of experiments. The word "experiment," like the word "experience," derives from *ex periculo*, out of peril. The Latin root suggests the acquisition of knowledge issuing from an ordeal to which the scientist subjects nature. Bacon understood this when he recognized that the inquiring scientist puts nature on the rack in order to discern what's there. Those who would know something experimentally put nature to the test—torture it, as it were—so that it will blurt out its secrets. The engineer attends to what shows itself through experiment and testing. This privileged access to nature generates responsibilities. The engineer is in a position to hear and to speak for what he or she has heard. Privileged access puts the engineer in the moral position of being nature's advocate. Nature is the engineer's client.

Further, engineering (like the art of healing) must consider not simply isolated entities but systems. Although scientists and engineers must provisionally abstract and isolate phenomena from the full-bodied world, their scientific inquiry reaches its practical completion only as it pushes out beyond the prefab ideas (and artifacts) in which most of us unalertly live and measures hypotheses and tests products against some larger portion of nature as originally received. Scientists and engineers must take in and acknowledge unabstracted nature as it blurts out in the applications to which they subject it. The O-rings cannot fool the cold weather. The engineer may create a product which fits into a complex artificial world, but not a world that can utterly transcend or vanquish with impunity the world as received. No product and no system of products comes into being out of nothing or vanishes into nothing. Its coming into existence rearranges something somewhere and its destruction never occurs without leaving a trace. And in the course of their functioning, most products and systems of products, however complex, imitate the simplest of organisms in that they must ingest and excrete. The car takes in gasoline and expels gases. However slick its design, it needs a mouth and an anus, which keep it tied, often disturbingly, to the external world. Thus in recognizing nature as their client, engineers must attend not simply to the integrity of the product they may be assigned to concoct—the perfect styrofoam cup—but the integrity of the ecosystem into which styrofoam cups by the billions are excreted.

Engineers and the Organizations

However, the disciplines that technique demands and that the integrity of nature requires have separated in the modern formation of engineers because institutions try to substitute themselves for nature (that is, they attempt to usurp nature's power to discipline, forgetting that we cannot disobey natural laws). The power structure of the large-scale organization defines the engineer instrumentally as an employee who delivers technical services but does not participate in decisions about the ends served. Engineers serve as the hammer and the computer, rather than the eye, the mind, and the voice, that fit the limited ends of the enterprise within the larger harmonics in which the enterprise should draw its being and end. Organizationally, professionals should resemble the free citizens of Athens more than the slaves who served them. Engineers should participate, and be educated to participate more freely, in decisions about the end of the *polis*, whether it be the Ford Motor Company, IBM, the Federal Government, or Genentech. The *Challenger* disaster exemplifies what happens when they don't have a voice in the *agora*.

The second reason why the engineering profession has separated professional ethics from environmental ethics is substantive rather than structural. It lies not in the subordinate status of the engineer as an employee in a hierarchical organization, but in the narrow definition which engineers have accepted for their profession. Engineers should profess not simply technique but a covenant with nature as gift to which the gift of technique, rightly understood, binds them. Faulkner's "Delta Autumn" embodies the sense of this covenantal receiving of one's skill and the perception of nature in wide lens which it affords.

But, even if young professionals in the course of their education have caught a glimpse of their further duties to the environment, the immediate ends of the organization which employs them tend psychologically to engulf them. The corporation relentlessly pursues a marketplace ethic of buying and selling at maximal profits. The organization perceives its own ends contractually, not covenantally. Contracts facilitate only buying and selling. Covenants include the further ingredients of giving and receiving. Contracts price everything: materials and energies are extractable, fungible; techniques, for sale; goods, loyalties, and products, convertible; whereas covenants establish indefectible duties. Professionals incorporated into institutions internalize the contractual ethic; they lose sight of the duties to their environment which their discipline covenantally entails.

The giant corporations that compete in the marketplace delude us into thinking that life fulfills us at its most absorbing and binding level when we buy and sell, not when we give and receive. The world of commerce dazzles the imagination, stirs the anxieties, and whets the appetites of the newly fledged professional. It dangles the bait of ownership and control rather than offering the nourishing duties of tenancy and stewardship; it thereby misses the human obligations to the natural world that resemble those of a guest to a host. Those obligations of tenancy should fall upon corporations as well as upon the professionals—the lawyers, the accountants, and the engineers—who work for them.

The authors of *Engineering Ethics*[45] have offered several modest and graded proposals (from the mandated to the permissible), as they seek to expand the engineer's responsibilities of advocacy and tenancy toward nature. At the level of the mandated, they believe that engineers should be required by their guilds "to hold paramount human health in the performance of their engineering work (including health issues that are environmentally related)." However, they do not believe that professional codes should require engineers to "inject non-health related environmental concerns into their engineering work." Nevertheless, on the latter environmental issues, the authors urge that the guilds recognize the right of engineers to engage in "organizational disobedience" toward their employers on matters affecting their own personal beliefs or interpretations of what professional obligation requires. Such "organizational disobedience" might involve either inaction or action contrary to or in protest against the plans and purposes of the employer. Specifically, the authors propose, the codes should assert: "Engineers shall . . . have the right to voice responsible objections to engineering projects that they believe are wrong, without fear of reprisal. Engineers shall have the right to support programs and causes of their own choosing outside of the workplace."[46] The concept of "organizational disobedience" is bold, but, as the authors are well aware, the guilds have not equipped themselves, with matching boldness, to protect the intrepid practitioner. Not that each and every engineer at the middle management level can become the "compleat engineer," the voice of conscience on behalf of a too fouled and fragmented and despoiled world. But somewhere within the full range of the profession, the work of advocacy for a sustainable earth must go on.

Owls vs. Jobs

Finally, in the promissory vision of things, the covenants with the earth and with humankind intersect. ". . . and then He created man to be His overseer on earth . . . not to hold for himself and his descendants inviolable title forever . . . but to hold the earth mutual and intact in the communal anonymity of brotherhood . . ." Eventually, defacing the land also violates one's fellows. It is no accident in Faulkner's "Delta Autumn" that the very hunter who, on an earlier trip into the wilderness, seduced a woman and then abandoned the son he conceived by her, on this final trip kills a doe. Faulkner has already prepared for this link between the two covenants in his account of how the boy was given his technique. He was not a hunter by natural talent alone. The skill partly comes to him through human givers; one of them, Sam Fathers, a walking symbol, as it were, of ethnic diversity. The community and not simply the wilderness helps create the hunter; correspondingly, the destructive use of technique abuses both the human and the nonhuman world. Faulkner's faithless hunter violates covenantal fidelity not only by killing a doe but by abandoning the black woman who has borne his child. Feckless technique is unfaithful; it violates professional discipline and betrays both nature and the human species. Finally, in the Faulkner story, the abandonment of the child nicely links environmental ethics with our moral relationship to future generations, themes which theologians have conjoined in the concept of stewardship and the ideal of a sustainable earth.[47]

This unitary vision of the natural and the communal has split in the current debate over environmental issues. The ideals of loyalty to one's fellows and responsible care for the environment have generated different, and oftentimes contending, causes. Historically, the environmental movement turned the attention of liberals and some activists away from the social causes of the late '60s and '70s—civil rights, economic justice, and the Vietnam War. A black professor of ethics once gloomily observed that white liberals had vanished as his colleagues in these social causes and reappeared on the wilderness watch. President Reagan shrewdly exploited a populist reaction to the environmental movement in appointing the egregious James Watts as his first Secretary of the Interior. Watts distinguished himself from the elitism of the environmentalists by calling for policies that would include a bit more public access to the national parks and, more to the point, justify aggressively selling public lands to developers and a general relaxing of the environmental regulations. He argued that these gifts to business interests would eventually trickle down to the people in the form of more jobs. The public relations specialists boiled down this right-wing populism to "jobs vs. the spotted owl."

The slogan "people-oriented" was specious, since the purported beneficiaries of these policies would surely have to breathe unprotected air, swim in polluted water, and live near sludge-dumping industries. Still, the right wing had a point. Well-to-do summer residents of the upper New England states fiercely defend the environment, but do little to attend to the plight of the jobless in the little cities of the North that depend upon lumber and paper companies. The cost of repairing and respecting the environment should not take jobs from some people to give pristine playgrounds to others. That's what the spin doctors made the issue appear to be when the environmentally alert said that they would like a little spotted owl in their definition of a forest.

Others have argued that the country need not face a stark choice between the covenant with community and with nature. If the nation's engineers develop intermediate technologies and industries that respect the environment, they will help create new jobs, and jobs that will give the nation a competitive edge, in an important sunrise industry. Varyingly, the Swedes, the Germans, and the Americans have responded to meet the needs for more environmentally sensitive and healing technologies. Further, the entire planet will suffer acutely if the Third World, with its huge populations, follows developers as recklessly and wastefully as those in the continents of Europe and North America.

In his book *Earth in the Balance: Ecology and the Human Spirit*, former U. S. Vice President Al Gore struck an optimistic note about our ability to respect simultaneously the double covenant. But the complexities of office made it clear to the Clinton administration that one cannot satisfy simultaneously the ideal demands of both the environmentalists and the advocates of full employment. Certainly, a combination of government and business investment in research on new fuels, technologies, and disposal systems will create new jobs.

But these jobs will not always aid specifically and directly those thrown out of work by environmental regulations. The lost jobs are usually low tech; the new jobs, high tech, often beyond the reach of those retooled in the most conscientious of retraining programs. While greater investments in R and D will help the country develop new technologies, such investments in the short run will siphon off financial resources from other enterprises; and many firms will continue to shift their operations overseas where they will face less constraining regulations.

How then can engineers help a government honor its double covenant, which in the Garden of Eden or in a fully redeemed world coinhere, but which, in a fallen world, limit and contend with one another? The answer lies in some sort of rough-and-ready compromise between the two covenants, a compromise which admittedly will not satisfy the one-eyed.

The word "compromise" has two meanings. When a clear distinction exists between right and wrong and one yields to the temptation to do wrong, one has compromised oneself in the sense of defecting from one's basic moral identity. The engineer who fudges on the test results, the hunter who kills the doe, the company that dumps lead into the soil which, in turn, destroys the brains of children—these actors harm others and compromise in the sense of diminishing themselves. But in many situations and in most of political life, one faces a clear distinction, not between right and wrong, but between conflicting goods—goods which from the final vantage point of the

eschaton coinhere but which, in an imperfect world, one must some-
how hold on to at the same time. Such compromises do not wholly
escape wrong-doing. We deal with them too lightly when we call
them tradeoffs. We cannot put behind us yesterday's compromise and
move guiltlessly into the future. The very best bargain we strike may
well generate still further duties of reparation as we imperfectly
honor the several covenants which are ours.

Thus a covenantal vision of things, with its notion of primordial
gifts and duties, hardly converts into casuistic principles for resolving
any and all quandaries or into a fixed social program or environmental policy. It eliminates neither the world of the marketplace nor the
need for governmental regulation and action nor the pressures under
which engineers and corporate managers work.

But it places the fallen world of buying and selling, taxing, regulating, and reforming within a wider horizon. It lets imperfect men and
women see the world for what it is and thus lets it become a little different from what it was. It places the familiar world that we know at
the distance of insight and corrective vision. The rituals of covenantal renewal keep us wakeful and alert.

> . . . he would not sleep tonight but would lie instead wakeful and
> peaceful on the cot amid the tent-filling snoring and the rain's
> whisper as he always did on the first night in camp; peaceful,
> without regret or fretting, telling himself that was all right too,
> who didn't have so many of them left as to waste on sleeping.[48]

A colleague who read this chapter challenged my resort to a story
about hunting for our clues and cues in dealing with nature. "Why
did you choose such an instrumental activity?" His question forced
me to reconsider why, in writing about engineering, the most instrumental of the professions, and about America, the most instrumentally organized of countries, I was drawn to the Faulkner story about
hunting. The story, I suspect, appealed because it offers a take on the
ritual activity of hunting that awakens the contemplative; Isaac lies
"wakeful and peaceful." In a narrative about an apparently instrumental technique, Faulkner lets both the instrumentally organized
world and the earth we are called to honor, lie exposed. That contemplative moment provides a point of moral reentry into the driven
world, in which, under the terms and conditions of modern life, professionals largely work: the corporation and the government. How-

ever, I would not want to deny the capacity of other stories and their interpreters to open up the contemplative moment, the reflective pause, that would encourage the most instrumental of God's creatures and the most instrumental of specialists among those creatures to take up their responsibility for advocacy and care.[49]

Notes

1. *Science Magazine*, June 20, 1986, 1489.
2. Ibid.,1488.
3. The distinguished physicist and Nobel Prize winner Richard P. Feynman, who served on the Rogers Commission and heard Robert Lund's testimony before the Commission, reports the testimony as follows: "A manager of the Thiokol Company named Mr. Lund was testifying. On the night before the launch, Mr. Mulloy had told him to put on his 'management hat,' so he changed his opposition to launch and overruled his own engineers." See Richard P. Feynman, *What Do You Care What Other People Think?* (New York: Bantam Books, 1989), 176.
4. According to Feynman, the White House did not in fact put NASA under immediate public pressure; the President did not plan to use this melodramatic line. See Feynman, *What Do You Care What Other People Think?*, 216–17.
5. For an account of the Greek sense of these two characteristic marks of the physician, see P. Lain Entralgo, *Doctor and Patient* (New York: World University Library, McGraw-Hill, 1969), 15–52.
6. See Walter Burkert, *Greek Religion* (Cambridge, Mass.: Harvard University Press, 1985), 167–68.
7. Feynman, *What Do You Care What Other People Think?*, 237.
8. Burkert, *Greek Religion*, 167–68.
9. Benjamin Farrinton, *The Philosophy of Francis Bacon* (Liverpool: Liverpool University Press, 1964), 27.
10. Farrinton, 28.
11. Farrinton, 54.
12. *Statistical Abstract of the United States*, 104th edition, (United States Department of Commerce, Bureau of the Census, 1984), 599.
13. Krause, *Death of the Guilds: Professions, States, and the Advance of Capitalism, 1930 to the Present* (New Haven, Conn.: Yale University Press, 1996), 61, 65.
14. Feynman, *What Do You Care What Other People Think?*, 224.
15. A quotation from the Rogers Commission Report cited in *Aviation Week and Space Technology*, November 14, 1986.
16. Feynman, 132 ff.
17. Charles Peter, in his April 1986 essay in *The Washington Monthly*, "Quagadongon to Cape Canaveral: Why the Bad News Doesn't Travel Up," 27–31, quotes the earlier prophetic comment, which Russell Baker and he had made in the first issue of the magazine published long before the *Challenger* disaster.
18. Krause, *Death of the Guilds*, 60.
19. Krause, 154.
20. Krause, 63.
21. Robert Perucci and Joel E. Gerstl, *Profession Without Community: Engineers in American Society* (New York: Random House, 1969). Charles E. Harris Jr. Michael S. Pritchard, and Michael J. Rabins have noted that engineers need not join their respective engineering societies or register with a State Registration Board as professional engineers. The latter public body, if membership were required, might actually establish legally enforceable standards to which engineers might appeal if pressured by their companies to engage in unprofessional

conduct. As it is, the guilds and state bodies can only promote, they cannot enforce, professional ethics. *Engineering Ethics: Concepts and Cases*, 2nd ed. (Stamford, Conn.: Wadsworth/Thomson Learning, 2000), 265–80.

22. See Harris, Pritchard, and Rabins, *Engineering Ethics: Concepts and Cases*, 265–80.
23. *Ibid.*, 270.
24. It should be noted that leaders in the field of engineering ethics have by no means conceded that the field should include the subject of "environmental ethics." For example, Robert J. Baum, in his survey book *Ethics and Engineering Curricula*, vol. 7 (Briarcliff Manor, N.Y.: The Hastings Center, 1980), insisted that "[t]he field of engineering ethics must be distinguished from the related but quite different field of the study of the ethical (and other) impacts of technology." While Baum favors offering courses in technology assessment and environmental ethics in the curriculum of a university, he does not feel that courses in professional ethics for engineers should consider such topics, except, marginally, in ethics courses for civil engineers. John Wilcox and Louis Theodore send a different signal in *Engineering and Environmental Ethics: A Case Study Approach* (New York: John Wiley and Sons, 1998). They organize over one hundred cases linking engineering specialists with environmental concerns. In the 1990s, the codes of three major engineering guilds (the American Society of Civil Engineers [ASCE], the Institute of Electrical and Electronics Engineers, and the American Society of Mechanical Engineers) either expanded or incorporated for the first time canons on environmental ethics. The ASCE code, as revised in 1996, affirms that "[e]ngineers shall hold paramount the safety, health, and welfare of the public and shall strive to comply with the principles of sustainable development in the performance of their professional duties." For substantial commentary on the provisions in the codes of the three engineering societies on environmental ethics, see Harris, Pritchard, and Rabins, *Engineering Ethics*, 208ff.
25. See Quentin Anderson's study of Emerson, Thoreau, and Whitman, *The Imperial Self: An Essay in American Literacy and Cultural History* (New York: Alfred A. Knopf, 1971).
26. William Faulkner, *The Wild Palms* (New York: Random House, 1939), 162.
27. Ibid., 163.
28. Ibid., 144.
29. Vianna Moog in *Bandeirantes and Pioneers* (New York: George Braziller, 1964) points out that Brazil's topical soils were poor, compared with the great plains of Europe and North America. Economically, the Amazon, as opposed to the Mississippi River, proved to be in Moog's memorable phrase, an "unpatriotic river." It brazenly washes out soil from Brazil and disgorges it later in the Atlantic where it "is carried along by the Gulf Stream to add new territories to Mexico and the United States, in the alluvial formations of Yucatan and Florida." The river resembles the mythic serpent who steals away treasure not its own. The land itself tends to encourage the spirit of the *conquistadors*.
30. Lynn White, "The Historical Roots of the Ecological Crisis," *Science*, vol. 155: 1203–7.
31. *Time Magazine*, January 5, 1981.

32. *Washington Post*, March 8, 1981.
33. Pico della Mirandola, "Oration on the Dignity of Man," found in *The Renaissance Philosophy of Man*, ed. Ernst Cassirer, Paul O. Kristeller, and John H. Randall Jr. (Chicago: Phoenix Books, University of Chicago Press, 1956), 223–25.
34. Juan Luis Vives, "A Fable About Man," found in *The Renaissance Philosophy of Man*, 387–90.
35. René Dubos, "A Theology of the Earth," in *Western Man and Environmental Ethics*, ed. Ian Barbour (Reading, Mass.: Addison-Wesley, 1973).
36. Cormac McCarthy, *The Crossing* (New York: Alfred A. Knopf, 1994).
37. The American theologian Sallie McFague appreciates this wild aspect of nature, while at the same time carrying forward (and reworking) the sacramental tradition. Appealing to Annie Dillard, *Pilgrim at Tinker's Creek*, McFague recognizes the terror as well as the beauty of nature; it does not tidily fit into the household of human purposes. See her *Super, Natural Christians: How We Should Love Nature* (Minneapolis: Fortress Press, 1997), 142–47.
38. William Faulkner, "Old People," in *Go Down Moses* (New York: Viking Books, 1973), 181.
39. William Faulkner, "Delta Autumn" in *Go Down Moses*, 351.
40. Ibid., 351.
41. Ibid., 354.
42. Ibid., 364.
43. Baum, *Ethics and Engineering Curricula*, 6.
44. Baum, 5.
45. Harris, Pritchard, and Rabins, *Engineering Ethics*, 227–30.
46. Ibid., 228.
47. The link between environmental ethics and our moral responsibility to future generations has received theological treatment in the concept of stewardship and the ideal of a sustainable earth. See, for example, the anthology of philosophical and theological essays on the subject: *Responsibilities to Future Generations: Environmental Ethics*, ed. E. Parkridge (Buffalo: Prometheus Books, 1981) and Edith Brown Weiss, *The Planetary Trust: Conservation and Intergrational Equity*, 11 Ecol. L. Q. 495 (1984).
48. Faulkner, "Delta Autumn," 343.
49. For example, Sallie McFague, taking advantage of Annie Dillard and other authors, argues for a horizontal Christian sacramentalism as the basis for an ethic of care. Medieval sacramentalism, in her judgment, was too "vertical." It pointed nature upward too instrumentally toward human ends and too symbolically toward God. While not rejecting the notion that nature provides us with intimations of God, McFague argues that a horizontal sacramentalism must first recognize things as subjects in themselves. "They are transparent to the divine; they are first of all themselves, and, as such, in the intricacy and uniqueness of who, what, they are, they speak elliptically of God." (*Super, Natural Christians*, 173.) The horizontal attentiveness of scientists and engineers to what is should provide its own elliptical service to the divine by staying the hand that would proceed too manipulatively and carelessly in reconfiguring the earth.

Chapter 4

Unacknowledged Public Rulers

Corporate Executives

A hundred years ago, professionals who acquired their skills largely worked as unencumbered solitaries. Doctors drove out in their buggies to see patients. Lawyers received clients in their digs. Individual inventors, such as Whitney, Edison, Bell, and the Wright brothers, worked in small shops rather than with battalions of anonymous engineers in the corporations. However, professionals today, for better or for worse, work increasingly for large-scale organizations. The doctor as a solo practitioner hardly survives today. Small group practitioners cannot insulate themselves from the provider organizations that supply them with patients, monitor their costs for services, and pay them. "Ninety-two percent of physicians have at least one contract with a managed care plan . . ." and "the number of physicians who are employees has grown from 24 percent in 1983 to 45 percent in 1997."[1] Huge law firms recruit directly the brightest, if not always the best, law school graduates; and corporations have established large in-house colonies of counselors. Eighty-five percent of engineers work for a corporation. The destiny of most professionals today works itself out on the stage of corporations, which, in turn, fiercely compete against one another.

These organizations form into two classes: some still identify themselves—at least officially—with the fundamental purposes of a profession (schools, universities, and many hospitals among the nonprofits, and, to some degree, law firms, newspapers, and accounting firms, among the for-profits); other institutions treat the stated goals of the profession as largely subordinate to an organizationally defined purpose. However, we can easily exaggerate the line between for-profit and nonprofit institutions. Almost all institutions feel, in one way or another, the pressures of the marketplace: if not in the struggle for profits, then for survival. If the nonprofits, for the sake of their public mission, neglect the bottom line, they soon discover themselves exposed to institutional martyrdom; they bear witness to their mission today but do not survive to carry out that mission tomorrow. No institution, public or private, profit or nonprofit, flies wholly above the hard economic necessities of the bottom line.

The task of management in such organizations has been professionalized. Corporations and service bureaucracies recruit most of their leaders either from practitioners of the traditional professions (who, as they rise in the organization, assume the burdens and coloration of managers) or from a growing company of administrators who acquire formal education in management at the universities. Although top jobs in management do not go exclusively to those who graduated from a professional school, graduates of liberal arts college—mere amateurs—perceive that by other routes few arrive at the executive suite.

The increasing concentration of professionals in huge and often commercial organizations has profoundly affected professional practice. A large organization permits professionals to specialize to a degree not possible before; it places a high value on cost-saving and efficiency; and it generally encourages a higher standard of technical performance than the solo practitioner can achieve. Identity with a large commercial organization also endows the professional's work with an obvious public significance that it does not usually acquire in smaller settings; and it has greatly magnified the power professionals exert on the society at large.

However, the move into large organizations has also tended to blur or dissipate professional identity. Doctors, lawyers, accountants, and engineers may eventually rise to the top and run some of the great corporations, but their ascent does not assure that they will shape the organization in the light of traditional professional ideals. In fact, their ascent as employees largely depends upon their internalizing a very different set of aspirations and skills than those traditionally associated with the professions. They must learn, above all, how to manage huge organizations and keep them from drowning in red ink, a skill which all such organizations prize, but which the professions have not, at least overtly, made a primary goal.

This chapter will not focus on whether leaders of corporations display the traditional marks of a professional—intellectual, moral, and organizational—which have surfaced earlier in this book. Such an exploration, while worthwhile, might suggest that only by positively identifying corporate leaders with a traditionally defined profession could a society hold such power-wielders accountable. Rather, we need to examine directly the moral underpinnings of the marketplace and the moral status of corporate leaders within it—leaders who, among the many powers they wield today, largely organize and monitor the production and distribution of professional services.

The Moral Underpinnings of the Marketplace and the Corporation

Some apologists believe that the marketplace and the corporation do not need moral underpinnings. They argue that the marketplace, as opposed to more utopian modes of social organization, spares us the need to place heavy moral demands upon people. It does not ask people to be idealistic or altruistic. It appeals chiefly to their self-interest. Some recent enthusiasts have adopted the heroic rhetoric of Ayn Rand and argued that greed is good. Others simply accept the cool reassurance of Adam Smith that knowledgeable, self-interested exchanges between individuals not only enrich both parties but contribute cumulatively to the wealth of the nation, without either party having to look out for the common good.

Similarly, the modern corporation, the winner in the modern marketplace, does not place heavy moral demands on its employees. It asks for merely skilled, not heroic, performances from its employees. Indeed, given its internal specialization of functions, the large organization would find heroic behavior extraordinary, idiosyncratic, and disruptive. It demands and enforces regularized procedures through which the corporation achieves efficiencies and economies of scale as it competes successfully in the marketplace. Thus the marketplace and the corporation deserve our respect, even our enthusiasm, not because they morally inspire us but because they accommodate realistically to human nature and mobilize the most fundamental drive within us—self-interest.

Others argue that the marketplace cannot function as a wholly impersonal mechanism that makes no moral demands upon us. At a minimum, it assumes the three personal virtues of industry, honesty, and integrity for the system to work. The marketplace needs industry (without which goods would not be produced), honesty (otherwise each would steal from the neighbor rather than exchange with him) and a modicum of integrity (truth-telling and promise-keeping, without which one could not count on receiving value in contractual exchanges). To these traditional three virtues, modern guardians of the marketplace add the virtue of fairness, especially required in exchanging equities. Prohibiting insider trading levels the playing field between buyers and sellers of securities. Together the four virtues help meet the demands of commutative justice, that is, justice in the dealings of one party with another.

Emphasis on these individual virtues alone, however, does not begin to touch the systemic issues of modern economic life. Preaching industry to the jobless hardly addresses the structural issue of the employable unemployed. Commending honesty and integrity to farmers and farm workers does not avert their financial ruin when a foreign country suddenly changes its wheat or rice import policies. Nor does the principle of fairness, if restricted to such issues as insider trading, address the sometimes coercive inequalities in the bargaining power of workers with employers. Moreover, these virtues hardly touch "externalities," such as pollution, injurious products, hazards in the workplace, or the decay of cities, which the marketplace often haphazardly exacts from society as undeclared costs of its operations.

Calling for these individual virtues alone also fails to respond fully to the internal needs of the corporation. An organization requires, beyond the individual virtues, the social virtues that dispose its members to work together. The philosopher, A. W. H. Adkins designated such virtues as the cooperative, as opposed to competitive, virtues.[2] For corporations to succeed, Lockean individualism must give way to the cooperative virtues teamwork demands.

However, even the virtues associated with teamwork will not suffice. The merely cooperative virtues are virtues of process rather than of substance. They do not derive from shared substantive goals but rather specify skills which the large-scale organization requires in pursuing any goal whatsoever, including those which may be quite immoral. Emphasis upon the cooperative virtues alone—those skills persons need to act in concert with others—systematically evades the substantive moral question which the corporation must face; namely, the aim and goal of the enterprise.

Given their power and privilege in the modern world, business leaders substantively and preeminently need the virtue of public-spiritedness. We have defined public-spiritedness as the art of acting in concert with others *for the common good*. This art includes both a subjective and an objective element. Subjectively, acting in concert with others summarizes the virtues of process. Objectively, the common good defines the goal which the leaders of the enterprise must pursue.

Why should the business leader keep in mind the public good? After all, business leaders head what we characterize as a *private* enterprise, its responsibilities traditionally restricted to private investors. Is it not, at the least, a distraction and, at the worst, a corruption of the enterprise to expect the leader, *qua* business leader, to act out of public spirit? Should we not, at most, concede the possibility of an occasional act of charity, a grace note of generosity, to ease the organization's way in the community at the level of PR, but no more?

On the contrary, I would argue that both the power and privilege of corporations (and the professionals who largely work for them) require us to rank public-spiritedness among the cardinal virtues necessary in the business leader. We mislead ourselves if we view the business community merely as one private interest group among others in a market economy. Today the business community wields a power that vastly exceeds that of any other group in our society—churches, synagogues, mosques, labor organizations, service organizations, and the like.[3] In a market economy, business leaders decide those major aspects of production and distribution which other societies might reserve to the government. Business people decide on industrial technology, patterns of organizing work, the locations of industries, market structures, the allocation of resources, and executive compensation and status. These decisions create momentous public impacts, for good or for ill, not only on investors, but also on workers, neighbors, consumers, suppliers, and satellite service industries, on the air we breathe and the water we drink and bathe in, and on the forests and lakes to which we would retreat on weekends. While engaged in what we call private enterprise, business leaders act, in effect, as "public officials" in a market economy. Taking the long view of Western history, Charles E. Lindblom has observed that two institutions—business and government—shape the modern world just as surely as the church and the state shaped the medieval world.

Further, the public power that business wields is not a power that business alone created. Business enjoys extraordinary public largesse in a modern democratic society. To cite but a few public gifts to business in the United States: road improvements, railroads, airports, enclosure acts, large tax credits for research and other investments, huge tax offsets (amounting to what *Time Magazine*, November 9, 1998, called in a cover article "corporate welfare"), the business rental of Defense Department plants at favorable rates, urban renewal projects to help retailers, special tax-free perquisites and fringe benefits for top management, and government investments to support the infrastructure of education and other services that enable business to recruit workers.

Business also receives special treatment at the hands of the law and government officials. Business leaders expect government officials to take seriously their judgment on any policy affecting the business climate. Even though the government can forbid some actions, it cannot directly command business to perform; hence it behooves presidents and prime ministers to confer with business leaders, who exert enormous formal and informal veto power in the society. Their capacity to create convulsive impacts on traffic patterns, school systems, parking accommodations, sewage plants, police and fire departments, and other public facilities—often without having to face the answering veto power of other groups—marks an extraordinary power that we can no longer define as wholly private. Business leaders function as unelected, even though carefully selected, public officials. Their power, privilege, and role demand the virtue of public-spiritedness.

However, the question remains: how should one define the substantive goal or goals which these putatively public-spirited officials should pursue? The question has provoked serious debate. The corporation (and other large-scale bureaucracies) are largely single-purpose institutions. Hospitals seek to heal; universities, to educate; and businesses, to produce goods and services for a profit. In practice, the large-scale organization can pursue multiple, related ends. (The university hospital not only *heals* patients, it also *teaches* students and *sponsors medical research*; the business conglomerate may span a number of businesses.) But these collateral goals usually combine in a single, inclusive, primary aim (such as health, education, or economic performance at a profit).

This tendency of a large-scale organization to aim at a single public purpose has generated both fierce critics and defenders. Radical critics from the Left in the late '60s in the United States protested against major organizations that, obsessed with their specialized tasks, failed to respond to those overriding moral challenges, which, the radicals felt, should test an institution's right to survive. At the other end of the spectrum, conservatives (and others) argue that a society functions best if each institution within it ordinarily pursues its own special mission.

The term "conservative" here loosely covers two very different visions of the social order. Classical conservatives (Edmund Burke, among others) held an organic view of the body politic and envisaged the great institutions of the society, the government included, working compactly for the common good (Japan Incorporated or Gaullism in France). This chapter will concentrate on a second, libertarian brand of conservatism (associated with Milton Friedman, Margaret Thatcher, and others). Modern libertarian conservatives argue for a minimalist state and believe that the allocative wizardry of the free market alone will best produce a multiplicity of goods. Far from subordinating self-interest to some notion of the common good, business institutions, in this libertarian view, can make no greater contribution to the society than to pursue, without distraction or moderation, the maximization of profits.[4] Otherwise, Friedman argues, corporations (1) stray from their competence (economic decision-making rather than social engineering), (2) abuse their power (as they paternalistically impose on others their notions of social and cultural good), and (3) exceed their authority (derived solely from stockholders).

Neither the New Leftists nor economic libertarians satisfactorily resolve the issue of institutional purpose. The Left's ideal of multi-purposed, decentralized institutions overlooked the prosaic advantages of specialization: efficiency and productivity. Further, despite its talk about community, the New Left of the '60s undercut one of the important features of community: reciprocity. A latent hostility toward community lurks behind the reluctance to specialize and the refusal to accept what specialization implies: a dependency upon the dedicated efforts of others. Mutual dependency in a differentiated society requires that institutions sustain a primary mission, a mission, moreover, that they must pursue across an extended period of time. (The New Left tended to collapse extended time both for persons and institutions and to substitute the urgencies of the present moment for a mission carried out over time.) Moreover, institutions forced to infinitize themselves and do everything produce anarchy. The educational institution must educate well; it cannot, in and of itself, respond to all the moral and political challenges served up to it before lunch on any given day. Making good on its primary purpose is part of the *public* responsibility of the institution.

However, Friedman's more influential libertarian ideal of maximizing profits also fails as a definition of corporate purpose. Although a mixed economy requires economic performance at a profit, maximizing profits for stockholders at the expense of all else converts a requirement into an imperial obsession. (While Friedman accepted the side constraints of ethical custom and the law, he held to a highly individualistic conception of ethical custom (no lying, theft, or murder) and a minimalist understanding of the law. He hardly meant by ethics, social ethics, and he hardly wanted from the law much more than the protections that permit one to pursue profits to the hilt.)

Some ethicists would uphold the principle of maximizing profits by distinguishing between the short run and the long run. Under the guidance of enlightened self-interest, large institutions will see that they cannot afford in the long run to neglect responsibilities to their workers and to the neighborhood and society about them. Corporations, universities, and hospitals eventually suffer if they wield the power of giants in their field but pretend to social and political impotence and let the cities around them fall to pieces. However, the sheer size of these institutions tends to weaken this appeal to self-interest. Their grandeur of scale institutions makes long-range perils seem, at best, remote. Short-term pressures to maximize profits for stockholders will overwhelm warnings of long-term perils unless other moral considerations accompany the warnings. Whether the corporation will ever suffer from its sins of omission and commission is historically problematical to business leaders. Why not maximize profits now and let the future take care of itself? Money and investments are often portable—from northern cities to the South, and from southern cities to investments overseas. If self-interest is the only issue, then staying in place and expanding the notion of corporate responsibility beyond the goal of maximizing profits will seem, at best, foolish, and at worst, illegitimate, unauthorized, and immoral. The ideal of corporate responsibility will seem but to squander stockholder's resources for the protection and benefit of those who have no rightful claim to these holdings. Appeals to enlightened self-interest alone will not suffice to dismiss or to modify the principle of maximizing profits. We need to counter each of Friedman's three arguments directly.

1. The view that corporate leaders are incompetent to make judgments about matters other than profit-making, exaggerates. In some areas of corporate responsibility, managers usually have more knowledge and competence than most others in the society. Certainly they should know a great deal more than others about product safety and about the harmful impacts of manufacturing processes on workers and neighbors. Corporations should accept responsibility by virtue of their knowledge of, proximity to, and complicity in such problems.

In other areas, certainly, the corporation may not be knowledgeable or competent. But moral responsibility in life extends beyond areas in which persons and institutions already have competence. Virtuosity in love-making does not always give a young couple the right to restrict their responsibility to that activity alone. Competent lovers may suddenly find themselves inexperienced, not-very-competent parents, morally obliged to acquire that competence. Economic prowess and competence sometimes generate responsibilities elsewhere. Economists have found a convenient way of excluding many issues from the manager's responsibility by writing them off as "externalities." But the externalities of water and air pollution, traffic congestion, neighborhood crime, unemployment, and the quality of education and culture in a host city have a way of obtruding on the moral and political agenda of citizens and their institutions and require business leaders to develop some measure of wisdom and even expertise in areas where previously they possessed none.

2. Friedman and other libertarian critics have also charged advocates of corporate responsibility with paternalism—a benevolent, but nonetheless oppressive, interference in the affairs of others. They argue that as the corporation exercises great economic power, it should forswear social, political, and cultural intrusions that diminish human autonomy and freedom.

The very word "paternalism" stirs a subtle mix of negative memories, including Victorian company towns and suffocating total institutions. However, modern industrial cities have suffered less from overbearing benevolence than from icy indifference. The callused self-interest of the powerful today threatens human autonomy and freedom far more than do misguided good works. Well-intended interventions, moreover, need not inevitably diminish the freedom of others; they may also expand opportunity. Freedom, responsibly exercised, is not a commodity of fixed bulk that automatically diminishes for some when exercised by others. To the degree that institutions such as the corporation open out beyond their immediate self-interest toward the common good, they may expand and nourish rather than diminish the civil rights of citizens, their economic opportunities, and their cultural resources.

3. Finally, some have sought to meet Friedman's most often cited argument from authority (that managers have a legitimate duty only to stockholders) by distinguishing between stockholders and stakeholders. Stockholders are important stakeholders in a company, but by no means the only ones. Workers, customers, neighbors, suppliers, and the public at large have varying stakes in its performance, sometimes, indeed, deeper stake than stockholders, who may dart in and out of their investments more easily than workers and neighbors, who, less mobile, depend fatefully on a company and its fortunes.

This familiar argument, however, rests on little more than the consonance of the two words—"stock" and "stake"—unless one can show why obligation should extend beyond the stockholders in an enterprise. The analytic concept of "covenant," introduced in the chapter on the engineer, identifies and clarifies the responsibilities of a corporation to its various stakeholders. A covenant ethic at once expands obligation beyond the limits of commercial contract (the stockholder's purchase) and takes corporate responsibility a notch deeper than token expressions of corporate philanthropy (contributions to the local community chest drive). A covenantal bond develops between several parties through a two-way process of giving and receiving, above and beyond the contractual buying and selling, paying and working, that may characterize the more transient and commercial contracts and contracts between parties. The covenantal bond also differs from the one-way flow of gifts that characterize philanthropy. Covenants evolve from extended exchanges between parties, from which permanent obligations and agreements arise that shape the future. This growing sense of responsibility between parties also broadens the membership of the community to include stakeholders whose investments in an enterprise do not necessarily take a commercial form. Much happens between two parties (between a corporation and its workers, a corporation and its neighbors, a corporation and its environment) that gives them a stake in what each does. They are covenanted together.

In contrast, the ideal of corporate philanthropy presupposes a one-way street from giver to receiver. The philanthropist gives; others receive. When the philanthropist loses interest, he moves on. Corporate responsibility reduced to philanthropy alone trivializes corporate ethics. The corporation obscures the depth of its obligation when it adopts the philanthropist's view. It cannot give as pure benefactor alone. It has already received much from the community—not only the investments of stockholders, but also the labor of workers, the ambience and services of the community in which it operates, the environment that supports it, the privilege of incorporation by the state, and all the protection bestowed upon it as a "person" under the due process clause of the Constitution. Its indebtedness to the society is great.

But not all this indebtedness can be noted up in commercial, contractualist terms. Certainly, the corporation pays its workers and its taxes (sometimes with the benefit of sweet deals on taxes) but these transactions also flesh out a life between people and institutions that goes deeper than transient marketplace contacts. Repeated transactions build up a relationship even when they "contract" to define the moral obligations of the corporation. Formally considered, the concepts of contract and covenant are first cousins: they both include an agreement between parties and an exchange; they look to reciprocal future action. But, in spirit, contract and covenant differ. Contracts involve buying and selling; covenants include further ingredients of giving and receiving. Contracts are external; covenants are more internal to the parties involved. Contracts are signed to be expediently discharged; covenants have a gratuitous growing element in them that nourishes rather than limits and terminates relationships. Contracts can be filed away, but a covenant becomes a part of one's history and shapes in unexpected ways one's self-perception and perhaps even destiny. The decision-making of a corporation is massively contractual. But that decision-making rests upon a covenantal base that charters its life, grants it protection, and endows its enterprises with a public significance and responsibility.

Workers As Stakeholders

The chapter on the engineer explored the consequences of a covenantal ethic as a guide for corporate responsibility toward nature. This chapter will develop the covenantal implications for a second stakeholder in the corporation—its workers. The stakes for workers reach deep. For better or for worse, corporate behavior profoundly affects a worker's essential identity. The Catholic Church has spoken most forcefully on this matter by referring to the "spirituality of work," a tradition that traces back to *Laborare est orare*—to work is to pray. John Paul II, in *Laborem Exercents*, and the American Bishops, in their Pastoral Letter on the Economic Order, have defined employment itself as a spiritual matter. Employment lets people participate in our common life. Just as voting lets citizens participate in the political order and encourage communal justice, earning a living allows them to participate in the economic order and encourages communal service. Unemployed workers lose confidence in their public identity; they become strangers and sojourners in their own land—*in* the society but not *of* it.

Earning a living entails two minimal moral standards: protecting workers' health and safety and paying a just wage. Without the protection of health and safety, workers cannot live healthily enough to work; and without a just wage, workers cannot earn enough to live—and to support those whose lives depend upon their earnings. Left to their own devices, corporations, in the early phases of industrial capitalism, often dealt recklessly with workers' health and safety and replaced the standard of a just wage with the marketplace law of supply and demand. Under the rule of the market, an oversupply of labor makes workers' bargaining power dwindle. Hence workers sought government regulations and/or collective bargaining to protect their health and safety and to secure decent wages. Corporations, in reaction, sometimes sought to reassert a superior bargaining power by breaking unions. Recently, they have also resisted pressure from government to treat workers (and the environment) responsibly by threatening to remove corporate operations to other cities and even other countries. The global scope of the marketplace today has made it particularly difficult for national governments to discipline corporate behavior. Housebreaking the global corporation is an underdeveloped art.

For the sake of survival and profits, corporations have also pled the necessity of downsizing the workplace. The commitment to downsize—"lean and mean"—turns particularly mean when boards of directors institute bonus and stock option schemes for top managers that tie in total compensation to earnings and stock prices. Firing workers often gives top managers the quickest route to the profits that hike their salaries and the value of their stock options. Such hikes can yield the CEO a bounty some four hundred times that of average salaries in the enterprise. This disparity can shatter institutional solidarity and loyalty in victims, survivors, and executioners alike. The directors are giving extravagant rewards to those who earn their pay by ordering shipmates to walk the plank, while the messy human consequences of this decimation lie hidden in the antiseptic term *reengineering*.

Apologists argue that the adrift worker can climb aboard other ships (in a period of high employment). However, data from the Congressional Budget Office warns that across a twenty-year period, the after-tax income gap between the upper one percent of the U.S. population and the bottom twenty percent has dramatically widened. "Among the bottom fifth of households, average after-tax [and inflation-adjusted] income is anticipated to fall nine percent from 1977 to 1999";[5] "whereas the top one percent will realize an 115 percent increase in after-tax and inflation-adjusted income. The richest one percent of the population is projected to receive as much after-tax income as the bottom 38 percent combined."[6]

Cumulatively, such disparities ensure that too many citizens have little or no apparent stake not only in the companies for which they work but in the society at large. A civilization cannot long endure if it creates an underclass, a proletariat of the rootless and stakeless, whom society commands but offers little reward or recourse.

Thus a particularly worrisome, second strategy of "lean and mean" emerges. Some (not all) devotees of downsizing insist on downsizing government also, thus denying to the government those taxes that would enable the government either to provide employment to workers who can find no employment in the private sector or to provide supplements to the working poor who cannot meet basic needs for food, clothing, shelter, and health care from their low wages. In effect, some leaders want to have it both ways. For the sake of profits, they deny their responsibility for continuing employment for workers (even those workers from whom they may have benefited from long-term service); and they would deny to the government, even as a last resort, the power to assure that citizens can survive and participate in the economic life of the nation.

In effect, extreme libertarians who recognize only shareholders as stakeholders deny a corporate responsibility to workers (other than living up to their contracts); and they would whittle down the role of the other major player in the modern world—government—to the task of protecting marketplace exchanges. Libertarians are willing to pay taxes for security (fire, police, and defense departments) and transportation (roads and airports) but resist government efforts to address the unmet welfare needs of citizens for food, clothing, shelter, and health care. They prize the law as it enforces commercial contracts (commutative justice); but they would pare down the law as it seeks, even minimally, to make good on an important aspect of the social covenant (distributive justice).

Recent changes in the corporation and the marketplace—mergers, takeovers, reengineering, downsizing, outsourcing, the instant transmission of news around the globe, accounting and policy maneuvers oriented solely to quarterly reports, and the near-cyclonic speed of changes in technologies and products—have spiritually affected workers and slipped the hold of their stake in the enterprise. "Temp work" grew ten times faster than overall employment in the 1980s; and a temporary employment agency, Manpower, surpassed General Motors as the largest private employer in the nation.[7] A sense of temporariness grips employees throughout the economic system. It includes not only those holding jobs flagged as temporary but also high tech professionals.

In his study of the shift from the old to a new capitalism, Richard Sennett has detailed some of these impacts on workers.[8] He sketches a shift from the relatively permanent, hierarchically organized institutions (Max Weber called them "iron cages") of industrial capitalism to the rapidly changing world of a service- and information-oriented economy. In the "new capitalism," the work world has transmuted from: hierarchy to networking, from a relatively defined job to a shifting participation in limited projects, from the specialized to the highly adaptive, from rigid work schedules to flex-time, from cumulative experience to staying ahead of the curve, from inside the cage to outsourcing with no fixed abode (indeed, the worker can feel like a nomad, even if she works within a given corporation), from clear lines of authority and responsibility to the survival principle of letting nothing stick, from boss to team leader, from a linear sense of time to broken field running, from relatively legible tasks to managing technologies whose inner operations are opaque, from relative security to a constant vulnerability—a steady state of always being at risk.

Sennett does not attempt to slide down the moonbeams of nostalgia to find gold in an earlier industrial capitalism. "None of us would desire to return [to a social world that was] . . . claustrophobic . . . and rigid."[9] He concedes that "a deadening politics of seniority and time entitlements ruled the unionized workers at Willow Run; to continue that mindset would be a recipe for self-destruction in today's markets and flexible networks."[10] Still, Sennett recognizes that industrial capitalism offered immigrant generations relatively continuous, if sometimes poorly paid, employment. The relative stability of corporate structures and clearly marked job identities supplied the objective, external casing in which a worker might form a character and a career path that supported, if ever so modestly, those enduring commitments to family and other communities that both fill out and mold a human identity.

Sennett identifies the spiritual problem that confronts our era: ". . . how to organize our life histories . . . in a capitalism which disposes us to drift."[11] An adult son who works in one of the "sunrise" industries said to his father: "In your day, Dad, people seemed transient and institutions permanent; but today institutions as well as people are no longer permanent; and that compounds a worker's sense of his own transience." A drifting impermanence in institutions compounds the individual's own sense of his impermanence and drift. Even having a distinct individual character can become baggage that one may need to drop to survive. Or, put another way, the worker adrift may need the character of a chameleon: light, agile, superficial; one's résumé, continually retinted; one's skills, repainted. Further, the breakdown of institutions and the stable self also threatens to break down community. In the work place, a defensive indifference and protective withholding replaces the give-and-take, the trust/mistrust, the angry protest and engagement that animates a genuine community. And, inevitably, other commitments become difficult to sustain—to wife, children, neighbors, congregation, and service organizations.

The picture of roving impermanence does not change in the setting of even the wildly successful sunrise industries. Stock options in start-up firms, intended originally to reduce initial salary costs, to motivate employees to be imaginative and daring, and to lead to long-term ties to the company, have played out differently. The huge profits employees hope to realize from stock options have led many employees to become very conservative, not wanting to rock the boat before they have acquired the stocks. But then, they are quite ready to quit the firm, after completing their several rounds of options, and look for yet another start-up opportunity.

The Religious Background

The religious issue in covenantal versus libertarian views of human life turns on their different understandings of the *imago dei* in humankind. Michael Novak in *The Spirit of Democratic Capitalism* (and Prime Minister Margaret Thatcher in her speech before the National Assembly of the Church of Scotland) justified the libertarian position religiously by associating the *imago dei* with human *creativity*. Novak writes:

Creation left to itself is incomplete, and human [beings] are called to be co-creators with God, bringing forth the potentialities the Creator has hidden. Creation is full of secrets waiting to be discovered, riddles which human intelligence is expected by the Creator to unlock. The world did not spring from the hand of God as wealthy as human beings might make it.[12]

According to libertarian Novak, traditional Christianity did not adequately appreciate the full meaning of the *imago dei* within us— our participation in the creativity of God. It took the revolutionary theorists of the late eighteenth century to remove the obstacles to celebrating creativity. "They [Montesquieu, Adam Smith, James Madison, Thomas Jefferson] saw themselves as agents of the progress which traditional religion, its towers blocking the sun, has passionately resisted."[13] Once modern theorists helped remove the religious restraints the church and state imposed upon the marketplace, capitalism unleashed the single most powerful revolution in human affairs, a "stream of sparks," a "continual stream of innovations," a "sustained growth" unmatched in human history.

The spirit of democratic capitalism is the spirit of development, risk, experiment, adventure. It surrenders present security for future betterment. In differentiating the economic system from the state, it introduced a novel pluralism into the very center of the social system. Henceforth, all societies of its type would be internally divided—and explosively revolutionary.[14]

Seizing upon the phrase of the economist Joseph Schumpeter, Novak gives a religious resonance to the "creative destruction" which capitalism inspires and celebrates—shades of Vishnu and Shiva! Novak regrets that intellectuals in the United States and elsewhere have failed to appreciate the prodigal talents of business executives, from whose accomplishments the society has so richly benefited. He complains that "their inventions and organizational innovations, their capacities for leadership and practical judgment, are assets which benefit their fellow citizens. Until their activities appeared in history, the human race was far poorer than it is."[15] Yet the public media have roundly criticized chief executives.

No one such as myself who cut his teeth in a privately endowed university and read there Pico Della Mirandola's "Oration on the Dignity of Man" can glibly deny either the importance of creativity in human affairs or the role of the marketplace in stimulating it. Yet, after celebrating a creativity so spectacularly displayed in some entrepreneurs, we have to ask ourselves whether, in fact, God's image displays itself solely or chiefly in creativity. Traditionally, of course, philosophers and theologians have associated the *imago dei* with the godly faculty of reason, the power for creativity, and the capacity of technical reason to subdue the earth. However, the church has carefully understood this participation in the divine creativity as a warrant, not for random liberty, but for a creativity directed to the common good: ". . . human beings achieve self-realization not in isolation but in interaction with others."[16] One must express the *imago dei* in oneself in such a way as to honor and empower it in others and thus serve our common life.

However splendid the power of creativity, the decisive scriptural passage on the *imago dei* does not mention it. "So God created humankind in his image, in the image of God he created them; male and female he created them." Taken at face value, this remarkable passage from Gen. 1:27 does not appear to assign the image of God in us to creativity alone or, indeed, at all. It establishes responsibility rather than confers creative license. The *imago dei* informs a relationship: "male and female he created them." Further, this relationship, as we have reason to know from many other passages, depends for its life on the covenantal dynamics of giving and receiving. Human beings may exhaust in acquiring, securing, anticipating, worrying, achieving, displaying, dominating, excelling, creating, vanquishing, and humiliating, but the essence of human life occurs in the transaction of giving and receiving—"male and female he created them." Inevitably, the prophets of Israel and the Apostle Paul employed the metaphor of marriage to explicate the promissory bond between God and humankind. And, eventually, the church attempted to honor and celebrate this relational life in the godhead itself when, in the Trinity, it resorted to the threefold name: Father—Giver; Son—Receiver; in the procession of the Spirit. The *imago dei* does not lie in a power which we possess in isolation but spreads across a relationship.[17] It displays itself primarily, not in creating, but in caring and preserving or, better yet, in a creativity that cares, a generative love. In his distinctive way, the twentieth-century Jewish thinker Martin Buber posits relationality at the heart of human existence (*I and Thou* and *Between Man and Man*), a relationality which God sustains as Creator in continuing dialogue with his creatures.

One should not move too deductively and glibly from the great affirmations of faith to the social systems under which we live. Still, those affirmations offer a horizon against which to interpret and assess the performance of the marketplace that has so much power to enhance or deface the image of God in humankind. Clearly, a society flourishes best when beneath all its buying and selling, it acknowledges the bonds that build up between people through giving and receiving. We need to find ways of putting the brakes on an economic system that encourages, to use Robert Reich's phrase, "the secession of the successful." The successful and powerful are tempted to withdraw into their "enclaves of good schools, excellent health care, and first-rate infrastructures—leaving much of the rest of the population behind."[18]

A reciprocal, donative element pervades in the upbuilding of a covenant—whether the covenant of marriage and friendship, or the covenantal ties of a professional to his or her client or a great corporation to the neighborhood, city, state, and country in which it works. Tit for tat characterizes a commercial transaction, one-way giving characterizes philanthropy; neither does justice to the covenantal ties between us by virtue of which we serve and draw upon the deeper reserves and lives of one another.

Criticism of Corporate Leadership

Critics of the corporation and corporate leadership include radicals and regulators, structural reformers and transformers. While their criticisms differ substantially, their remedies sometimes overlap.

Radical Critics. The social and political programs of the Old Left appear less radical today than formerly. The Old Left would have supplanted the managerial elite of capitalism with an elite of its own under state auspices. Theoretically, this change would have oriented productive and distributive systems to the public good. However, the older socialist and communist countries faced huge difficulties in this undertaking—hubristically trying to plan centrally the production of almost all goods. The new inequities that arose in the distributive system, the military orientation of national budgets, the bleak effects of state management on the quality and attractiveness of goods, the informal reappearance of inefficient cost-price markets in countries that tried to do without them, and the repression of those civil rights that might have made political leadership more accountable disfigured and destroyed most socialist societies.

Meanwhile, the Old Left proved far from radical on the subject of large-scale organizations. Lenin and Stalin built them. If anything, the Left exacerbated the defects of the corporation developed under industrial capitalism. It generally encouraged single-purpose institutions to remain fixed upon a primary task to the point of rigidity; and it elevated hierarchical principles of organization to a quasi-religious status. No wonder that the historian of political thought Sheldon Wolin, in seeking to describe the overarching theme in modern political thought, turned to the phrase, the "Age of Organization."[19] Although East and West differed in substance, they shared the basic form of the large-scale institution.

Reacting to bureaucracies on the Left and Right, leaders of the New Left, in the '60s and '70s, made a truly radical move. For a feverish interlude, they wanted to dismantle the bureaucracies. Huge, single-purpose institutions had built a destructive and doomed system. These institutions could not innovate or invent; they could not respond flexibly.[20] Their vaunted productivity had blighted the environment. Their hierarchies oppressed workers; their officialdom entrapped citizens; their aims deformed national purpose. Their standardized products, from large automobiles to fast and fatty foods, endangered health and survival. These and other charges spilled out of books and TV talk shows, books and shows that huge corporations funded and controlled. The noise of the '60s eventually abated, but its echoes reverberated beyond the '60s in those who would lower expectations and scale down institutions to a more modest human compass.

Small may be beautiful, as humanists from Jefferson to Schumacher have reminded us; but not always, and not in all things. The United States may, in fact, be heading toward an era displaying two types of social organizations, including large, geometrical, relatively single-purpose institutions and small, informal, somewhat more spontaneous communities that both supplement, counterpoint, and criticize the first type of organizations, but also experiment with new forms proleptic for the future. (Herbert Read, in *The Grass Roots of Art*, notes that Egyptian civilization, at an important stage of its development, produced two kinds of art—one the formal, geometrical art of the pyramids, and the other, a more naturalistic, lyrical, spontaneous tradition of craft arts.)[21] The dialectical relationship between these two types of social organization already shows up in human services. In education, health care, and the care of the elderly and retarded, one needs not only the larger institutions that can fund and organize the talents of professionals, but also smaller-scale groups—religious congregations and other voluntary communities—that can mobilize amateurs to serve human need.

A comparable mix of large and small institutions has begun to appear, and often with tonic effects, in commerce as well. Students in the late '60s often inveighed against corporations, but they did not altogether abandon the marketplace. Some of them launched a variety of small businesses in the vicinity of campuses (in order to forestall their departure from *alma mater*) and thereby improved the ambience of college and university towns. Business schools have recently promoted programs in "entrepreneurship" in response to the need for small-scale capitalism. Charles Hendy has heralded "the age of the elephants and the fleas" and notes the importance of the Internet in multiplying the latter. "The Internet offers low entry costs, virtual offices, and global reach, and many have been lured away from elephant careers to try their luck with the fleas."[22] But, while small may be beautiful, it is not inevitably virtuous. Hendy concedes that "the fleas" can be "self-absorbed, even self-obsessed" with "little time for community or for politics, sometimes even for relationships."[23]

Regulators and Reformers. The coexistence in our society of smaller organizations and corporate giants hardly solves the problem of regulating or reforming the latter. American society has more often tried to regulate corporations than to reform them and uses as its chief regulatory systems the marketplace and the law. Although the marketplace seems to offer the energies of freedom and initiative, in contrast to the government which restrains, the marketplace also regulates. As Lester Thurow pointed out in the *Zero Sum Society*, the marketplace relies on a very elaborate set of rules and agreed-upon signals and government sanctions in the course of its operation. "Without government regulations, there are no property rights and without property rights, there is no free market."[24] One chooses not between two unregulated and regulated systems but between right and wrong regulations. The marketplace as a major and largely positive force in directing corporations to social responsiveness and responsibility cannot, unregulated, do the job alone. For example, the give-and-take of buyers and sellers in the marketplace arena does not, in and of itself, effectively curb corporate social injury.

> . . . those who have faith that profit orientation is an adequate guarantee of corporations realizing socially desirable consumer

goals are implicitly assuming: (1) that the persons who are going to withdraw patronage know *the fact* that they are being "injured" (where injury refers to a whole range of possible grievances, from getting a worse deal than might be gotten elsewhere, to purchasing a product that is defective or below warranted standards, to getting something that produces actual physical injury); (2) that they know *where* to apply pressure of some sort; (3) that their pressure will be *translated* into warranted changes in the institution's behavior. None of these assumptions is particularly well-founded.[25]

The law, through a set of discrete prohibitions, disincentives, and constraints, provides a second resource for curbing socially irresponsible corporate behavior. No agency other than the federal government and no instrument other than federal law can challenge the power of corporations. In some cases, these corporations exceed in economic power all but the largest of nations. Not until recently have the courts begun to require of the corporations a responsibility to balance their privilege as legal "persons." However, Christopher Stone and other critics have doubted the capacity of the law alone to produce corporate social responsibility. The escape hatch of limited liability, the frustrating diffusion of managerial responsibility, the reactive rather than the preventive nature of the law, and the myriad difficulties in passing and enforcing laws make some critics look elsewhere than to the courts for help. Quite apart from the difficulties in detail, which Stone has specified, the strategy of relying on external regulation *alone* falters at a crucial point. It generates a latent antinomianism—a barely repressed spirit of lawlessness—in the regulated. Regulations usually enforce minimal standards. But the regulated often turn these standards upside down and use them as guidelines to mark out for themselves the maximum of what they can get away with.

Professional guilds, at least in theory, might also help restrain and civilize corporate behavior. Unlike large-scale bureaucracies, which usually develop hierarchical patterns of super- and subordination between employees, the guilds foster collegial relations among their members. Traditionally, professionals accepted patterns of super- and subordination among themselves only as temporary phases of training and education. Eventually, apprentices master the guild's defining body of knowledge and skill and relate to other professionals as equals, colleagues, and peers. Thus independence marks the fully fledged professional; and independent colleagues appropriately work with one another chiefly by persuasion rather than by command.

In principle, the collegial and the hierarchical modes of identity conflict; however, in practice, professionals can succumb to the institution that hires them or retains them. The hierarchical pattern of authority and advancement prevails and discourages independent professional conscience. Organizational stairs and risers mark the social architecture of the university, the hospital, and the corporation. While clambering up these stairs toward a partnership, a job as chief of service, a full professorship, or a vice-presidency, the professional's commitment to the independent judgment that characterizes professional colleagues can weaken.

But what of professionals who have not simply dissolved into the corporate hierarchy? The doctor disturbed by a treatment delivered so hastily as to leave her patient in the lurch without adequate support for healing? The lawyer troubled by his firm's habit of aggressively racking up the client's billable hours? An engineer pressed to ignore defects or build obsolescence into a product? The assistant professor who spends time teaching rather than yielding to the institution's pressures to publish? Unfortunately, professionals who have exhausted alternative remedies can no longer look to their guilds to back them in challenges against the institutions for which they work.

Elliott A. Krause in *Death of the Guilds*[26] examines the history of four professions (medicine, law, engineering, and the professoriate) from 1930 to 1995 in five countries (the United States, Great Britain, France, Germany, and Italy) and concludes that for one reason or another the power of the several professional guilds has dwindled to the point of extinction in each country. Certainly the professorial guilds vary in their willingness and power to back members who challenge the large institutions for which they work. The American Association of University Professors (AAUP) has established investigatory and legal defense funds to protect its members against violations, and restrictions on academic freedom, and, occasionally, has applied sanctions against offending institutions. Other professions, such as engineering and nursing, have proved timorous by comparison, deserting guild members and leaving the individual professional to face a conflict alone, without financial or legal aid. Until recently, the guilds have not backed professionals with legal funds to pursue cases against corporations whose misbehavior threatens to bend professional ethics. Further, an engineering society, as compared with the AAUP, must surmount special obstacles to conduct investigations and protect its members against corporate pressures. A corporation owns the research of its employees; academic research eventually finds its way into the commonwealth of learning. Thus the AAUP can more easily uncover the information it needs to return a judgment against an offending institution than an engineering guild.

Guilds have also been lax and erratic in disciplining defective practitioners. Usually, the corporations for which professionals work, rather than their professional guilds, discipline professionals through personnel policies governing hiring, firing, salaries, promotion, and termination. Such corporate disciplinary standards emphasize the professional's technical contribution to the goals of the corporation rather than encourage substantive professional criticism of corporate goals and strategy. However, recently, socially responsible corporations have taken to developing a corporate code or covenants. The very idea of adopting a code reflects the influence of professional guilds on corporations. Sometimes such documents serve as little more than company manuals, posting the rules of the road; at other times, as bare exercises in PR. But, in some notable instances, such as Johnson & Johnson and Borg-Warner Security Corporation,[27] corporate codes reflect an earnest effort to think through and state the substantive goals and responsibilities of the enterprise.

Inasmuch as the marketplace, the law, and professional guilds have not fully succeeded in regulating and civilizing corporate behavior, critics such as Peter Drucker and Christopher Stone have argued for reforming corporate structure rather than imposing discrete, substantive regulations as the way to develop corporate social responsibility. Structural reformers fall into two patterns. One group would decentralize the corporation in order to distribute responsibility more widely. Drucker, for example, identified four basic designs for decentralizing large companies,[28] but whatever the structure, top management dominates the organization. Only four or five people share the uppermost levels of power. More boldly, some structural experiments would include workers in decision-making. The move toward industrial democracy emphasizes the well-being of the workforce as a central goal of management. Skeptics worry, however, that industrial democracy would not provide the flexibility, efficiency, and rapid response that survival in an intensely competitive economy requires. Other critics question whether a large group of essentially self-interested employees will respond any more sensitively to other issues of social conscience, such as environmental concerns, than do the traditional handful of self-interested top managers.

A second group of reformers has turned away from efforts to decentralize authority and sought instead to increase responsibility at the top—the board of directors. To this end, Stone would provide the board of directors of a corporation with its own staff to keep it from rubber stamping for upper management. Stone would also allot a sliding percentage of seats to outside public directors who would defend the public interest on the boards of our largest corporations. In a company with special problems—pollution, product safety, and so on—additional special directors would strengthen its conscience and competence in making relevant decisions. Stone's reforms extend beyond the board. He also recommends various changes in the managerial structure to increase the flow of information upward and downward in the corporation. Too many managers get off the hook by pleading ignorance. Increasing knowledge will increase individual accountability.

The rationale behind these reforms suggests that the corporation needs to develop a more interior sense of responsibility than will emerge from the external threats from the law or pressures from the market. We can frame no better image for this interior sense of responsibility than that supplied by the human person. Stone and others use the legal status of the corporation as a person to try to build ingredients analogous to personal knowledge and conscience into its life. Even more specifically, Stone develops a Freudian model that draws a structural analogy between the functions of the ego, the superego, and the id in personal life and the roles of top management, the board, and the profit motive in the corporation. The rational decision maker in personal life—the ego—corresponds to top management. The unconscious drives, libidinous and otherwise—the id—correspond to the profit and other motives that make workers and managers tick. Finally, and most crucially, the conscience that in personal life internalizes the dictates and demands of parents in particular and the society at large—the superego—finds its corporate analogue in the board of directors. Hence the importance of reforming boards in Stone's proposals.

Formally, Stone's work suffers from inconsistency. He works hard to show why the "law can't do it," why external threat and sanction do not work to civilize corporations. And yet, he himself urges that the law mandate far-reaching changes in the corporate structure. In effect, the law can't do it; but the law must do it. He means, of course, not that "the law can't do it," but that discrete, substantive laws directed to the content of behavior cannot do it alone. He proposes instead even more invasive laws that would reform the corporate structure.

The compulsory legal ingredient in his proposals leads to a second problem. Public directors, staff troubleshooters, and ombudsmen, imposed on the corporation from without, will, of themselves, hardly lead management to interiorize responsibility. They will form an isolated and stigmatized in-house KGB unless other, deeper transformations of the corporate ethos proceed simultaneously.

Finally, Stone rightly insists that the corporation needs a better "information net." The provision of "hot lines" to ethics officers, along with assurances of confidentiality, represents one effort to strengthen the information net. However, for several reasons, bad news tends not to flow upward. Underlings do not want to bear it nor authorities hear it. Neither group wants to acknowledge innocence sullied. But knowledge—not just technical, but morally relevant, information—will not flow within the corporation unless the corporation accepts the manager's role as leader and teacher.

Leaders, Consultants, and Middle Managers As Transformers. The very word "management" emphasizes the custodial—the manager handles a volume of business through rational, impersonal routines. But no corporation can afford to restrict itself wholly to routine. The business corporation must cope with the market—which forces its managers to deal daily and relentlessly with uncertainties—fickle customers, the volatile costs of raw materials, transportation, and energy, and sudden changes in taste and habit. Thus some analysts would reserve the term "bureaucracy" for nonprofit service organizations or public institutions, arguing that any business organization, large-scale or otherwise, working in the market, must maintain flexibility and adaptability, to survive. Indeed, the effort of a bureaucracy to eliminate uncertainty through routine produces its own uncertainties. The effort to eliminate risk itself risks creating rigid, inflexible, interminable procedures. Management must seek not to eliminate risk but to figure out the right risks to take.

Seeking to estimate risks, today's management seeks to act less custodially, more proactively. It adopts the language of leadership. The term "leadership" itself invokes etymologically the image of a journey. But a journey going where? Into the unknown. Into the not-yet-fully-revealed. Into the kaleidoscopic future. Thus business seminars invariably link leadership with the decade—the century—ahead: leadership connects the present to a relatively opaque future, partly self-determined and partly determined by forces and factors beyond rational control.

Leadership consists of what the German philosopher Martin Heidegger called *Vorlaufen* (literally, running ahead of oneself; less literally, anticipation). Anticipation in our specific context combines several ingredients: first, selecting a goal or destination; second, determining the route to this goal; and third, as the Old English root for the word "leadership" suggests, convincing others to go by showing the way. In business, top management assumes these tasks as its chief responsibilities.

Leadership requires facing the uncertainty of the future, that ultimate uncertainty which, Heidegger (and John Dewey and William James) felt, no rational creature can wholly eliminate or ignore. But, in everyday practice, leaders seek to reduce uncertainty to a minimum. From time immemorial, those bearing great responsibilities have sought to reduce risks by rendering the future as transparent as possible. Thus the Greek general, responsible for decisions and consequences, resorted to an oracle who read the entrails of birds to discern the future and make it seem more knowable and psychologically manageable. The revolutionary leaders of the nineteenth century similarly resorted to prophetic theories to escape mystery. Karl Marx prevailed over other socialist prophets chiefly because he placed revolutionary action within the context of a philosophy that predicted the future. He confined fate to the iron tunnel of historical necessity. Thus those very events—war, depression, famine, and the collapse of markets—that previously convinced the proletariat of its powerlessness, Marx treated as signs of the imminent collapse of capitalist society and the triumph of the proletariat.

The outside consultant or advisor to top management acts as oracle for twenty-first century corporate society. No less prey to anxiety before fate than the Greek general or the European revolutionary, the manager today seeks omens from the outside counselor/oracle. Consulting has become a modern growth industry. It offers academics opportunities to moonlight and other professionals handsome careers. Modern advisors/consultants claim to examine something more relevant than the eviscerated entrails of birds: they offer *hard* data. In practice though, modern experts, like the Delphi Oracle, have devised ways to hedge their bets. In earlier, more epistemologically optimistic days, modern experts talked about predictions; later, and more modestly, projections; and still more recently, scenarios, to help protect themselves against recalcitrant fact.

The consultant offers an important psychological service through cognitive distance. The very nature of managerial work produces myopia. Managers pull up their daily round of responsibilities close to their eyes. They collapse psychic distance and watch only where they plant their feet, not where the road leads. In this close-up, they also lose critical perspective on their colleagues and the advice they offer. Thus outside consultants provide them with a little focal space in which to maneuver; they help bosses recover a little of the discretionary power routines have swallowed, a chance to see afresh a world grown overly familiar. This detachment, after all, partly distinguishes the professional from the amateur. Physicians do not take care of their own families because they might succumb to emotion and fail to offer the most effective help to their own people. Similarly, the corporation draws the manager so completely into its inner life and rhythms that he or she risks losing the distancing eye of a professional. Ideally, professional detachment allows for the possibility of moral transformation; it offers the space and distance required to move in a new direction.[29]

Finally, the consultant provides top managers with some of those benefits of collegiality that a hierarchical organization often denies them. Isolation on top of the heap forces managers to look outside the corporation to consultants for uninhibited discussion of issues difficult to raise inside. However, in an era of downsizing and reengineering, consultants play a somewhat more sinister role; they protect community within the organization by serving convincingly as scapegoats: the manager can blame a consultant for unpopular changes. The consultant draws lightning away from those who will continue to work in the organization after ripping up the fabric of community.

Within the corporation, a new breed of middle managers—experts who serve in staff rather than line positions—has developed to provide some of the services that the outside consultant offers. These knowledge experts work on special tasks and advise top executives rather than take responsibility for leading others who report to them. These staff "middle managers" nest in the hierarchy, but they work somewhat professionally and collegially. They derive authority less from position than from knowledge; they rely less on command and obedience than on research, reflection, and persuasion.

Like the eighteenth-century *philosophes*, these midlevel employees exercise power by whispering in the ear of the powerful. Inevitably their power suffers two limits. It depends upon a receptiveness at the top—the king must wish to learn; advisors cannot outvote him. Further, the king may want only technical advice—in which case, the knowledge expert or professional lacks opportunities to transform that her access to power apparently offered. Already housebroken, advisers tend to reduce professional responsibilities to offering only technical competence. In effect, they say to the boss: "Tell us what your goals are; and we will tell you, as lawyers, as engineers, as accountants, or as management experts, whether and how you can attain them."

A different opportunity, of course, presents itself to the middle manager/adviser if the corporation defines the managerial task to include critical judgment about goals and not just tactical cunning in attaining them, if managing carries with it some obligation for moral substance, and not just instrumental intelligence. Those *ifs* imply a transformational rather than a transactional understanding of business leadership.

A contractual ethic of the marketplace tends to produce a transactional understanding of leadership. The transactional leader (whether functioning as a professional, a manager, or a politician) accepts at face value the wishes and interests of people and offers them services that gratify their explicit aspirations for power, money, or relief from distress. Thus patients and clients buy help from professionals in pursuing their own goals. Political leaders in the social contract state acquire power by gratifying the desires and interests of their citizens. Managers contract with owners to maximize profits by satisfying the desires of customers. All of these transactions amplify the client's powers, but leave unaltered the client's character and commitments. Whims, desires, and interests escape untouched, untransformed.

A covenantal understanding of institutional and professional responsibility, as suggested in earlier chapters, implies that the leader will transform, not simply gratify. Such leadership helps move citizens out of their private, everyday lives into a more spacious community devoted to public purposes.[30] A society whose frontiers and gross national product are expanding, with an abundant supply of energy and of places to dump waste, may not notice its need to transform national habits. Such a society can waste—indulging desires—because the economy will grow enough to gratify the many presently unmet desires. But a minimum growth democracy eventually must choose one of two courses. It can develop into a veto-ruled society, in which each power group protects its possessions through its very considerable defensive capability. In such a society, no serious, coherent program to solve any major problem can prevail; one interest group or another will nibble each part of a program to death. Vetoes will paralyze such a society. Alternatively, the society will find some way of reordering its priorities and habits in order to address and meliorate its fundamental problems. The latter is the task of transformative leadership. A democratic country needs this second kind of leadership from its politicians, but it will fail to cultivate such leaders if it never sees redirecting leadership exercised by its professional classes and by the leaders of the great corporations that have so thoroughly recruited and organized professionals in their service.

The Business Leader/Manager As Teacher. Redirectional leadership depends on effective teaching to achieve enduring convictions and not supply grudging compliance with decisions. Leadership that teaches does not simply bend people against their will, or dazzle them out of their faculties, or manipulate them behind their backs, or indoctrinate them without illuminating. Rather, it widens the horizon against which colleagues see a given world of practice and therefore opens up a freedom to perform in new ways.

The top manager heretofore has tended to control his or her world by commanding those within and by manipulating and pressuring those without. But managers have greatly exaggerated the necessity of inscrutability and secretiveness outside the corporation; they also overlook the cost of these two tactics. When leaders govern within exclusively by commanding rather than persuading, they control behavior rather than lead people and they fail to prepare a new generation to lead. Further, coping with the outside world exclusively by seducing (aggressive advertising) and bullying or manipulating (aggressive lobbying) generates distrust. False claims produce skepticism and resentment; false threats, grudging compliance or defiance. Neither customer nor government can hear the merits of the case. Top management should accept a responsibility to teach both citizens without and workers within.

It would be foolish, of course, to exaggerate these prescriptions. No large-scale institution, public or private, can wholly substitute persuasion for command. No president of the United States can afford to restrict his decisions wholly to what he can explain or defend by persuasion. A corporate board meeting or an executive committee does not resemble a seminar. The board must end discussion and decide long before everyone has understood or yielded to persuasion. But leaders of the corporation cannot mend their "information net" other than superficially unless they demand substantive, as well as technical, intelligence and discussion.

Junior colleagues, especially staff, must accept implicitly a corresponding obligation as advisors to teach their superiors. Such teaching, of course, in a purely contractual setting means transmitting information that the boss can use instrumentally to reach pre-established goals. A great deal of teaching in professional life does and should do just that. But in a covenantal setting, the advisor needs to raise substantive moral questions about goals. Otherwise, the meaning and social justification for the professional, the knowledge expert, dwindles. Presumably, the professional generates power through placing knowledge at the service of human need. It would be odd to so restrict the scope of this professional service in the corporation as to provide the staff advisor with less moral power than Balaam's ass, which posed an awkward question or two about the direction in which his master rode (Num. 22:22–35).

This brief review of various efforts to increase corporate responsibility has emphasized the limitations of each type of response, but not in order to demolish them all. It argues the deficiency of each simply as a sole and sufficient remedy. Taming the corporations may require responses on multiple fronts. The interior transformation of corporate culture does not eliminate the need for radical innovation or for external regulations and reforms. Radical experiments can venture beyond the institutions currently in place to develop those forms that may be proleptic for generations to come. Regulations can help post "off-limits" signs to ban outrageous behavior, can level the playing field, and can somewhat shift incentives. The threat of regulations can also help companies move beyond good intentions and PR. Structural reforms, in the relations of boards, managers, and workers, can better equip huge institutions to identify and pursue their proper ends. But experiments, regulations, and reforms without interior changes will also founder. The untamed opportunist in each of us ducks and dodges and will find a hundred ways to maneuver around regulations and reforms unless the interior constraints of covenant and calling begin to discipline the powers we wield.

Notes

1. Thomas Bodenheimer, "The American Health Care System—Physicians and the Changing Marketplace," *The New England Journal of Medicine*, Feb. 18, 1999, vol. 340, no. 7, 584–88, based on statistics supplied in *Socioeconomic Characteristics of Medical Practice*, 1997/98 (Chicago: American Medical Association, 1998).
2. A. W. H. Adkins, *Merit and Responsibility: A Study in Greek Value* (Oxford: Clarendon Press, 1960), describes the shift from the early Homeric, tribal emphasis on the competitive virtues to the later Athenian, urban emphasis on the cooperative virtues. Thus practical wisdom replaces courage as the preeminent virtue in Plato's *Republic*. In a well-ordered society, the warrior class no longer rules.
3. For what follows in these two paragraphs, see Charles E. Lindblom, "The Privileged Position of Business," chap. 13 in *Politics and Markets* (New York: Basic Books, 1982).
4. Milton Friedman, "The Social Responsibility of Business Is to Increase Its Profits," the *New York Times Magazine*, 13 September 1970.
5. Isaac Shapiro and Robert Greenstein, "The Widening Income Gulf," prepared for the Center on Budget and Policy Priorities (http:/www.cbpp.org), September 4, 1999, on the basis of data supplied by the Congressional Budget Office, Summer 1999, 1.
6. Ibid., 2.
7. Michael Lind, "The Next American Nation," in *The New Nationalism and the Fourth American Revolution* (New York: Simon and Schuster, 1995), 202.
8. Richard Sennett, *The Corrosion of Character: Personal Development in the New Capitalism* (W. W. Norton & Company, 1998).
9. Sennett, 117.
10. Ibid.
11. Ibid.
12. Michael Novak, *The Spirit of Democratic Capitalism* (New York: Simon & Schuster, 1982), 39.
13. Novak, 45.
14. Novak, 183.
15. Novak, 175.
16. *Pastoral Letter*, par. 65.
17. The ultimate Trinitarian root of such thinking about the image of God shows up in the full sentence from the passage previously cited: "Christian theological reflection on the very reality of God as a Trinitarian unity of persons—Father, Son, and Holy Spirit—shows that being a person means being united to other persons in mutual love." *Pastoral Letter*, par. 64.
18. Robert B. Reich, *The Work of Nations* (New York: Vintage Books, Random House, 1992), 291.
19. Sheldon Wolin, "The Age of Organization and the Sublimation of Politics," chapter 10 in *Politics and Vision* (Boston: Little, Brown & Company, 1960).
20. The Berkeley student leader complains, "As bureaucrat, an administrator believes that nothing new happens. He occupies an a-historical viewpoint." See Mario Savio, "An End to History," in *The New Student Left*, ed. Mitchel Cohen and Dennis Hale (Boston: Beacon Press, 1967), 248.

21. Herbert Read, *The Grass Roots of Art: Lectures on Social Aspects of Art in an Industrial Age* (Cleveland: World Pub. Corp., 1961).
22. Charles Hendy, "Tocqueville Revisited," *Harvard Business Review*, January 2001, 61.
23. Hendy, 62.
24. Lester Thurow, *The Zero Sum Society* (New York: Harper & Row, 1975), 89.
25. Christopher Stone, *Where the Law Ends: The Social Control of Corporate Behavior* (New York: Harper & Row, 1975), 89.
26. Elliott A. Krause, *Death of the Guilds: Profession, States, and the Advance of Capitalism, 1930 to the Present* (New Haven, Conn.: Yale University Press, 1996).
27. See Patrick E. Murphy, *Eighty Exemplary Ethics Statements* (Notre Dame, Ind.: University of Notre Dame Press, 1998).
28. Peter F. Drucker, *Management: Tasks, Responsibilities, Practices* (New York: Harper & Row, 1974).
29. For more on the place of anticipation and the need for space in corporate decision-making, see Charles W. Powers and David Vogel, "What Is Business Ethics?" in *Ethics in the Education of Business Managers* (Hastings-on-Hudson, N.Y.: The Hastings Center, 1980), chap. 1.
30. James McGregor Burns writes: "That people can be lifted *into* their better selves is the secret of transforming leadership and the moral and political theme of this work." James McGregor Burns, *Leadership* (New York: Harper & Row, 1978), 462.

Chapter 5

Politics

The Despised Profession

I ronically, the entire world needs good political decisions coming
out of the United States at a time when Americans scorn politics
as a vocation. This scorn shows up variously. In ordinary talk, the
words "politician" and "bureaucrat" send off negative charges like
static electricity snapping off cheap clothing. The word "politician"
fairly crackles with the opportunistic, personally ambitious, glad-
handing and underhanded, overpromising and underperforming.
Such negative signals reverberate still more loudly when we qualify
the noun "politician" with the adjective "professional." Normally the
adjective "professional" heightens status. We signal our respect for
musicians, actresses, or accountants when we call them "professional," but not for politicians. The professional politician has merely
picked up the tricks of a somewhat grubby craft. Meanwhile, bureaucrats—the permanent employees of government—fare little better
than politicians. We dismiss bureaucrats as officious, rigid, by-the-
book paper shufflers, and time-servers; they seem distant from the
human condition and unresponsive to human need.

The political system itself generates some of this contempt for
politicians and bureaucrats. Politicians tear bark off one another in
the course of electoral campaigns. Legislators heap scorn on bureaucrats in the executive branch of government and, in the name of
accountability, swamp them with rules, procedures, and reporting
requirements that multiply the paperwork bureaucrats must perform.
Dismissing them as paper shufflers, legislators nevertheless increase
the bales of paper they must shuffle. Hence bureaucracy happily
metastasizes under the care of its suspicious monitors.

But, deeper even than the self-inflicted wounds from which politicians and bureaucrats suffer, an ideological suspicion of government
undercuts it from many quarters. The old Marxist revolutionary Left

discredited all government on the grounds that it merely enforced the interests and power of the property classes. The student protesters of the '60s condemned government as a military-industrial complex up to no good on foreign soil. The far Right in the '50s saw the U.S. government as infiltrated and corrupted by communism (McCarthyism). In the '80s and '90s, it opposed government as if it were a foreign power, a vestigial remain, if you will, of King George III, not our government, an instrument of national purpose.

Less stridently, others on the Right advocate an economic libertarianism that would radically shrink the sphere in which the government could operate. Libertarians do not oppose all government. They would support taxes to fund the fire, police, and defense departments in order to protect life, liberty, and property. However, they usually oppose any other state regulations and welfare. Under the banner "get the government off our backs," they oppose regulations that require safe products and safe working conditions and that protect the environment; and they would dismantle welfare programs that support jobs, housing, education, health care, and child care. Such Robin Hood activities, they complain, rob the hard-working and the well-to-do and corrupt the poor. To solve most problems in life, libertarians look to the marketplace rather than government, and they would privatize, as rapidly as possible, education, health care, and social security.

Supply siders in the '80s theorized that the government actually created the chief problem the poor face: a lack of jobs. They argued that redistributive taxes lead to a stagnant economy and fewer jobs, from which, in the long run, the poor suffer. The government needs to get out of the way and reduce taxes. Cutting back taxes on the wealthy will unleash the power of the marketplace to create more wealth. Increased production, rather than burdensome redistributive taxes, will lead to plenty for all.

As it turned out, the trickle-down theory of supply siders proved wrong. The conservative advisor to the Republican Party, Kevin Phillips, noted that the Reagan tax policies of the '80s created huge budget deficits and dramatic transfers of wealth to the upper one percent of Americans, and cut the real income of workers and the poor.[1] However, despite the collapse of supply-side theory, some conservatives supported Reagan's tax cuts because they thought that the ensuing huge budget deficits would prevent the government from offering welfare to the poor. Thus, win or lose at the level of theory, the enemies of government would win—except, of course, as Kevin Phillips warned, they would lose the White House to the Democrats in the '90s.

Although not associated with the right, Peter Drucker found yet another way to diminish the role of politics and politicians in human affairs.[2] Surveying in an *Atlantic Monthly* essay the whole of the twentieth century, he noted that the United States has undergone three great social transformations in the past hundred years. The country has moved from an agricultural society through an industrial society and into an information age. These transforming events have occurred, Drucker notes, almost without friction, "with a minimum of upheavals."[3] However, at the same time, the twentieth century has also been "the cruelest and most violent in history, with its world and civil wars, its mass tortures, ethnic cleansings, genocides and holocaust."[4] These darker events Drucker attributes to three political geniuses of the twentieth century: Hitler, Stalin, and Mao. He then concludes without recognizing the fact-defying leap he has made: "Indeed, if this century proves one thing, it is the futility of politics."[5]

The futility of politics? Drucker fails to notice that politicians such as Churchill and Roosevelt, not Henry Ford or Joseph P. Kennedy, shouldered the immensely difficult task of organizing the Western World to defeat Hitler. Then, shortly after the war, a general, George C. Marshall—secretary of state under Harry Truman, not a CEO—devised the Marshall Plan to reconstruct Europe. The single most important piece of legislation at the end of World War II, the Marshall Plan, contained Stalin's empire and set the course for the eventual decline of communism in the twentieth century. Similar wise political decisions leading to the reconstruction of Japan contained the power of Mao in the East. Further, the United States would hardly have been in a position to pull off these accomplishments in foreign policy from 1940 forward, if the "New Deal" in the '30s had not provided a safety net to protect the country from some of the harsh, divisive consequences of a worldwide depression. Only earnest ideologues extract from the twentieth century the lesson that politics has failed. Quite the contrary, the century has proved the necessity of politics, its care and nurture, in order to protect the world from those tyrants who would collapse politics altogether and impose the military state.

However, it fell to entrepreneur Ross Perot in the 1992 election to express the most brusque disdain for the profession of politics with his snappy solution to any of a series of issues facing the nation—"just lift up the hood and fix it." The metaphor obscures a complexity. Three hundred million people own the car; and they disagree about what needs fixing and who ought to pay for it. Further, the rules of the shop do not authorize a single, specific mechanic to perform the repairs. The mechanic in the White House must try to work, while simultaneously listening to two large bodies of elected representatives of the three hundred million owners and submitting to a review board of judicial experts, who will scrutinize his tools to see whether they conform to shop rules. Finally, while he has his head ducked under the hood, the mechanic must hold a wrench in one hand and hold out the other to raise the money needed to campaign against other mechanics for his job. For all Perot's patriotism, a deep hostility to the Constitution and its separation of powers shaped his image of himself as the Mechanic empowered by electronic plebiscite to bypass representative government, take his own direct read on the people's will (which he would interpret to his own satisfaction without the distractions of mediating representatives), and then translate into policies executed through subordinates in military-style haircuts.

The media today have also contributed to popular scorn for government, less through their hostility to particular politicians than through their cumulative redefinition of the active citizen as a passive onlooker. The mid-nineteenth-century development of the telegraph, the daguerreotype, and the penny press and the twentieth-century wiring of the globe have cumulatively turned the recipient of information from decision maker into spectator. Politics deteriorates into a blood sport—who's winning? The media lock on freefalling scandal more readily than on tangled information that might help citizens reach complex political judgments. Citizenship is the art of deliberating and acting in concert with others for the common good; our modern fortuitous concatenation of spectators does not readily make up a body of citizens, capable of identifying, discerning, and accepting responsibility for the work of effective political leaders.

Types of Political Leadership

Three ancient cities symbolize three different forms of leadership: Jerusalem, Sparta, and Athens. The founder of Jerusalem, King David, symbolized leading by *charisma*. David, a man of transcendent gifts and charm, a poet, a musician, a great strategist, a sometime adulterer and betrayer of his men, also founded a nation and supplied a prototype for personal, kingly rule.

American democracy rejected this notion of personal, charismatic leadership. George Washington refused to be king; the founders agreed. They insisted on a government of *laws*, not of *men*. The genuine oil of charisma anointed a few of our presidents—Andrew Jackson, Abraham Lincoln, Teddy Roosevelt, and Franklin D. Roosevelt. However, today, only a sad counterfeit of charismatic leadership shows up in modern celebrities. Instead of the hero's deeds, we get a *People Magazine* glitz, and a disposition to choose presidential candidates only from those who pass the camera test for office.

Ancient Sparta, a military society, symbolizes the second type of leadership: *command*. Military leaders need not use many words; Sparta embodied a society given to taciturnity. It depended upon the bark of command and the grunt of obedience.[6] Leaders of the Spartan type abhor the messy give-and-take of political compromise; they prefer clear military organization to shifting political coalitions.[7] They prize hierarchy.[8] We still partly depend on such leadership today. Our President is commander in chief, and corporations appoint CEO's to command; but a democracy requires more than commands from its leaders.

Athens symbolizes a third type of leadership: *persuasion*. Athens relied on *logos* (that is, the *word* or rational *persuasion*). Democracies are inherently *wordy*. They build *parliaments*, literally houses of *words*. The American presidency may no longer be a bully pulpit, but it must be a bully blackboard to the nation. The President must lead by persuasion. You cannot lead for long, you cannot even command the armed forces for long, unless you bring the people along.

As symbols, none of the three cities symbolizes an important fourth ingredient of political leadership, an ingredient that Machiavelli described in detail. He knew that politics also requires the rough and tumble of bargaining, maneuvering, and manipulating upon which political survival and accomplishment often depend. To the three ancient cities therefore we need to add a fourth—Florence—and its successor cities the world over, run by their princes and ward bosses well acquainted with the power of self-interest in human affairs. In addition to charming, commanding, and persuading, political leaders must also bargain, manipulate, and maneuver.

The modern theologian Reinhold Niebuhr tried to strike a balance between the cities, if you will, particularly between Florence and Athens. His famous and often borrowed dictum puts it: "Man's capacity for justice makes democracy possible; man's inclination to injustice makes democracy necessary."[9] Politicians underestimate humankind if they do not appeal to the image of God within us; they overestimate humankind if they neglect the darker side of human nature, the power of self-interest in human affairs. Presidents surely must bargain, manipulate, and maneuver their constituencies. Only a species of sentimentality about human nature would deny them the strategy of leading through bargaining. At the same time, effective presidents must address what Lincoln called the "better angels of our nature." They must teach the nation. As Erwin C. Hargrove put it prosaically, they must "teach reality to the public and their fellow politicians through rhetoric."[10]

Teaching and persuading do not always take a rhetorical form. Upon the death of the master rhetorician, Franklin Delano Roosevelt, people winced at the speeches of his flat-voiced, prosaic, midwestern successor, Harry S. Truman of Missouri. But Truman supplied the country with a series of wise political decisions in the aftermath of the war (the Marshall Plan for the reconstruction of Europe heading the list). Good decisions and legislation have a way of tutoring a nation. Action often requires previous insight, but wise actions can also give insight as dividends. A leader need not always be a Jefferson, a Lincoln, a Theodore Roosevelt, a Woodrow Wilson, or an FDR to teach well.

Basic Cultural Ideals

Just what deep cultural ideals must presidents and other political leaders address if they would teach well? I have difficulty with the answer that Hargrove gives to this question in his book on *The President As Leader*. He identifies liberal individualism as our defining cultural ideal. Like other political scientists,[11] Hargrove defines liberal individualism broadly enough to include both economic libertarians and democratic egalitarians. Economic libertarians (read Republicans) gain power when government becomes too burdensome; egalitarians (read Democrats) win elections when the free play of the market economy begins to exclude too many people from the fundamental goods of American life. Libertarians and egalitarians duke it out in our politics, but, still, both groups are individualistic, not communitarian.

Hargrove, in my judgment, is diagnostically wrong in limiting American culture wholly to the parameters of liberal individualism; and he is morally and politically wrong in limiting leadership automatically to teaching whatever the culture has established as its conventional parameters. First, diagnostically, the American tradition is communitarian, not simply individualistic. All three major religious traditions—Protestant, Catholic and Jewish—relied on their communal origins as they made their way into this country: Jews and Catholics, explicitly. Jews disembarked in this country under the triple banner of God, Torah, and Israel. Catholics defined the church as the body of Christ, its communicants joined inseparably as members of that body, and affirmed the common good as the defining goal of a Catholic social ethics. Although Protestants eventually succumbed to the rhetoric of individualism, they did not at first embrace that creed. The early Protestant immigrants, entering into their shipboard covenants, understood themselves as bound together in "the ligaments of love," defined their several callings as the way in which God ordained them to serve the common good, and tutored themselves in the arts of democratic citizenship as they deliberated in the local congregation.

Furthermore, the eighteenth-century founders of the country did not entirely distance themselves from the communitarian heritage of the country. Certainly, they emphasized individual liberty more than any other ideal. However, the phrase "public virtue" ranked second to liberty as the most often invoked term at the time of the revolution. The founders defined public virtue as the readiness to sacrifice self-interest to the common good.[12] Why public virtue? Instrumentally, the revolutionaries recognized the need for sacrifice in winning a war of independence. But they also recognized that, long after the urgencies of war concluded, the country would need public virtue in its citizens to sustain its character as a republic, *a res publica*. Liberty itself would not long survive unless, in the uses of their liberty, the American people sustained a readiness to serve the common good. The framers of the Constitution carried forward this sense of community into the first words we uttered as a nation: "We, the people." The preamble to the Constitution does not proclaim, "We, the factions of the United States" or "We, the interest groups of the United States" or "We, the individuals of the United States," but "We, the people." Individualism may be the primary language spoken in the United States, but it is not, as Robert Bellah and his colleagues pointed out in

Habits of the Heart,[13] the only language. Communitarian language ranks second to the language of individualism in American life. Communitarianism is a native, not a foreign, tongue. In "teaching reality," leaders can speak this second language.

Furthermore, even if the language of individualism exclusively defined the American character, it would be morally wrong to restrict leadership entirely to what Americans have hitherto found acceptable as conventional wisdom. If dominantly individualistic, Americans may need to learn how to compensate for the weaknesses of individualism. For individualism, while in many respects admirable, does not help us recognize and respond adequately to the dilemmas we face in a complexly interconnected and interdependent world. Individualism has helped create a world in which individualism alone cannot survive.

Individualists of both kinds also overlook the complexity of the judgments about social goods and priorities that citizens through their leaders must make. Libertarians and egalitarians resemble one another in that they suspend (or reduce to a minimum) the question of the good or goods a society ought to pursue. Libertarians fiercely oppose the intrusion of the state upon the liberty of its citizens.[14] Each citizen in his liberty can pursue whatever goods he chooses, as long as he does not interfere with the similar liberty of others. In this libertarian setting, the poor can, at best, hope for charity from their fellows. They cannot appeal to a principle of distributive justice for help in meeting basic needs. Meanwhile, egalitarians insist on fairness as the pre-eminent principle of justice, but they do not examine deeply enough the question of the fundamental and high goods a society ought to pursue.[15] In effect, the principle of equality insists chiefly that everyone get a fair share of the pie, whatever the pie may be.

In my judgment, a society must examine more closely and critically the question of the contents of the pie—the common goods men and women ought to pursue—however much a consumerist society may be disposed to neglect the issue. The goods constituting the common good are surely plural in number. The first good of a society is that of belonging, not only because belonging supplies the ticket to other goods, but because belonging is a good in itself. Additionally, a society and its members need a range of fundamental goods crucial to survival—food, clothing, shelter, safety, basic education, and health care; and they need a set of higher goods that permit its members not simply to survive but to flourish—art, culture, higher education, work, love, friendship, citizenship, honors, and play.[16] While we can rely partly on the marketplace for generating and distributing many of these goods, some of the high goods (such as love, friendship, and honors) we cannot buy or sell without corrupting them; and other fundamental goods (such as food, clothing, shelter, health care, public safety, and education) are so basic to life that we cannot treat them exclusively as mere commodities. The marketplace may go a long way toward distributing basic goods. But a decent society must find ways, at an adequate minimum level, to provide its members with access to the necessities; and a fully flourishing society encourages and supports the pursuit of the higher goods.

Since no philosopher, no expert, no pundit or politician can supply a society with a fixed hierarchical ordering of these goods, a society also needs the goods of process—the principles and procedures, appropriate civil rights and rules—it can use to reach fair decisions about priorities. It also needs leaders who, working within the constraints of these procedures, reach wise decisions. Lawful procedures alone do not ensure equitable outcomes.

The Politician and the Uncommonly Difficult Pursuit of the Common Good

The diversity and vertical range of the goods that comprise the common good make politics among the most difficult of professions. Each of the professions serves an important human good difficult to pursue: the doctor, healing; the lawyer, truth and justice under the law; the business executive, abundance at a profit; the teacher, education. The politician differs from other professionals in that he or she purportedly serves not a particular good, such as health care, education, and abundance, but the common good. (That is why, from Aristotle forward, many moralists saw a powerful connection between ethics and politics. Ethics describes the fitting pursuit of the good; politics, the common good. They form two sides of the same coin.)

Serving the common good is uncommonly difficult compared to serving a particular good, such as education or health care. The common good, inconveniently enough, breaks out into competing substantive goods, both basic and higher. Further, interest groups pressing for (or neglecting) any particular good always strain the prior good of community. Finally, the necessity for procedural restraints upon decision-makers, as they disagree about priorities, inevitably leads to delays, obstacles, disappointments, frustrations, and adversities with which political leaders, even with the best of intentions, find it difficult to cope.

In pursuing the common good, political leaders face two types of moral problems: temptations and quandaries. Temptations include cases in which a clear distinction divides right from wrong and the politician chooses wrong; he takes a bribe, steals, lies, self-deals, fails to recuse himself in conflicts of interest, or harasses sexually. In such breaches, the politician puts his private interests or the interests of his owners ahead of the common good.

Quandaries include cases in which no simple distinction exists between right and wrong. The politician must choose between competing goods and/or competing evils, so that, no matter which way she turns, she must forfeit or limit support for some good or impose some evil or loss. In yielding to temptation, she rationalizes; in resolving a quandary, she deliberates, weighing goods and principles constrained by limited resources. Sargent Shriver once observed that by the time a policy decision reached the desk of his brother-in-law President Kennedy, it posed an ethical question in the sense of a quandary. It demanded a judgment about priorities. Quandaries about using time, money, and other resources vex all leaders, administrators, professionals and, for that matter, parents.

The word "compromise" carries a different meaning in the setting of temptations and quandaries. In yielding to temptation, politicians compromise their identity. To accept a bribe erodes the core being of a public servant, who serves his private good rather than the common good. In a quandary, however, an agent must choose one good at the expense of another or support both goods at a level far short of the ideal. In this case, a compromise does not denigrate. One seeks a compromise that offers the best possible approximation of the ideal in an imperfect world.

Just where one must strike the balance in a particular case often rouses disputes; the task of seeking a balance can provoke good-faith differences on both sides. However, the turbulence of politics and policy-making often confuses the two types of moral problems. The policy-maker sees a quandary, where the fierce advocate, the single-issue citizen, sees only a clear distinction between right and wrong and accordingly accuses the policy-maker of a base compromise. It does not help when single-issue groups rail against politicians as unprincipled "relativists" for failing to accede fully to their requests. Policy-makers seeking a compromise may simply be pluralists rather than relativists. Their accommodation, when multiple goods (and principles) conflict, may offer the best possible approximation of the ideal in difficult circumstances. Not all is awash in the sea of the relative when politicians seek earnestly to strike a compromise.[17]

On the whole, politicians who take seriously their calling to serve the common good fall into two types: some primarily seek justice; others, order. Reformers and progressives tend to criticize the established order in the name of justice. Setting their faces against injustice or tyranny, they would reform and transform the society for the sake of the oppressed or those treated unjustly. Conservatives, meanwhile, tend to prize order and stability. Setting their faces against instability and anarchy, they fear that liberals, reformers, and radicals threaten ordered society with their disruptive campaigns on behalf of justice.

In striking a balance, wise leaders recognize both justice and order as basic social goods, injustice and anarchy as evils. No one wrote more eloquently (or campaigned more persistently) on behalf of those deprived of justice than Martin Luther King Jr. But his "Letter from a Birmingham Jail" detailed a strategy for civil disobedience that also respected order.[18] He insisted that his followers seek to negotiate with their opponents before engaging in civil disobedience, undergo a discipline to keep that disobedience nonviolent, disobey only as a last resort, and even then, lovingly and openly and with the final intent of resuming negotiations. Adlai Stevenson, the liberal Democratic candidate for President in 1952, similarly recognized the importance of reconciliation and order in the midst of national transformations. He only reluctantly accepted the nomination in 1952 because he recognized that an Eisenhower victory might advance the good of harmony and stability in the United States. It would let the Republicans and the business community ratify most of the social changes of the thirties and forties which, out of office, they had opposed. Similarly, moderates hold dearly to the good of order, but some have wisely come to accept legislation on social security, minimum wages, housing, and other issues of social justice. They recognize that a failure to remedy injustice, as they retreat into private schools, private neighborhoods, and private security services, will eventually undercut the stability which they prize.[19]

Leadership and the Virtues

Whether politicians aim to reform or consolidate, they undertake a complex task that calls for a set of virtues, above and beyond the skills associated with charisma, command, bargaining, and persuasion.

Leading a democracy differs from *managing* an organization. The manager, whether working for the government or a corporation, works toward *preset* goals. The leader faces the more difficult task of choosing goals, not just operating on preset rails. Leadership usually entails breaking new ground, whether in the cause of reforming or consolidating a community. It poses the vexing questions of destination. Political leadership requires choosing goals wisely (and the balance between them which the culture has not entirely preset) and the means to honor them (about which further serious differences of judgment may exist).

So the leader needs especially the virtue of practical wisdom or, what we might call today, discernment. In order to know what to do, leaders must see what is out there; they must see clearly both the cultural/political context in which they must, shrewdly, work and also the corrections needed in prevailing ideals to which they must persuade the country. Discernment requires more than the tactical cunning to which Machiavelli reduced the classical virtue of prudence. Discernment includes practical wisdom about ends, not just the adroit choice of means to reach culturally predetermined ends.

To help them set priorities and deploy resources in the pursuit of goals, modern political leaders rely heavily on advisers and consultants. But, no matter how much wisdom and information leaders take in, they cannot resolve all doubts or eliminate all risks. At best, they choose wisely what risks to take. So, in addition to wisdom, the leader needs courage. A rough patch of trouble usually follows hard choices. Most decisions that cross a president's desk are hard choices and thus provoke a coefficient of adversity. Thomas Aquinas defined courage as firmness of soul in the face of adversity. Such courage has two aspects: active and passive. Active courage attacks problems, rather than dodging or ducking them. However, defeat calls for the equally important, if somewhat more passive, courage of endurance or resilience—the ability to get up off the floor and carry on. (Our modern political campaigns test endurance to the point of cruelty.)

Leadership also requires temperance. Plato once noted that to govern others, one must first govern oneself. Runaway desire can drive institutions lurching out of control. Plato also recognized that the greater long-term danger to a Republic's integrity comes from the intrusion and corruption of cash, not sex, into its political life. On the take is even worse than on the make. Such corruption besets not simply the individual but a society so ordered that it yields power to ravenous interest groups and their lobbyists.

Leadership in a democracy also requires public-spiritedness, what the founders of the country called "public virtue," a readiness to sacrifice self-interest to the common good. So defined, public-spiritedness is the indispensable source of distributive justice. We cannot distribute well or wisely for the good of all, if we do not exact responsibly and proportionately from the bounty of each. Without public-spiritedness, we deny ourselves the possibility of enduring structural solutions to deep structural problems: poverty, a badly educated populace, some eighty million citizens with little or no health care insurance, and the disturbing creation of a permanent underclass in our nation. One cannot irregularly hand out charity to persons suffering from deep structural problems and expect the problems to evanesce. We need also the government to serve as the major instrument of distributive justice.

But the breadth of power-wielding in a country of mixed economy calls for the virtue of public-spiritedness not only in politicians but in the leaders of corporations and other huge organizations. We may have strong presidents only intermittently in our national political life, but we depend regularly on CEOs in our corporate life. In large part, such organizations pursue their own interests under the leadership of a corporate president, but the country will not long survive and flourish if leaders in the "private" sector do not spare at least a walleye for the common good.

So what does political leadership in a democracy require? The Greek art of persuasion, certainly, but also the ancient virtues of wisdom, courage, temperance, and public-spiritedness. And we will not get enough of these virtues if we demand them of our political leaders alone. The leaders of other powerful institutions in the society must evince these virtues as well.

Good Citizenship

Gary Wills, in *Certain Trumpets: The Call of Leaders*,[20] emphasizes followership as a key element in leadership. Does the tree falling in the forest make noise if no one is there to hear it? Has the trumpet sounded, certain or uncertain, without an audience to attend to its lead? We mistakenly associate followers with passivity. Wills rightly emphasizes (though he does not elaborate on) the active responsibilities of followers. Political (and ecclesiastical) leaders must bet a lot on the followers they draw. Passive followers do not inevitably hold an exalted view of their leaders. On the contrary, their passivity tempts citizens to heap disproportionate blame on their leaders since passive bystanders accept no responsibility for their community's failures. Active citizenship requires that citizens develop the art of acting in concert with others for the common good. As the founders defined it, such public-spiritedness requires a readiness to sacrifice at least some immediate self-interest to the common good. Lacking that readiness, people tend to look to their leaders to gratify only their private self-interest. They do not think of themselves as public beings with public responsibilities. They quickly grow angry, petulant, and resentful when leaders fail to gratify their appetites.

A great ineffectualness afflicts a nation when the energy of resentment alone drives its politics. A private and therefore dangerously volatile emotion, resentment spills out into the streets and sweeps everything before it into the gutters but then itself sinks again into the sewers. Resentment produces a torrent, strong enough to wash the rascals out, but not steady enough to sustain policies that might remedy some of the fundamental problems the nation faces.

Many have pointed to evidences of a decline in the role of the citizen today. Voter turnout at elections has dwindled. As membership in political parties has declined, participation in politics between elections has also diminished. Michael Walzer noted decades ago that Americans have shifted from a "Greek" notion of active citizenship, which highlights continuing duties, to a Roman understanding of citizenship as passive, which emphasizes entitlements.[21] More recently, the citizen, with the help of the media, has slouched even deeper into the couch of passivity. Professional marketeers of leaders and leaders themselves tend to look upon citizens as customers or consumers. The citizen before his television set feels little sense of complicity in or responsibility for the decisions political leaders make or fail to make. Such citizens attend, almost exclusively, to their daily business of "food, sex, love, family, work, play, shelter, comfort, friendship, social esteem, and the like."[22] Politics lies at the "outer periphery of attention." Interest in public affairs flickers, at best, only occasionally at election time.

Not all have viewed such passive citizens with alarm. Classical Conservatives, from Edmund Burke to the early William Buckley, believed that a country is working best when politically sleepy, when people unvexedly preoccupy themselves with their private lives. Progressives, to the contrary, have tended to view with alarm the dwindling of the ideal of the actively engaged citizen. A Republic requires that citizens exercise their liberty, in some degree, to serve the common good. Still others offer a more complex view of gains and losses. Michael Schudson, in *The Good Citizen: A History of American Civic Life*, identifies no less than four successive and, in varying degrees, still persisting notions of citizenship across three centuries.

Colonial society cultivated the notion of the deferential citizen. The colonial tradition of deference to town and church elders persisted in the constitutional provision for representatives who must sift "raw opinion through deliberative legislative processes."[23] However, the rise of Jacksonian democracy in the nineteenth century encouraged the citizen as party member and movement activist. This more populist notion of the citizen persists to this day in a political rhetoric that courts public opinion and invokes "the people" and in procedures that select candidates for office increasingly by direct primaries. The Progressive Era at the end of the nineteenth century proposed a third ideal, the informed citizen. This ideal granted to reporters and journalists writing for newspapers a high vocation; and it also defined one of the major missions of public education. The McGuffey Readers would provide civic lessons in the classrooms reinforced by give-and-take on the playgrounds. In the setting of public education, pupils would learn how to move beyond the confines of the family, open up to strangers, and become citizens.

However, unlike other commentators, who have read the past fifty years solely as a fall from deference to incivility, from massive participation in politics to voter lethargy, from the ideal of the informed and active citizen to the reality of the citizen as passive spectator, Schudson hails a fourth positive stage in the history of citizenship.[24] Since the 1950s, the United States has dramatically widened the web of citizenship. The Supreme Court decisions in the '50s to desegregate schools and buses; the 1957 Civil Rights Act which legislatively extended citizens' rights to include women's rights in the workplace. Successive legislation and, perhaps even more important, litigation helped establish the rights of women (and children) to welfare and to their protection from abuse in the family and from sexual harassment in the workplace. Society also set in place the rights of the handicapped in schools and public places, gay rights, regulations protecting the environment, and, most recently in the 1990s, patients' rights.

Thus the last fifty years have shifted emphasis from the active to the rights-bearing citizen, especially those citizens who previously did not enjoy full access to the life and opportunities of the society. Legislation, especially the social legislation of the 1960s, reinforced, expanded, and extended the reach of such rights; but citizens have looked even more to the courts than to the voting booth to secure these rights.

Schudson concedes that the ideal of the informed citizen has weakened today. People chiefly focus on their own daily lives and pay only marginal and fitful attention to the life of the commonwealth. They rely on headlines and sound bites for their knowledge of politics. Still, he remains somewhat hopeful. Even though sound bites do not produce informed citizens, they allow for what he calls "monitorial citizens." Headlines and sound bites alert citizens to problems and excesses that the *polis* must address and redress.

The Schudson portrait of the rights-bearing citizen does not fully reassure one about the health and well-being of citizenship in America. The courts have properly served to identify and protect previously abused rights-bearers and thus to widen the web of citizenship. Rights are a start. However, resolving political issues in court comes at a price; such resolutions are inherently adversarial. They do not in and of themselves reweave that web of community which the litigant frays. Litigation can make it clear that the common good includes my good, not simply your good, and your good, not simply mine. But litigation does not of itself deepen a sense that your good is not simply something court writ sticks me with. I need to know that your good deprived diminishes the common good and, ultimately, me. That discovery comes only as rights-bearers begin to act on those rights in the complex business of coalition building, bargaining, and persuasion that forms the commerce of politics.

The image of the monitoring citizen—one who scans headlines and catches sound bites—also does not completely allay worries about the health of the republic. The image assumes that the citizen need only occasionally stir and get exercised. She normally concentrates on her own private enterprises and largely overlooks public business. Occasionally a troubling problem blips on her radar screen—the state of the schools, a local bond issue, safety in the streets, a corrupt officeholder. It catches her attention and impels into the public forum or the streets to vote, to give money, perhaps to protest. The monitoring citizen supplies occasional outbursts of indignation or resentment to energize politics. However, resentment is too volatile, fitful, and private an emotion, too preoccupied with immediate costs and inconvenience, to supply a nation with lasting remedies to its problems. In 1968, Hubert Humphey called for a Marshall Plan to address the problem of rehabilitating American cities. Invoking the Marshall Plan, he nostalgically recalled the public program that helped solve a pressing and fundamental problem—rehabilitating Europe after World War II. The Marshall Plan's benefits, however, would not become visible for ten years. In the interval, informed Americans had to sustain a highly visible financial commitment in order to acquire an almost invisible long-term benefit, a reconstructed Europe. A Marshall Plan for American cities today would require such informed, not merely tax-watching, citizens to succeed.

The image of the monitoring citizen encourages single-issue politics—such as the welfare of hardwoods in the Northwest or pro-life versus pro-choice legislation. Monitoring citizens raise up leaders who are powerful advocates and lobbyists for a particular cause. They do not encourage political leaders who can move citizens beyond sound bites to context, beyond simple preferences and raw anger to complex judgments about competing goods. Professional politicians in a democracy must lead chiefly by persuasion. But persuasion grows more difficult—and increases the leader's temptation to resort solely to slogans and manipulation—if citizens raise only the issues that agitate them. Followers must know enough to recognize the complex array of ends and causes that enter into a policy judgment about the common good if the politician is to lead them, not perfectly, but well.

The Limits of Politics

Given the scorn for politicians in our time, this chapter has pled for the dignity, the complexity, and the indispensability of politics as a vocation. In the course of the discussion, I have partly characterized the political leader as teacher and urged a more adventuresome view of what such a leader can teach than that proposed by Hargrove in his book on presidential leadership. Still, I must acknowledge two obstacles to such adventurous leadership—one, circumstantial, the other, intrinsic. Earlier, I suggested that the United States, like Athens, depends on leadership by persuasion. But, circumstantially, leaders need access to a place where they have a chance to persuade and teach citizens. In ancient Athens, leaders had free access to the marketplace, the *agora*. In ancient Israel, the prophets frequented not only the court but the marketplace when they sought to speak the truth to kings and the people. However, in the United States today leaders need access to the television station; and the ticket of admission to TV is astronomical—over a billion dollars in the 1996 election, still more in 2000. One politician seeking his party's nomination as candidate for the presidency in 2000 raised $60 million over a year before the election.

Because political access to the *agora* costs so much today, we use words differently than did the Athenians or the prophets. We no longer arrange them in extended arguments to make clear all the factors that shape complex political judgments. We dice them into bits, intended not to inform and persuade but to manipulate. Thus money today threatens to corrupt not simply leaders but our language and our political discourse. Improving such discourse requires systemic reforms, such as shortening political campaigns and negotiating more free access to television for those who would conduct the people's business of governance. As things stand, we have reversed the relationship of campaigning to governing. Leaders today do not campaign occasionally in order to govern. They have to campaign constantly and govern only occasionally.

Our political discourse suffers a second, intrinsic, sometimes tragic, limitation. In response to F. G. Bailey's cynicism about political discourse (*Humbuggery and Manipulation: The Art of Leadership*, Ithaca, N.Y. Cornell University Press, 1988), Hargrove asserted that presidents can successfully *simplify* without distorting a required political message and the cultural ideals that justify it. In transcendent moments that may be the case. Lincoln surely accomplished that incandescent simplicity which fully honors complexity in his Gettysburg Address and his Second Inaugural. Others have sometimes succeeded. But, even with the best of intentions, language pointed toward programs and policies inevitably sloganizes; it recoils, in advertiser's horror, from the full complexity of experience. It abstracts; and, although its abstractions can clarify portions of the total consciousness of a people and help organize the government for action, they also distort, neglect, and marginalize other interests and ranges of experience and conviction. Politics traffics only in the possible and the doable, not the altogether. Its slogans inevitably denature reality; they grow distant and spectral; they captivate some followers but disconnect from other citizens. Such limitations have hampered political discourse long before the advent of the TV sound bite.

The inevitable distortions and sloganizing of politics led the philosopher R. G. Collingwood to argue that a society needs its artists as well as its politicians.[25] Through the exploration of image, metaphor, and symbol, artists retrieve and freshen language and perception, and thus enrich and clarify the public consciousness that political slogans leach and muddy. Artists help counter the artful manipulations of propaganda. In freshening language and consciousness, they help us recover community in its entirety, which politicians risk sacrificing for the sake of immediate action.

The peculiar contribution artists make to the common good calls for some restraint on the part of patrons, foundations, and governments that support them. Criticize what artists create. Don't foolishly confuse kitsch with art. But also don't expect artists simply to illustrate favorite ideas and tidily package favorite causes. Their explorations with paint, words, sounds, and materials help move us beyond formulae and routines to enliven consciousness and thus rescue community from its inevitable but impoverishing fixations. Wise supporters of the artistic enterprise need to suck in their breath, give artists some money, but then take a deep breath and think before trying to tell them what to do and to say. Otherwise they deny artists the freedom of language and discovery through which, partly, a society renews itself.

Religion, as well as art, can similarly serve the political health of a people. Religion serves politics partly through the particular advice and counsel it offers when prophets speak up to authority directly and boldly; but religion can also serve indirectly by addressing the spacious reach of human experience beyond the cramped arena of politics. As Samuel Johnson put it,

> How small of all that human hearts endure,
> That part which laws or kings can cause or cure.[26]

In addition to making their modest contributions to immediate action, churches and synagogues have a further responsibility to recognize and serve the vast territory of the spirit that lies beyond the reach of politics. Serving this wider domain should not lead religious leaders to diminish or despise the limited arena of politics or to dismiss the huge distinctions they must make between honest and demagogic discourse, between the politician as teacher and the politician as artful illusionist. It should simply remind them that the health and vigor of the political arena itself requires further assists from the spirit upon which inclusive community depends.

Notes

1. See Kevin Phillips, *The Politics of Rich and Poor Wealth and the American Electorate in the Reagan Aftermath* (New York: Harper Perennial, 1990), especially chaps. 1–4.
2. Peter F. Drucker, "The Age of Social Transformation," *The Atlantic Monthly*, November 1994.
3. Drucker, 54.
4. Ibid.
5. Ibid.
6. M. I. Finley tersely observes in *The Ancient Greeks* (New York: The Viking Press, 1963) that the Spartans' ". . . famed 'laconic speech' was a mark that they had nothing to say," 64. J. B. Bury notes in *A History of Greece*, 4th edition (New York: St. Martin's Press, 1975) that the Spartan "Assembly did not debate, but having heard the proposals of kings or ephors, signified its will by acclamation," 92. In effect, ". . . strict military obedience was the primary virtue." M. I. Finley, *The Ancient Greeks*, 66.
7. "Sparta was a large military school." Bury, *A History of Greece*, 97.
8. Economically, Sparta was egalitarian. Private luxury was forbidden. Subject peoples (the helots) did not serve private owners; their labor was civic property. However, politically and militarily, hierarchy obtained in the ordering of the city and of subject peoples. Finley, *The Ancient Greeks*, 64.
9. Reinhold Niebuhr, *The Children of Light and the Children of Darkness* (New York: Charles Scribner's Sons, 1972, originally published in 1944), xiii. Without attribution of the idea to Niebuhr, Clinton Rossiter in his "Introduction" to *The Federalist Papers* (New York: A Mentor Book, 1961), xiv, xv, writes: "No one can read these pages without being reminded powerfully of both the light and dark sides of human nature—*of man's capacity for reason and justice that makes free government possible, of his capacity for passion and injustice that makes it necessary*" [italics mine].
10. Erwin C. Hargrove, *The President as Leader: Appealing to the Better Angels of Our Nature* (Lawrence, Kan.: University Press of Kansas, 1998), vii. In the course of the text Hargrove writes, "politicians must try their best to describe the world and their plans for dealing with it in the most accurate terms they can master. In short, they must teach reality," 42.
11. See, for example, Louis Hartz, *The Liberal Tradition in America* (New York: Harcourt, Brace & Co., 1955).
12. Gordon S. Wood, *The Creation of the American Republic* (New York: W. W. Norton & Co. Inc., 1972), 65–69.
13. Co-authored by Robert Bellah, Richard Madsen, William Sullivan, Ann Swidler, and Steven Tipton, *Habits of the Heart: Individualism and Commitment in American Life* (Berkeley: University of California Press, 1985).
14. Robert Nozick, *Anarchy, State, and Utopia* (New York: Basic Books, 1968). John Stuart Mills' "On Liberty" and Friedrich A. Hayek's *The Road To Serfdom: A Classic Warning against the Dangers to Freedom Inherent in Social Planning* (Chicago: Phoenix Books, University of Chicago Press, 1944) provide the background to Nozick's libertarianism.

15. John Rawls, *A Theory of Justice* (Cambridge: Harvard University Press, 1971). John Rawls settles for a so-called "thin theory of the good," that is, a minimalist account of necessities upon which the least advantaged can build life.

16. For a good account of the plurality of spheres in which we live and the plurality of goods in our common life, see Michael Walzer, *Spheres of Justice* (New York: Basic Books, 1983). For a careful account of the distinctions between fundamental and higher goods, see William Galston, *Justice and the Human Good* (Chicago: University of Chicago Press, 1980).

17. The hard-pressed pluralist differs from both absolutists and relativists. On the face of it, absolutists and relativists seem irreconcilably opposed. Absolutists argue that the validity of a principle depends on its universality (there can be no exceptions). Relativists have discovered exceptions, and therefore would deny the principle. At a deeper level, absolutists and relativists agree. Both subscribe to the view that the validity of a principle depends on its universality; the value of a good depends upon its supremacy in all circumstances. Neither has yet discovered the wisdom of Aristotle's observation that moral principles are true for the most part. They are true for the most part in the sense that they reach their territorial limit in those cases where they must yield to another principle or good, the more stringent, more urgent in the case.

18. Martin Luther King, *Loving Your Enemies, with Letter from a Birmingham Jail and Decloration of Independence from the War in Vietnam* (New York: A. J. Muste Memorial Institution, 1981).

19. In his jeremiad on the white overclass, Michael Lind complains that it has devised ways to insulate itself from "rotting cities, poor jobs, crumbling urban public schools, wandering maniacs, crime" by conceiving "the public good as the aggregate of private goods—private schools, private neighborhoods, private security services." Ultimately, the specter of anarchy lurks behind his final image: "The ideal of the white overclass . . . is not a city on the hill but the mansion behind the wall." *The New American Nation*, 214.

20. Gary Wills, *Certain Trumpets: The Call of Leaders* (New York: Simon & Schuster, 1994).

21. Michael Walzer, *Obligations: Essays on Disobedience and Citizenship* (New York: Simon & Schuster, 1970), ch. 10.

22. Robert Dahl, *Who Governs?* (New Haven, Conn.: Yale University Press, 1961), 279, quoted by Michael Schudson in *The Good Citizen: A History of American Civic Life* (New York: Martin Kessler Books, 1998), 240.

23. Schudson, *The Good Citizen*, 294.

24. Schudson, *The Good Citizen*, 247. For what follows in these paragraphs, see chap. 6, "Widening the Web of Citizenship."

25. R. G. Collingwood, *The Principles of Art* (Oxford: Clarendon Press, 1938).

26. Samuel Johnson wrote the lines for Goldsmith's *Travellor*, cited by W. Jackson Bate, *Samuel Johnson* (New York: Harcourt Brace Jovanovich, 1975).

Interlude:

The Shaping of Public Happiness

The professions covered in the last three chapters of this book belong together. These professions bear chief responsibility for cultivating the ethos of the nation; they play the role of teacher. Taking the long view of history, we can identify three successive teaching authorities in Western civilization—the church, the public education system, and increasingly, today, the media. Each of these institutions has shaped our perception of the world and supplied us with our cues for behavior.

Until the Enlightenment, the church exercised magisterial authority. The church has not altogether disappeared today as a teaching authority, but it yielded increasingly from the eighteenth century forward to a secularizing education system that served as the dominant teacher until the third quarter of the twentieth century. The professoriate, in its turn, has not disappeared, but it has increasingly acceded to the media its power as the source of information and the shaper of language and attitudes. The media, in the form of newspapers and pamphlets, played a significant role in the founding of the Republic and expanded still further in power from the middle of the nineteenth century forward. By the end of the twentieth century, the media had come to define the era itself as the Information Age.

Before exploring these three professions, specially charged with the task of tending to the ethos, we need to identify the deep fault in the culture to which the several teaching professions contribute and with which they must contend if they would help develop a sense of public responsibility in professionals. In my judgment, the divorce between the public and the private, between inner life and outer forms and institutions, is the deep problem, what the Germans would call the *Ur-problem*, that underlies all others which break the surface as social problems. Let a haunted Japanese novelist strike the theme.

In a Dostoevsky-like novel, *The Temple of the Gold Pavilion*,[1] Yukio Mishima describes a Buddhist acolyte's obsession with the temple he serves. The beautiful building stands for the entire realm of outer forms—those made by men and the gods—obdurate and indifferent to the acolyte's impotence.

Mishima uses a fine image to convey the split the acolyte feels between his own inner life and the outer world. He stutters. Other men pass easily through the doorway between the inner and the outer, but every time the hero of the story attempts to pass through the door, he turns the key only to discover rust in the lock.

The young acolyte both loves and hates the beautiful temple. He resents it and yet feels drawn to its cold beauty. Eventually, he sets fire to the sanctuary, in an ecstasy of destruction.

Once again, Mishima uses a fine image to describe the deed. He tells us that the young incendiary does not think of himself as starting a fire; rather, he releases those fires already *latent* in the universe.

The first of Mishima's images exposes the problem which the last three chapters in this book address. Toward the whole world of outer forms, institutions, and ceremonies today, we sometimes feel like Mishima's stutterer. We cannot pass easily from our interior life to those external forms that dominate the public scene. The public realm seems almost alien to our private happiness. Entire institutions—schools, churches, synagogues, corporations, governments—seem to interlock, reinforce one another, and persist without touching and nourishing inner lives; or, if religion sometimes addresses inner life, it often disconnects from the public realm.

At first glance, this divorce between the inner and the outer seems to have begun in the middle '60s. The radicals called the public realm they repudiated the "establishment" or the "system." In the late '60s, young radicals protested against a system they resented because they believed it mutilated lives. The most savage statement of this protest came not from an American under thirty, but from the then-forty-year-old Scottish psychoanalyst R. D. Laing, who, in *The Politics of Experience*, denounced the brutalities of our modern educational system. Parents, maneuvering their children to succeed in a harsh world, pressured them to become efficient overachievers, shrewd little connivers, clever in cadging the grades that would open the doors to the best schools, clear the way to the best jobs, turn the keys into the best houses, and open the plots in the best cemeteries—all part of a career path that would let one's progeny succeed in and secede from the public realm. Parents pressed for this achievement in the name of a tough-minded realism about the outer world. Laing compared them in their frantic realism to the London beggar who maimed and mutilated his children in order to equip them to succeed in the family trade.[2]

Laing employed Gothic exaggeration comparing a high-powered educational system to the low cunning of a Fagin. But many people over forty remembered only too well some of the psychic mutilations of an educational system and lifestyle that included too much insomnia and hypochondria, too many tranquilizers and too much alcohol, too many broken homes and burnt out cases, to deny altogether Laing's charge against their generation.

The militant protests against the system in the '60s gave way in the early '70s to withdrawal. An illustration from the field of religious studies may illuminate this complicated subject. The '70s saw a striking interest in non-Western religions— much of this interest positive and often for good reasons. However, the interest shifted restlessly from year to year. One year students exalted Zen Buddhism, another year, Krishna Consciousness, still another, Transcendental Meditation, or the Religion of the South Dakota Sioux, or Sufism, or Kundalini Yoga. In fact, a single, questing spirit provoked this restlessness in religious studies and practice across the decade. These traditions enjoyed one important common feature: they were *somebody else's* religion, *not* one's own and *not* the religion of one's parents. Enthusiasms shifted but the driving force endured, a religious version of the impulse behind the cult of romantic love, the fascination with the faraway princess. Students responded to the lure of exotic traditions, under whose social and political fallout they had not had to live. They saw too clearly the warts, goiters, hair curlers, and pot belly of Christianity and yearned for the less clear faraway possibilities. They wanted to have little to do with the church T. S. Eliot once compared to the hippopotamus.

For similar reasons, students in the early '70s eventually withdrew from politics in general and political parties in particular. The purity of their ideals forbade them to deal with anything so warty and earthy as a political party, appropriately symbolized by the most prosaic of farm animals—the donkey—and the most ponderous, the pachyderm.

Clearly the responses of protest and withdrawal in the middle '60s through the early '70s marked a profound dissatisfaction with the public realm. But the radicals of the counterculture mistakenly supposed that they had invented the split between inner meaning and outer form. Two decades earlier people had already sensed this split and summed it up with the word "conformity." Metaphors from the 1950s—the "windmill," the "grind," and the "rat race"—betrayed the fact that people expected to find little happiness in the public arena. Facing an outer world which they found unfulfilling, people in the 50's responded by passively conforming to the society's demands while pursuing their careers. Meanwhile they reserved for themselves— behind a shelter of thoughtful sermons on conformity, or jokes in the New Yorker—a sanctuary of private life which was their own.

Only the solutions have changed. Successive generations tried conformity in the '50s, rebellion in the '60s, and withdrawal in the early '70s; and they returned in the '80s to an atomistic careerism through which they hoped to fulfill a dream of private happiness through accelerating consumption. All these responses betray considerable suspicion of public life. Whatever happiness people think they can pursue and attain they associate with their private lives.

We have lost a sense of connection between inner life and outer forms and institutions that led the American Revolutionary thinkers to declare this country a republic (*res publica*, a public entity). John Adams at the time of the American Revolution saw *public* happiness as the most important political principle. Adams accepted as a political axiom "no taxation without representation" *not* because taxes would reduce his purse and thereby subtract from his *private* happiness (the taxes against which Adams and others protested were minuscule), but to being "without representation." That state of affairs deprived him of his *public* happiness, his right to be seen and heard, and to make himself felt in public forum and in political commerce with his fellows. Without the freedom to live and act in concert with others in public happiness, the merely private life—as variants of the word itself suggest—becomes the diminished life—"privative," "deprived," impoverished.

The political philosopher Hannah Arendt has argued that the day when the great phrase "life, liberty, and the pursuit of happiness" gradually came to mean, exclusively, "private happiness" marked a great misfortune for the republic.[3] From that day forward, we began to treat the public realm as a necessary evil, as though it merely served private ends. We did not expect or enjoy happiness in the public domain.

Liberals, radicals, and conservatives—all for their different reasons in the past century—have inveighed against imperialistic and oppressive institutions. But they have not recognized that beneath the growth of imperialistic institutions often lies an equally imperial concept of the self. Literary critic Quentin Anderson, in his study of Emerson, Thoreau, and Whitman, defines the imperial self as the self that accepts no limitations upon itself, at the hands of others.[4] Half indifferent to and resenting the public realm, the imperial self refuses to invest in growing strong, nurturing, and self-restraining institutions. For the latter task, we must cultivate the civic self.

The civic self, as opposed to the imperial self, understands and accepts itself as limited and amplified by others. The civic self recognizes that it enjoys an expansion of its life in and through its participation in community. The civic self, as noted earlier, includes both a subjective and an objective element. Subjectively, the civic self requires the citizen and society to cultivate the ability to work in concert with others. Objectively, this working in concert with others must serve—at least in part—the common good. Certainly men and women must pursue their own private good. We are not angels. Self-interest and group interests have their place in the polity. But a society wholly driven by self-interest would tear itself to pieces, no matter how ingenious its constitutional safety mechanisms. Therefore, the leaders of the revolutionary and constitutional periods in American life, recognized the importance of "public virtue" in a citizenry. "No phrase except 'liberty' was invoked more often by the revolutionaries than the 'public good.'"[5] Public virtue implied some measure of readiness to sacrifice one's own self-interest for the common good.[6]

John Adams recognized that the constitutional republic which he and his colleagues had devised would not long survive the corrosion of self-interest without the active engagement of two institutions in the formation of the American character: religious institutions and educational institutions. We will need to consider teaching professionals in both institutions, but not before exploring yet a third set of institutions which exercise a well-nigh dominant teaching authority in the modern world: the media.

Notes

1. Yukio Mishima, *The Temple of the Golden Pavilion*, trans. Ivan Morris (New York: Alfred A. Knopf, 1959).
2. See R. D. Laing, *The Politics of Experience* (New York: Ballantine Books, 1967), especially chap. 3, "The Mystification of Experience."
3. Hannah Arendt, *On Revolution* (New York: Viking Press, 1963), 124–37.
4. Quentin Anderson, *The Imperial Self: An Essay in American Literary and Cultural History* (New York: Alfred A. Knopf, 1971).
5. Mortimer J. Adler and William Gorman, *The American Testament* (New York: Praeger Publishers, 1975), 87.
6. See Gordon S. Wood, *The Creation of the American Republic* (New York: W. W. Norton & Co. Inc., 1972), 68.

Part II

Chapter 6

Media Professionals (and Celebrities)

Unordained Teaching Authorities

Western societies have lived under three successive teaching authorities. By teaching authority, I mean the institution that chiefly supplies people with their perceptions of the world and themselves and gives them their clues for behavior. For twelve hundred years after the inception of Western civilization, people looked chiefly to the church as their teaching authority. From the seventeenth century to the twentieth century, Western societies turned increasingly to the university for their organized interpretation of the world and themselves and their intellectual resource for world mastery. However, increasingly today, media professionals (and celebrities) have overshadowed religious leaders and academicians as the authorities to whom people turn for their views and cues.

How people currently spend their time illustrates this transfer of teaching authority. Religious institutions can usually snare no more than an hour or two of a student's time on the Sabbath—except for those young people who attend parochial schools. The schools—public and parochial—still command up to thirty-five hours a week during the school year, but, as studies have repeatedly noted, children now spend more time in front of TV and computer games than in the classroom. The lives of the saints go unread and the deeds of heroes unsung. Both have faded and yield today to talking heads and celebrities who define with giddy self-importance what is worth aspiring to.

Various religious and educational institutions today betray their lack of confidence in the substance they offer. They rely increasingly on celebrities, anointed by the media, to lure the attention of children and parents. Evangelists will often recruit and display star singers, actors, and athletes to impress the young and sway them toward conversion. Telegenic, free-lance preachers orbit among the movie stars and rely on the magic of the box to suffuse their message with a glow and a glory it apparently lacks on its own. Colleges and universities

193

also rely increasingly on the camera to acquire a larger public significance than they can manage on their own authority. They look to their athletes to keep them in the spotlight; and they sponsor lecture series designed to bring celebrities to campus to dispel the obscurity that shrouds the institution. Universities thus squander some of their public opportunities to identify voices with something to say to the community. They reveal their marginality when they obeisantly hand over such public teaching occasions to media-crowned celebrities.

Meanwhile the media form and color our perception of the world and ourselves through the routines of sitcoms and dramas, through the selection of news events that fit into a pre-fab frame, and especially through the vignettes and images of advertising. Cumulatively, they cue us to what we should want and how we should behave as workers, lovers, consumers, parents, friends, and citizens. In a sense, the news media exceed the descriptive power of mere teachers: They do not passively report on events; their very focus often instantly alters or creates them. Since, moreover, media leaders perceive themselves as merely marketing stories, news, comedies, talking heads, authorities, and celebrities, they accept little responsibility for the impact of their selections and ordinations. While media conglomerates today concentrate power, they diffuse moral responsibility.

In keeping with the focus of this book, this chapter will cover chiefly print and television reporters and journalists—the most obvious of professionals who occupy the media spotlight and exercise teaching authority. However, it must be conceded at the outset that a swarm of other experts—accountants, camera operators, financers, computer engineers, lawyers, marketeers, advertisers, account executives, hairdressers, costumers, directors, and producers—also toil and spin the media web. Further, the technology of the medium itself, irrespective of the content it delivers and its major professional players, affects the knowledge and the knowledge-based power that the medium transmits. The scholarly Walter J. Ong detailed this insight in his account of changes from the oral to the written mediation of cultures;[1] and the aphoristic Marshal McLuhan popularized the claim that "the medium is the message"[2] The prevailing technology by means of which messages arrive alters the world and even human sensibility. It is no surprise that John Chambers, CEO of Cisco Systems, expansively predicts that the technology du jour, the Internet, "will change everything. . . . It will have every bit as much an impact on society as the Industrial Revolution . . . [And] it will happen over seven years."[3]

Some of the prophecies today rise to the eschatological. The Internet will bring an end to the world as we know it. The Internet has already launched companies and users into cyberspace without ties to the surly bonds of earth. The Internet will let people choose their own information services and thus bypass books, newspapers, the TV networks, and cable systems. Economically, the Internet will help solve the energy problem by letting employees work at home and by carefully monitoring markets and thus limiting inventories of energy-expensive products. Politically, the Internet will render national boundaries permeable, thus denying to dictators the total control of information in their countries. It will provide international companies the information flow they need to manage globally and, at the same time, aid and abet the instant messaging upon which protest groups depend to inconvenience efforts at global management! Some have predicted that the Internet will eventually liberate politicians in democracies from having to raise money (e-mail will reduce their heavy costs for direct marketing and television programming); and Ross Perot campaigned on the dream that an electronic democracy, channeled through Mr. Perot as its medium, would increase the people's influence on governmental decisions.[4] Finally, the Internet has begun to boil middlemen or "intermediaries" out of society,[5] a somewhat nasty prospect for travel agents, stock brokers, lobbyists, government bureaucrats, and perhaps professionals of varying stripes.[6]

Perhaps the deepest of all the changes that the media have wrought in an educational setting bears on the human perception of time. Traditionally, religious and academic institutions have lived by an agricultural calender. Teaching entails the planting of seeds and the tending to growth, which the etymological root for seminar as a seed box retains. The liturgical and the school years mark growth across the ordeals and the yields of the seasons. However, the industrial revolution replaced agricultural time with the clock. The rule of mechanical time leads to productivity schedules, punching the clock, time and motion studies, and quarterly reports; and it imposes upon educators the engineer's goal of turning out products in the light of stated objectives and teaching plans. The Internet further speeds up time. It thrives on instant access and instant feedback. It calls for "heads up," not heads down in a book, and it always aspires to "staying ahead of the curve."

Clearly, those who would lead in such a world must cope with much greater volatility. Wisdom itself loses its roots in time. The term "conventional wisdom" no longer refers to the sifted wisdom of the ages; it describes the general take of commentators on a particular event; and with the news accessible 24 hours a day, it speeds up still further into "ever-faster shifts in prevailing opinion."[7] In these rapid cycles of change, a special creature of the media emerges to give a somewhat wavering continuity to the public scene—the celebrity. Only occasionally encumbered by knowledge, the celebrity helps signal to the people what it looks like to be in the know, what attitudes to adopt, and what to prize and what to despise in the course of managing their lives. The two figures of the professional and the celebrity coalesce in television journalists, who, as professionals, knowledgeably connect with the fast moving world they describe and who, through their regular appearance on camera, acquire a celebrity status. Still, we need first to turn off the klieg lights and focus on journalism as a profession.

Journalism and the Marks of a Professional

Law, medicine, and the ministry—the classical learned professions—tidily exhibit the characteristics we have identified as marking the professional. Intellectually, professionals profess a body of knowledge; morally, they profess that knowledge on behalf of someone—the client, the patient, the parishioner—or some institution—the hospital or the government. Organizationally, they accept, at least in principle, a guild discipline that defines and more or less imperfectly enforces responsible professional behavior. Journalists resemble, but also partly differ from, traditional professionals in each of these three particulars.

Organizationally, journalists, like other professionals, form guilds. Press clubs abound. An Association for Education in Journalism and Mass Communication links professional schools. Newspapers have developed codes of ethics that attach penalties to violations of basic standards; and the Pulitzer Prize has emerged to honor distinguished performance. Journalists, in their own manner, imitate the model drawn by Abraham Flexner, when he noted that professionals organize for self-improvement, not just self-promotion.

However, efforts at professional self-regulation and discipline in journalism face major obstacles, constitutional as well as commercial. The doctrine of freedom of speech and press, enshrined in the First Amendment to the Constitution, denies both to the government and to a professional guild the power to prevent journalists from publishing their work—however badly or irresponsibly they write. The guild cannot enforce professional standards by denying the incompetent or the unethical the right to practice. It cannot stop malpractice; it can only criticize malpractice through the work of other practitioners.

As a practical matter, however, regulation and discipline come from another source. Journalists and reporters need commercial sponsorship to publish their work; and therefore publishers and owners of networks have in practice defined and enforced their organizational standards on journalists through their powers to hire, fire, and promote, and to accept and reject manuscripts and other materials. These corporate disciplinary powers partly enforce, but also partly weaken, professional standards.[8] Some managerial regulations and decisions overlap with professional purpose; others serve the company's bottom line rather than support professional excellence. In his novel *Lucky You*, Carl Hiaasen, who writes a twice-weekly metropolitan column for *The Miami Herald*, casts the cold eye of a satirist on the deterioration of newspaper standards in allocating time, money, and talent.

> The downsizing trend that swept newspapers in the early '90s was aimed at sustaining bloated profit margins in which the industry had wallowed for most of the century. . . . The first casualty was depth. . . . Cutting the amount of space devoted to news instantly justified cutting the staff. At many papers, downsizing was the favored excuse for eliminating such luxuries as police desks, suburban editions, foreign bureaus, medical writers, environmental teams (which were always antagonizing civic titans and important advertisers). As newspapers grew thinner and shallower, the men who published them worked harder to assure Wall Street that readers neither noticed nor cared.[9]

Thus while the Constitutional principle of freedom of the press limits the ability of the professional guild to regulate its members, the First Amendment does not prevent news corporations and/or the conglomerates that control them from regulating professionals or freelance writers who work or contract with them. Organizationally, journalists—as a guild—wield very limited power, hemmed in by the very Constitution that exalts them and by the marketplace that pays them.

Morally, the journalist's role differs from that of members of the several "helping professions" who serve individual clients, patients, parishioners, or students. As William Lee Miller has observed, the journalist has no corresponding one-on-one tie—whatever the journalist may mean by "dear reader."[10] However, journalists do not fail to qualify as professionals just because they lack individual clients. Only some professionals directly serve individual clients; others, such as the armed services, the civil service, and the church (conceived not just as a collection of individuals but as an institution with a public mission to perform) serve a larger social purpose. To uncover the specific good such professions serve requires identifying the *telos*, the goal, the mission or purpose of the institution as a whole. What "good" justifies the press? To what purpose, a *free* press?

The question of purpose asks the press to move beyond a negative to a positive concept of its freedom. Negative liberty means freedom *from*—freedom from external interferences and from compulsions from within. Positive liberty refers to a freedom *for*—a freedom directed to its attracting end.[11] Clearly, the media have tended to define their freedom negatively as a freedom from interference by the government and by political parties.[12] The media have paid less attention to freedom for; that is, the positive ends or purposes free media must pursue to justify their freedom from restrictions on their liberty.

In its most orotund justifications of itself, the profession appeals to the First Amendment to the Constitution and largely looks to the Constitution as a shield to protect its negative liberty. Clearly, the First Amendment emphasizes a negative freedom from interference: "Congress shall make no laws . . . abridging the freedom of speech or the press." But to what positive purpose this negative liberty? The several freedoms enumerated in the First Amendment also point the press to something further and positive. The freedoms to speak and assemble and worship, along with freedom of the press, taken together, should enhance, to use William Lee Miller's phrase, "the deliberative process" in a democracy.[13] Freedom of speech and the press and the freedom of assembly, religious and nonreligious, supply members of a society with indispensable opportunities to talk, reflect, and interact with one another. They create the possibility of vigorous public life in a republic. The prohibitions against an established religion and a controlled press clear space in which people can deliberate for purposes, moral and political, apart from which the life of a republic would wither. The First Amendment does more than mark out a sanctuary of privacy into which the state cannot enter—although it does that. It also recognizes that a republic cannot flourish in its public life unless its people can know what is going on, deliberate with one another, and form their own judgments free from official compulsion or threat. The Amendment invites and protects the continuation of that deliberative process which led up to and contributed to crafting the Constitution itself. The Amendment does not simply protect the people and their institutions *from* government, it makes possible their self-governing. In brief, the Constitution protects and encourages the press to augment the public good through an *informed citizenry*.

Even so, the First Amendment does not establish an absolute freedom of the press. Other constitutional rights limit it. For example, in 1997, *The Dallas Morning News* published a transcript it had acquired of Timothy McVeigh's confession of guilt to his defense attorney in the bombing of the federal building in Oklahoma City the previous year.[14] In the uproar that followed publication, distinguished journalists defended *The News* for doing what journalists ought to do when in possession of a major news story—publish, and publish without apology. Journalists exercise thereby their First Amendment right, including the corollary right to protect their sources of information. An informed citizenry, so the argument goes, shores up the deliberative process in a democracy.

However, critics of the decision to publish argued that the newspaper had undercut McVeigh's constitutional right under the Sixth Amendment to a fair trial and its immediate corollary, the protection of confidential exchanges between attorney and client. In effect, the freedom of the press to support the deliberative process in a democracy is not absolute. In criminal cases, the Constitution specifically assigns deliberation to the courtroom and vests responsibility for that deliberation in an impartial jury, a body difficult to protect from pressure if the press, in effect, conducts a prior public trial by newspaper. Each side in this dispute flailed the other with the Supreme Law of the Land.

In publishing its article on the McVeigh case, *The News* acted chiefly on behalf of its sense of its privilege and responsibility under the First Amendment. In not exploiting the transcripts thereafter as a huge mother lode from which to extract article after article, *The News* also may have recognized, partly out of respect for the Sixth Amendment, that it had made a close call.

Historically, the free press, in the United States has depended upon a second underpinning—not only the Constitution but the mid-nineteenth-century development of the penny press, which provided the newspaper with its economic base.[15] This second underpinning led to a different understanding of the aim and purposes of a free press. Until the 1840s, the press needed the patronage of governments, political parties, or merchant guilds. Editors were little more than secretaries "dependent upon chains of politicians, merchants, brokers, office seekers for their position and bread."[16] But technological developments (steam-driven presses, cheap paper, railroad transportation, and the telegraph) and the increasing literacy of the population converged to provide the newspaper with a new financial basis. Newspapers could offer more news at lower prices to a large body of readers—a readership, which, in turn, attracted many retail advertisers who replaced direct patrons, and thus made a *free* press possible, that is, a press independent of patrons, parties, and governments (though not free of the internal institutional constraints of owners and advertisers and the desires and interests of readers).

These two effective sources of a free *press* have produced two different definitions of the reader and of the basic purpose of journalism. The Constitution anticipates the reader as *citizen*; the marketplace pursues the reader as *consumer*. The Constitution associates the reader with public assembly, with politics, the difficult art of acting in concert with others in pursuit of the common good; the marketplace directs the reader toward private consumption; the Constitution hopes to foster deliberation and the clarification of judgment; the marketplace aims at generating and gratifying desires.

These two competing definitions of the audience which the media address shape the ideals that professionals state as their own. The stated ideals of journalists have a Janus look: reliability but also sparkle; information and interpretation, but also entertainment; accuracy, completeness, and timeliness, but also liveliness; the facts, but also the story that will play. Clearly, these ideals need not exclude one another. To inform, the journalist need not stupefy the citizen with dull writing. But, just as clearly, the goals often conflict. For example, papers tend to place the sensational but inaccurate story on page one, and, much to the dismay of the injured party, locate the *erratum* on page thirty-three not simply because editors find it hard to confess error, but because yet newer stories command more attention. The media treat readers and viewers as consumers.

Clearly, however, the founders of the nation did not have the amusement of consumers but the deliberative life of citizens in mind when they chose to grant this underpaid profession a privileged place in the Constitution. For this reason, the standard of "accuracy, accuracy, accuracy" has tended to overshadow others in professional practice.

Intellectually, journalists have emphasized the formal standard of accuracy. Reporters must tell the truth. However, the journalist's intellectual mark differs strikingly from that of the classical professional. The learned professions of law, medicine, and ministry have each produced a huge body of literature, which practitioners master and apply to human needs. Whatever intellectual disputes emerge in the professions, their bodies of knowledge remain relatively objective and esoteric in the sense that each discipline generates its established methods and procedures for resolving disputes—without relying on external referees.

Journalism, however, lacks a body of organized knowledge from which it derives authority; and thus journalists have vacillated as to whether their work qualifies them intellectually as professionals. Some have insisted that journalism is simply a craft or skill. Indeed, they often look with a jaundiced eye upon those professions that claim such knowledge-based authority and dismiss other professionals and experts who appear on TV shows as "talking heads" or as members of the "chattering class." True, Pulitzer emulated the learned professions by establishing a school of journalism in a university; and Watergate helped flood such schools with too many applicants. But, as Michael Schudson observed, "Nothing in [journalist] training gives them license to shape the other's views of the world."[17] Journalism is an "insulated profession,"[18] lacking the proprietary authority derived from a relatively inaccessible and rationally organized body of knowledge.

Others have sought to counter this designation of journalism as a skill by linking journalism with the intellectual ideal of objectivity. While the journalist does not command a stable body of objective knowledge, Walter Lippmann believed that objectivity can inhere in method rather than content. Journalists should free themselves from the warp of their biases and interests and cultivate the habit of "disinterested realism." Across the decades, however, the journalist's confidence in the possibility of attaining the ideal of disinterested realism declined. The journalist of the 1890s depended upon a double confidence: that a reporter could get at the facts and that the facts would carry their own moral significance. In this century, however, journalists have increasingly realized that they cannot attain the ideal of disinterested objectivity. The journalist falls short of objective reporting not simply because of personal bias, incompetence, or malicious intent, but also because of the constraints of the organization, its deadlines and customs.[19]

This heightened appreciation of the obstacles to objectivity and accuracy later produced, if not cynicism, a shift toward investigative reporting that is frankly subjective and adversarial.[20] Some interpreters of the shift may have too quickly surrendered the ideal of objectivity. The mere fact that one inevitably falls short of an ideal does not in and of itself invalidate it. The theologian Reinhold Niebuhr observed that one must try to approximate an ideal even though one cannot fully realize it. He compressed this moral demand in the phrase, the "relevance of an impossible ethical ideal."[21] The cynic mordantly dismisses an ideal because no one can attain it. The idealist naively assumes that he can attain it and thus undercuts the transcendent ground for self-criticism. The realist needs to recognize both its relevance and its transcendence.

The problem of objectivity in journalism poses too many complications to discuss satisfactorily in one corner of a chapter. However, it may help to comment on two confusions: first, some reporters tend to confuse objectivity with neutrality; second, some journalists tend to confuse criticism with adversarial combat.

The simple equation of objectivity with neutrality assumes that *all* value judgments are *subjective*. To report objectively the journalist must abstain from expressing her own judgments. This self-imposed abstention can spring from intellectual modesty, but it can also result from a positivist and relativist philosophical outlook. Positivism relegates all judgments about value and worth to the merely emotive, subjective, and therefore arbitrary. Values do not inhere in things; we read them into things. Thus those who would occupy the high ground of objectivity can report only facts (including the fact that various parties hold opposing views on a given issue); all else slides off into mere opinion. Objectivity demands neutrality on all questions of values.

In practice, this association of objectivity and fairness with neutrality leads reporters to defer unduly to authorities. To keep himself from becoming the tool of one authority on a subject, the skeptical reporter casts about for quotations from others with opposing views: ". . . one can quote speakers in positions of recognized authority; one cannot independently evaluate what they have to say, except by quoting another acknowledged authority."[22]

This neutered objectivity, combined with a nose for the melodramatic, leads TV journalists to distort the public debate. Producers of TV news programs satisfy both the time constraints under which they operate and their desire for melodrama by framing any given debate into two opposing views. This format simplifies a story sufficiently to seem comprehensible to an audience in thirty to forty-five seconds and exaggerates the drama (especially if both sides shriek absolutist and uncompromising slogans). For example, TV tends to dramatize the debate on the environment as a contest between wild-eyed tree-huggers and dollar-blinded developers, when, in fact, the most plausible view on the subject would endorse neither position in its absolute form. Equating objectivity with neutrality betrays objectivity at two points: It assumes that all parties to a debate express only their subjective opinions; and it panders to the voyeur in us all by stating the rival subjective opinions in their most vehement, confrontational forms.

A deepened respect for objectivity may require journalists to assess the merits of a case without always masking their appraisals by recruiting an opposing authority as mouthpiece for their own views. The media may have an obligation to offer critical judgments that transcend mere opinion. The painstaking efforts of a Walter Lippmann or a Samuel Johnson to get at the full truth of an issue, its moral truth, were pursuits of objectivity, not mere exercises in expressing opinions. Reporters—and the inquirer in all of us—must, of course, still leave room for the clear statement of alternatives on the grounds, not that the truth exists nowhere, but that it will most likely emerge through rigorous public conversation.

We must also not confuse an independent and critical press with an adversarial press. Some morally passionate professionals push for a media relentlessly opposed to the government and other authorities. Adversarialism assumes that the press must choose between only two alternatives: either to serve as the tools of power (in effect, as PR servants to the mighty) or to oppose any and all articulations of power. Adversarially defined, the press sets its face against the government and other authorities as though they were an enemy.

This negative definition of the press's task often follows from a field-of-force theory of politics which holds that the government does nothing but articulate and exercise power on behalf of political interests and that the press must counter those interests on behalf of other voiceless interests. A mocking press often helps throw the rascals out, but it can fail to provide sustained support for people and policies that would justify removing the rascals in the first place. Such relentless adversarialism grows cynical and resentful toward all political and social power.

Whatever the momentary justifications for cynicism, we should not confuse it with criticism, for cynicism eventually implodes critical judgment. It shirks from making discriminate judgments as to worth and value. The cynic levels the high and the low, the noble and the squalid, the authentic and the counterfeit—he sees all as equally low. Criticism presupposes making discriminate judgments, both positive and negative. A cynical adversarialism trashes everything equally. Aristotle helpfully identified two ways in which we fail telling the truth. We err by excess and defect: by exaggeration and by belittlement. Advertisers and public relations specialists indulge in the art of enhancement through puffery, air blowing, and gilt by association; other media experts make their mark through indiscriminate mockery. Criticism, not cynicism, is the clear-eyed antidote to puffery.

Teaching Authority

Journalists and other media specialists today exercise more power as teachers and transmitters of prevailing cultural ideals than does any other professional group. Earlier we spoke of the constitutional role of the press in supporting the deliberative process in a democracy by informing citizens. Perhaps even deeper than their purported service to deliberation, the press and other media give to citizens a sense of belonging. To belong, people need to feel clued in. They want to know what's up, what's new. At its worst, this justification for a free press panders to voracious curiosity. It intrusively and wantonly breaks through the hedges of privacy. Still, by reporting the news, by creating a sense of belonging, the media, since the mid-nineteenth century, have served an incredibly diverse immigrant nation well.

Joseph Pulitzer long ago recognized the journalist's teaching role when he declared that he wanted the New York *World* "to be both a daily school-house and a daily forum—both a daily teacher and a daily tribune."[23] In casting the newspaper as teacher, Pulitzer had in mind the immigrant society of his time. In 1900, some twenty-six million citizens had parents who had immigrated; another ten million citizens were themselves immigrants. With a touch of shrewd condescension toward readers who did not command the English language, Pulitzer emphasized bold headline type, cartoons, pointed story lines, and other tabloid devices still with us to acquaint immigrants with their new world.

In a sense, we have not left Pulitzer's world of newcomers behind. The once-immigrant nation now perpetually migrates. From the farms to the cities, from the cities to the suburbs, and from the North to the South and to the West, Americans move, on the average, once every five years. The media, in such a world, continue to serve us as immigrants and migrants.

At a still deeper level, the media—emphasizing, as they do, what's new, what wasn't there yesterday—continue to make immigrants of us all. They redefine us daily as the newly arrived, those who need constant reorientation. When we have been too busy and distracted for a few days to read the newspaper or watch TV, we talk about catching up on the news, as though we have lagged in a caravan that moved off ahead of us into unfamiliar terrain. Or, more accurately, as though the landscape itself has changed while we slept.

Everyday, at breakfast, we face the question at the door: what's up? what's new? what strange turns has the world taken since yesterday? The media tell us and commentators advise us on how to interpret the day's explosive events. Framing our day, the media wield an extraordinary power. Journalists need not meanly envy the power of other professionals. Nor should they stridently invoke the privileges of a free press without acknowledging the very considerable moral responsibility such teaching power entails.

Unquestionably, the teaching power the media wield is peculiar; and it is fraught with both promise and danger for a republic. Journalists do not transmit their own knowledge to a wider audience but rather the knowledge that other professionals and leaders tend to hoard and command as their own. This dependency creates its antagonisms. Other professionals often prefer to sell services rather than share their special knowledge with others. As media specialists expose knowledge to the public, they threaten government and business leaders and other professionals with a hemorrhage of their authority, power, and livelihood. The latter fear a loss of control. The press threatens to take war out of the President's exclusive hands, and health care, out of the doctor's and the insurance company's grip. This laicizing of professional authority produces a structural adversarialism, deeper than the combativeness of a Sam Donaldson, to the degree that politicians find it convenient and other professionals find it profitable to store their knowledge in cellars to which they alone have keys.

This antagonism against the journalist's second-hand teaching through reporting need not inevitably arise. (I leave aside the interviewee's legitimate annoyance with incompetent reporters who garble their stories.) A reasonably self-confident political and professional leadership need not fear competent reporting in a democracy, which, in any case, requires the widespread distribution of knowledge. Doctors, lawyers, and presidents, in doing their work with patients, clients, and citizens, must teach; and the journalist's prose, the TV camera's image, and the multimedia's ingathering of text, image, and sound can stimulate and amplify that teaching.

Today, however, an irony is in the making. The technology of the Internet increasingly places a wildcat power to write and publish within the reach of admittedly uncredentialled, undisciplined, and unfinanced nonce-journalists. The guild says accuracy, accuracy, accuracy, but Drudge and his copycats, with only occasional salutes to fact, write and publish as they please. Websiters can pass on rumors, fabricate news, concoct schemes, and peddle tips, medical treatments, and snake oil. The Information Superhighway branches out into countless rumor byways; and the famously uncredentialled profession of journalism finds itself hard put to distinguish the freelancer from the freebooter. In effect, the Internet now threatens to hemorrhage the universe of those professionals who earned their living by hemorrhaging the universe of all other professions.

The Media and Politics

Ironies aside, the media cannot, on their own, teach a republic or tutor its citizens. As teaching shifts in loci today from the church and the academy to media conglomerates, the sources of information move from public to private and from nonprofit to for-profit institutions. The media have also redefined the recipients of information, especially in the arena of politics, somewhat more passively. Earlier we highlighted the role of the media in giving a perpetually immigrant people a sense of community, a sense of belonging. But, at the same time, the mass media have tended to define those whom they "clue in" as passive spectators, not as active, responsible agents. A community composed entirely of onlookers transmutes into what the prophetic Soren Kierkegaard of the nineteenth century called a "phantom" community—a public—"that abstract whole formed in the most ludicrous way, by all participants becoming a third party (an onlooker)."[24] Kierkegaard recognized that such spectators, who bear no continuing responsibility themselves for actions or events, inevitably seek amusement. "This indolent mass which ... does nothing itself, this gallery, is on the look-out for distraction and soon abandons itself to the very idea that everything that anyone does is done in order to give it (the public) something to gossip about."[25]

Denying responsibility for what they see, spectators look to the print and screen voyeuristically. They judge the passing parade of athletes, actors, politicians, and players in the day's events as performers. All fields slump into entertainment, politics included. Kierkegaard's *Attack on the Present Age* anticipated by 140 years Neil Postman's *Amusing Ourselves to Death: Public Discourse in the Age of Show Business.*[26] In due course, the role of experts commenting on politics inevitably changes to suit the interests of spectators. As James Fallows has noted, political experts handle not substantive but observational and predictive questions: who's winning? who's likely to win? which horse has lost ground? since last they offered comments to spectators in the coliseum about the races they are watching.[27] In their eagerness to win their own speed races, the networks in the presidential election of 2000 mischievously jumped the gun several times in declaring a winner.

Deliberation—which takes time—suffers. Politics in a republic traditionally depended upon the capacity of citizens to follow, in newspaper, pamphlet, or essay, if only roughly, an extended line of reasoning that consummates in political judgments. But recently and especially with the advent of television and the Internet, the media have increased our impatience with complexity and ambiguity. *USA Today* has led the way in the art of abbreviating. Stories shrink into a couple of paragraphs, not much longer than the headlines that draw attention to them. The reader can scan them, like TV images, at a glance. Other newspapers and the older national magazines, *Time* and *Newsweek*, have copied *USA Today* in their formatting of material. None of this packaging alarms consumers on the hunt for fast food stories to go with a fast food lunch. But such franchised, deep-fat tidbits do not provoke reflection to help citizens in a democracy reach complex judgments about issues fateful for the common good.

On the whole, the pressure to simplify stories and ideas encourages a single-issue politics. That phenomenon, along with other impacts of the media, tends to diminish the moderating role of political parties in America. Political parties, traditionally, took some of the hard edge off the combative position of a particular interest group, as parties organized their various constituencies into a comprehensive political program. Candidates today are selected to run for office, not by their political peers (in smoke-filled rooms), but by direct primaries. The candidates desperately need and therefore look to well-financed single-issue groups to win their party's nomination. Financial backers and telegenic campaigners, rather than political peers, determine who the party nominee will be. Every politician tends to become his or her own political party. Party discipline weakens, affecting not only the tenor of political campaigns but the quality of the governance to follow.

It is too early to tell whether the recently developed and much heralded "interactivity," which the Internet makes possible, will reverse the long decline in the citizen's active participation in politics. Even so, it may simply encourage activity in short, fevered, reactive spurts rather than lead to a more sustained engagement.

The Media and Education

The media have affected education even more than politics. As they format events and ideas, the media influence education far beyond the particular impacts of professional reporters, journalists, and commentators. To appeal once again to Flannery O'Connor: you know a people by the stories they tell—and hear. Collectively, the media, not only through news reporters but through every orifice, pour out a veritable torrent of stories—sit-coms, soap operas, game shows, daytime talk shows, mini-biographies of athletes, dramas sited in the crisis locations of hospital, police station, and law office, and the polished vignettes which advertisers tell and retell to sell their products. In the midst of all this retailing of stories, the media have served up a new figure—larger than life—whose presence and aura bestow a kind of teaching authority.

The successive teaching authorities in the West relied on exemplary figures, not simply ideas, to transmit their ideals and furnish people with their cues for behavior. The moral life communicates largely through stories. The church looked to its saints and the larger society to its heroes and heroines for inspiration. The saint offered words and deeds that pointed believers toward the transcendent ground of their lives. Heroes and heroines risked themselves and their careers and goods as they expended themselves for a cause that transcended them. Today the media give us celebrities rather than heroes. The saint or the hero enlarges you, helps you stretch. The celebrity doesn't. He diminishes you because you simply tend to envy the celebrity's glow. At best, others borrow a momentary significance by placing themselves somewhere in the vicinity of the celebrity's radiance. They gawk rather than learn.

The hero and the celebrity resemble one another at only one point. From the Homeric epic forward, heroism took two: the warrior to perform the deed and the poet to celebrate it; the mother to show the courage and the daughter to honor it and transmit it to her children. Today we have replaced the hero with the celebrity and the poet with the media. The media latch onto, not deeds, but a glow, style, or shine, which the camera loves. And what the media puff, they can eventually deflate. Thus media cynicism inevitably follows media enthusiasm. Cynicism brings down the celebrity as speedily as the click of a camera shutter, the arching of Johnny Carson's eyebrow, or David Letterman's giggle.

Protectively, young people need to pass through cynicism as they shed their naïveté, their clumsy enthusiasms, and their inevitable disillusionment with some of their values umbilically received. However, cynicism, when it becomes fixed as a style, endangers the young; it blocks education; it wastes the public realm. It withers, like some Agent Orange, the growing mind. To educate means to lead out, to enlarge the mind and the soul. But the cynic dries up the impulse to be educated at its root. In trashing everything, the hard-wired cynic thereby quells his impulse to be enlarged by anything. Thus the third teaching authority founders pedagogically in the cynicism it has industriously created; and the young abandon the pursuit of wisdom for a beady-eyed knowingness.

The dangers of the media need not lead to a Luddite demolition of the technology. Not even radical critics of the media, such as Marshall McLuhan and Walter J. Ong, believed that modern technologies irreversibly alter and dumb down the human mind. The media, despite the conglomerates that own them, the technologies that transform them, and the uses that degrade them, have managed to produce some practitioners of distinction and to generate some intramural distinctions in performance between cynics and critics and even some capacity for self-criticism.

Further, the earlier teaching authorities—the church and the academy—are still with us; and they have a job to do. Churches and synagogues, when they do their work well, help—along with other voluntary associations—to convert some of the passive amorphous mass of onlookers, of which Kierkegaard complained, into discrete bodies of public-spirited citizens. The academy, when it works right, must do more than assimilate the gadgetry of high-tech information systems into its operations or produce technicians who will fill the jobs a computerized society opens. The academy must cultivate critical intelligence and thus help break the thrall of a media age that oscillates wildly between mindless enthusiasms and uneducable cynicism. Only as it cultivates critical intelligence will the academy adequately form both professional leaders who wield a knowledge-based power and citizens who must make discriminate judgements about the quality of that leadership in its service to the common good.

Notes

1. Walter J. Ong, *Orality and Literacy: The Technologizing of the World* (New York: Methuen, 1982).
2. Marshal McLuhan, *Understanding Media: The Existence of Man* (New York: McGraw-Hill, 1965), ch. 1, "The Medium Is the Message," 7–21.
3. James Fallows, in his review article on "Internet Illusions," *The New York Review of Books*, 16 November 2000, 29, quotes and dates John Chambers' prediction, 1998.
4. The glib analogy of Ross Perot's electronic democracy to participatory democracy fails. Participatory democracy requires that citizens directly engage one another, not simply file their preferences in the data bank of the leader.
5. Dick Morris, *Vote.Com: How Big-Money Lobbyists and the Media Are Losing Their Influence and the Internet Is Giving Power Back to the People* (Los Angeles: Renaissance Books, 1999) reviewed by James Fallows, "Internet Illusions," *The New York Review of Books*, 16 November 2000, 29.
6. Fallows, Ibid., 28–32. James Fallows detailed these and other prophecies about the future that the Internet would create, only to observe that by the end of 2000 not many of these displacements in the seven-year revolution had in fact occured. However, the Internet has already produced or aggravated a series of moral and political issues with which some of the institutions, old and new, will have to cope: the threat to confidentiality; the dangers of monopoly; the pirating of music, movies, and books; the growing gap between rich and poor; and the exemption of e-mail order firms from state sales tax, which, in effect, releases such firms from the general duties of citizenship. Media moguls have also found their way to the trough of corporate welfare. They have secured the rights to the digital spectrum without paying anything to the government for the use of this public commons—either the $60 billion or more of its worth or the contribution of free time for public programming.
7. Ibid., 30.
8. *The Dallas Morning News*, for example, has published News Department Guidelines on forty-one practices. Some of its guidelines cover substantive ideals, such as fairness and accuracy in the use of words and images. Ten guidelines fall into the category of professional temptations, such as plagiarism, accepting freebies, drinking on the job, and conflicts of interest. Many other guidelines comprise corporate rules of the road, such as keeping up one's passport and going through the company machinery of referral patterns for decisions and assignments. However, since managers design such operational handbooks, they reserve to themselves the heavyweight moral decisions, which the institutions face; namely, priority decisions in allocating money, time, and talent.
9. Carl Hiaasen, *Lucky You* (New York: Alfred A. Knopf, 1997), 21.
10. William Lee Miller, "Notes Before Beginning a Journalism Ethics," an unpublished essay revised and published as "Journalism as a High Profession in Spite of Itself," Occasional Paper No. 3, Cary M. Maguire Center for Ethics and Public Responsibility, Southern Methodist University.
11. Isaiah Berlin distinguished between two concepts of liberty, negative and positive, in *Four Essays on Liberty* (New York: Oxford University Press, 1969), ch. 3. Long before Berlin, Immanual Kant distinguished between negative and

positive freedom. See the third section of Kant's *The Fundamental Principles of the Metaphysics of Morals*, especially pp. 65–66, in the English translation by Otto Manthey-Zorn (New York: D. Appleton-Century Company, 1938).

12. Critics of the media have recognized more recently the compulsions from within that limit freedom, that is, the internal constraints of organization, timing, and money that journalists face at the hands of the newspapers and networks for which they work.

13. For what follows, see William Lee Miller, *The First Liberty* (New York: Alfred A. Knopf, 1985), especially pp. 344–55, "On the Underpinnings of Republicanism."

14. Pete Slover, *The Dallas Morning News*, March 1, 1997, Section A, 1–23. See also the follow-up article by Gayle Reaves and Steve McGonigle on March 5, 1997.

15. Edward Jay Epstein, *News From Nowhere* (New York: Random House, 1973) and Michael Schudson, *Discovering the News* (New York: Basic Books, 1978).

16. Schudson, *Discovering the News*, 116.

17. Schudson, 9.

18. Ibid.

19. See Epstein, *News From Nowhere*, Part 1.

20. Schudson, *Discovering the News*, chap. 5.

21. Reinhold Niebuhr, *An Interpretation of Christian Ethics* (New York: Harper & Brothers, 1935) chap. 4.

22. Schudson, *Discovering the News*, 186.

23. Schudson, 98.

24. Soren Kierkegaard, *The Present Age: A Literary Review*, found in *A Kierkegaard Anthology*, ed. Robert Bretall (New York: Modern Library, 1936), 267.

25. Ibid.

26. Neil Postman, *Amusing Ourselves to Death: Public Discourse in the Age of Show Business* (New York: Viking Penguin, 1985).

27. James Fallows, *Breaking the News: How the Media Undermine American Democracy* (New York: Pantheon Books, 1996), 31–33.

Chapter 7

Ministers

Ordained to What Public Purpose?

This chapter on the role of religious institutions and their professional leaders in the formation of public character covers only the Christian ministry and even there, most recognizably, although not exclusively, the Protestant ministry. I have restricted focus partly for reasons of my own limited competence and partly because the Protestant clergy, more than their peers in the rabbinate and the priesthood, have tended to associate religious life with a purely private happiness. Students of Judaism, Catholicism, and Eastern Orthodoxy will readily identify the similarities and differences their leaders face in meeting their public obligations.

A healthy marriage encompasses both its private and public aspects, both the secrets that pass between two lovers and the public responsibilities that the couple, still nourished by their inner life, assumes. Lovers obsessively seek to withdraw from the world; but spouses resolve to face outward toward the world as they participate in and contribute to the community. Our architecture embodies this doubleness: A home has its private chambers, where two people come to terms with and enjoy one another, but also its public rooms, the dining room and the living room, where they receive friends and strangers. Middle-class Americans signaled their shift toward a more private understanding of marriage when they emphasized the family room at the expense of the conventional public rooms in a house.

The church similarly lives in two realms. The church enjoys its own interior life; but it betrays its mission if it cannot turn outward toward the world. The church's relationship to God resembles a marriage partnership more than a love affair. It enjoys through word and sacrament the presence of God, but it cannot lead a disembodied life apart from the world. Indeed, each of the churches faces out toward a very specific external world that partly shapes its obligations and the public duties of its ministers.

213

The external world, as we have suggested, suffers chronically from a split between the private and the public, between inner life and outer forms and institutions. This split between the inner and the outer does not create a discrete social problem of the kind that usually makes the headlines, such as urban blight, downsizing, unemployment, racial tensions, violence, homelessness, deficit spending, and bureaucratic red tape. It constitutes rather a "deep fault" that precedes and affects all the other problems. It shapes the way in which we perceive discrete problems and fatefully affects proposals for their amelioration.

The church (and therefore its leadership) must undertake some responsibility for bridging the split between interior life and public institutions. The combination of the church and other voluntary communities, such as synagogues, parent-teacher associations, citizens' projects, and cause-oriented movements, constitute a distinctively American social resource. Edmund Burke once referred to voluntary communities as "the little platoons" among us, which are "the germ," as it were, of "public affections."[1] Modern sociologists less elegantly name these voluntary communities "intermediate institutions." They occupy a middle ground between the solitary citizen and the "mega-institutions" of state and corporation. Whatever their name, they help bridge the distance between the public and private in a culture that has created a gulf between the two. As such, they constitute publics within the public at large.

Intermediate institutions can help cultivate the citizen in two ways. First, objectively, they sensitize the citizen to the common good. Although a church or a service organization follows its own special interests, it must also keep an eye focused on the common good. To that degree, the organization functions as a public within the wider public and not simply as an interest group engaged in promoting itself. The good of the public at large cannot long flourish if it merely comprises the overlapping interests of groups, such as the National Association of Manufacturers, the American Federation of Labor, and the Cattleman's Association. Groups, solely defined by their interests, can underlap, as well as overlap, or exhaust themselves in profitless competition. The public at large depends upon determinate publics within it that help it focus, however fuzzily, on questions of the common good.

Second, voluntary communities, behaving as publics, not only point their members objectively to the common good, but also tutor them subjectively in the art of acting in concert with others. They tease people out of the bottle of private preferences, desires, and interests, and immerse them in a community which the mega-institutions cannot or only limitedly provide. They introduce people to what John Adams called "public happiness." The very voluntariness of the community challenges each member to learn how to get along with others, engage in debate, cope with friends and opponents over policy differences, and overlook personal slights and grievances for the sake of common goals.

In meeting public needs, such voluntary communities, the churches included, face several major difficulties. First, the government has reneged on many of its responsibilities for public welfare, which it previously discharged, and dealt them to the "third sector." The churches and other voluntary communities have not been able to expand their resources sufficiently to shoulder these new loads. They depend heavily upon their members for the donation of money and time. But long-term inflation until the last decade and changing tax laws threatened their income; and the advent of the women's movement dramatically reduced the time their volunteers contribute. More women have taken jobs, partly because careers have opened to them and partly because low wages and salaries have made two incomes necessary to support a family. Meanwhile, the huge corporations for which they increasingly work consume much of their time and energy, leaving little for their families and still less for service in voluntary communities that previously relied upon, to say nothing of exploited, women for free services. In losing women, the churches have often lost the entire family, because the church, as a traditional "outlet" for stymied women, not only took advantage of their talents, but annexed their spouses and children through them. Justice forbids turning the clock back, but prudence requires congregations, at a minimum, to think through theologically and sociologically how to design a church that no longer need rely on sexist patterns in the society at large for its support.

Some basic elements in the church's understanding of its mission should charge its leaders with wider duties than service to the interior needs of its members and more reliably than occasional, crisis-driven forays into public action.

The Church As Mission and Community

The Protestant denominations, most particularly the free churches, tend to think of the church in noninstitutional terms. They define the church as an existing community, a fellowship. Only secondarily do they characterize the church as structured and equipped to perform specific functions. This state of affairs explains the episodic, hit-or-miss character of actions. Social action in the congregation often flourishes only as long as a church happens to have a powerful minister concerned with such matters and often dries up with his or her departure. The church may need to reverse this relationship between community and function, fellowship and action. Instead of thinking of itself first and foremost as a community engaged in a variety of occasional activities, the church may need to ask itself what the essential functions, the essential activities, of the body of Christ are, and then form a community around them.

To use an analogy from another field: A powerful sense of community can develop in a theater company that dedicates itself first and foremost to its essential activity, putting on a play. The action exhilarates and sustains members to the point that they feel a letdown when the curtain falls on the last performance. Ordinary isolated life seems stale after people have merged themselves into a meaningful action. Conversely, a theater group deteriorates and its high standards and morale collapse when it thinks of itself first as a society that happens incidentally now and then to put on plays.

Analogously, expending a church's energies in its essential activities brings it to life; it trivializes as a community when it lacks a shaping mission. A complementary and reinforcing, instead of a contentious, relationship can exist between order and vitality, function and power, structure and dynamism, body and spirit. Too often, however, in American Protestant church life, liberals, evangelicals, and radicals alike have assumed that structures invariably constrict and oppress rather than supply the forms through which the energies of the people of God can bloom. If the churches accept a symbiotic relationship between the vital and the organic, they still face a critical question: What are the vital functions of the body of Christ that define the church's public mission and the minister's responsibility?

The essential functions or actions of Christ himself give an enduring answer to this question of mission. The theological equivalent for function is "office," the specific forms of which the church derives from the scriptures of Israel. Serious reflection on ministry must explore the three great offices in the work of Christ: priest, prophet, and king.

The priestly office of Christ authorizes the church's liturgical action; the prophetic office, its teaching function; and the kingly office (as Jesus defined kingship), its service function. The church apprehends God's triune inner life as self-expending love—Father, Son, and Holy Spirit. The offices of Christ and the functions of the church provide three ways of participating in God's self-expending love: worship, its festive celebration; teaching, its clarification; and service, its practical expression in sharing. These three substantive actions define the work of the minister. On the principle that form follows substance, we must first deal with these functions and only then with various further contending images of the minister as leader. The formal articulation of the minister's power and responsibility follows from and must confine itself to substance.

The Minister As Priest

In exploring the minister's larger public obligations, it would seem sensible to bypass the activity of worship and concentrate on the minister's social service, on the grounds that the latter bears most directly on politics. Politics seems far removed from the liturgical. Politics defines the world of means subordinate to ends, of instrumental complexes, of conflict, disputation, and strife. In contrast, worship refers to an action which is an end in itself; it offers, at best, some measure of respite from those political conflicts that threaten to tear a society apart.

Put even more forcefully, do we not run the risk of corrupting worship if we begin with the political implications of the liturgy? Men and women worship God because God is. They corrupt worship if they bend worship to some other goal: peace of mind, career advancement, family unity, better health, moral improvement, or political cause. Some such secondary goods may follow from worship but if these become the aim and purpose of worship, the worshiper instrumentalizes God to other ends, thus diminishing God to what God is not, the great slot machine in the sky. "To celebrate a festival means to do something which is in no way tied up to other goals; [it] has been removed from all 'so that' and 'in order to.' True festivity cannot be imagined as residing anywhere but in the realm of activity that is meaningful in itself."[2]

While one corrupts worship if one reduces it to the "so that" and the "in order to" of politics (or to the goals of the marketplace or psychic health), secondary implications, including the political, do flow from worship. The Catholic moralist Dietrich von Hildebrand sketched in *Liturgy and Personality*[3] a portrait of the liturgically formed person, the person who takes the liturgy seriously, who does not corrupt it for reasons of self-improvement, self-advancement, or any other secondary gains, yet who reflects secondarily the shaping power of the liturgy on character. Similarly, one may ask what liturgically formed citizens might look like, that is, citizens who take seriously the sacraments of the Lord's Supper and Baptism and the ordinary prayers of the church as an influence on their interactions in the *polis*, even though they do not exploit worship for political goals. (Protestants need to learn here from other faith traditions. Whereas the Protestant usually asks, "What is the scripturally formed person like?," the Catholic [and Eastern Orthodox] believer asks, "What is the liturgically formed person like?")

The Sacrament of the Lord's Supper. In a pluralistic country, this sacrament cannot directly provide the basis for societal unity. To impose the sacrament on others would convert it into what it cannot be and still be itself: an intrusive creed that divides. But Christian congregations must take the Eucharistic vision seriously in fulfilling their responsibilities as a public within a public at large.

This central act of Christian worship reenacts the meal Jesus shared with his disciples before his imminent and violent death. Even that meal in its human details did not offer a respite from the violence to follow. The disciples squabbled over which of them was the greatest; but Jesus undercut their game of king of the mountain by reversing the world's understanding of royalty. "The kings of the Gentiles lord it [leadership] over them. . . . But not so with you; rather the greatest among you must become like the youngest, and the leader like one who serves. . . . I am among you as one who serves."[4] In the course of the meal, Jesus rebuked Judas, who would betray him, and Peter, who, despite his grandiloquent profession of loyalty, would deny him. Yet, at this same meal, Jesus took bread and wine and distributed them to his errant, defecting disciples. He would proceed thereafter to fulfill his own indefectible purpose—despite outright betrayal, the apathy of disciples in Gethsemane, the shiftiness of political leaders, the fickleness of crowds, and the violence and isolation of the death which he knew would follow. Subsequent generations of Christians, repeating his words, take bread and wine as their way of "making present" (*anamnesis*) his self-expending and nourishing love.

In its sheer violence, Jesus' death resembles the liturgies of violence endlessly repeated in the modern media, but points in the opposite direction. It arouses awed love rather than fear, creates community rather than isolated onlookers; it invites people to join and share, not to watch alone at a distance through satellite TV. The reenactment of the Eucharist would reclaim the sorry past, but in mercy rather than vengeance; transform the future without deforming the present; and extend charity outward to the needy, the stranger, and the enemy, while it presses judgment and mercy inward to that dark corner where self-pity and malice fester. This event impels Christians both to come together and to go out to others in self-expending love.

Participation in this event is an end in itself; it transcends the political, but the "making present" of the Eucharist does not withdraw celebrants from the rough terrain of the political; it brings to the surface those conflicts with which the political order must cope. The sacrament acknowledges those threats to life to which the dark pessimism of Hobbes and the social contract, theorists testified. However, it also states that the deepest taproot of community among us is not a *Summum Malum* that forces fearful, self-interested men and women into the social contract, but a *Summum Bonum* that breaks and limits the hold of fear upon us and invites us into the covenant of undaunted, self-expending love.

In a sense, modern-day terrorism represents a liturgical reaction to the social contract theory of the state. Terrorists intuit that the modern social contract relies heavily upon the power of fear to hold things together. But fearful self-interest that draws people together can quickly drive them apart. In wielding violence, terrorists trigger the disintegrative power of fearful self-interest. In receiving (and accepting into one's own life) the Savior who lays down his life for others, the Eucharist offers the social order the leavening power of self-donative love.

The prominence of the terrorist's cult of blood from the '70s onward exposes at once the insatiable hunger of modern people for the liturgical and the deprivations of a politics that springs from a lack of liturgical substance. The ritual of terrorism parodies the sacrament of the Eucharist. Luther called the Christian sacrament the enacted word; the modern terrorist substitutes the propaganda of deed. The Christian rite remembers a figure who serves at once as high priest and sacrifice. The terrorist action distinguishes the high priest from his victims. However, if the terrorist holds his ground, he must be ready to die, if not for his victims, with them.[5] His readiness to kill and die creates the power he exercises over the society that watches raptly on television.

Like the traditional act of worship, the terrorist's attack goes beyond the ordinary limits of political means and ends. Politically, the deed often seems counterproductive, self-destructive, and irrational. It doesn't seem to make any sense as a means directed to an end. As the Bogside Catholic MP John Hume long ago complained about terrorism in Northern Ireland, "The Provos bombed themselves to the conference table and they bombed themselves away again."[6] The action is ecstatic in the sense that it stands outside the causal nexus of means and ends; it juts out religiously as an end in itself. It does not look beyond itself to a further justification. Shi'ite terrorists express this ecstatic element mythically in their expectation that the martyr will be directly translated into heaven.

Terrorism offers a festival of death, a celebration that has its own priest and victims and that carries with it the risk that the priest himself will become a victim. Others con-celebrate in this liturgical action through the medium of the media. Thus the media respond to the human thirst for ritual, the need for ecstasy, the desire to be lifted out of the daily round. Through violent death, their horror before it and their need to draw near it, the event relieves liturgically bereft men and women of that other death, boredom; and it momentarily strips the state, founded in self-interest, of its protective power.

The Sacrament of Infant Baptism. The folksy domestic sentiment with which we surround the sacrament of Baptism obscures its daring as a public rite. This sacrament acknowledges, on principle, that the church welcomes the disconcertingly strange, the future in all its squirming uncertainty, into its life. The sacrament asks parents to relax their obsessive hold on their child. It invites those most inclined to deal myopically with the infant, most tempted to seek its good at the expense of others and to crush it to the bosom in apprehensive love, to hand over their child into the hands of another. Baptism asks parents to see their child at a disquieting, yet quieting, distance; that is, to accept it as a child of God. Taken seriously, the rite requires parents to prepare their child for something more than a domestic significance and to free the child for a public identity beyond their final reach and control.

The Prayers of Invocation and Adoration. These prayers at the outset of worship distinguish the Ruler of the Universe from those principalities and powers that normally lure the human heart and command allegiance. The prayers of adoration block idolatry; they leave no doubt as to the status of the government, and indeed, all political causes; humanly important, but not ultimate. The citizen cannot pray to an eternal God and take a temporary state too seriously. God has allowed the state for both the good that it can do and the evil that it can prevent, but, in the setting of adoration:

> Even the nations are like a drop from a bucket, and are accounted as dust on the scales. . . . All the nations are as nothing before him; they are accounted by him as less than nothing and emptiness.[7]

Yet, this metaphysical/religious vision should not end in political detachment. As it strips political leaders and activists of vanity and illusion, it should also free them to wield power under God and in the service of God's creatures. The prayers of adoration help let the air out of inflationary political rhetoric; and thus they ought to reduce the violence and divisiveness which that rhetoric tends to inspire.

Intercessory Prayer. Usually these prayers, whether in worship or personal devotions, include petitions for four overlapping groups of people: intimates and friends, public authorities, enemies, and the needy. At first glance, prayers for family and friends would seem to contradict the meaning of public life. They seem to presuppose a kind of deity of the hearth. They ask God to extend the parent's loving and partial hand. The supplicant asks God to treat those in the circle of intimacy preferentially, to act like a legislature that passes a private bill or like a president who occasionally suspends general laws to intervene in a special case.

The supplicant should pray for those she loves. But the Lord's Prayer qualifies such intercessions and subjects them to the Son's petition: "nevertheless not my will but thine be done." Intercession forces supplicants to take those nearest and dearest, the beleaguered objects of their worry, and to see them at a distance and in a strange light, and to recognize that their ultimate well-being does not depend upon their own efforts to contrive their good. Intercession, so understood, moves those one loves from a private closet into the open air; it ought to continue what baptism began as it releases those one loves into a more spacious life.

The church also offers intercessory prayers for public authorities, both ecclesiastical and political. At a minimum, this particular prayer reminds worshipers that prayer cannot simply dwell on the turmoil of private life. The church's prayers and its actions must also extend to queens and presidents, bishops and vicars, deans and sheriffs, garbage collectors and safety inspectors, and all others who bear the burden of office. The petition for political leaders in one of the Protestant orders of worship reads: "Mighty God, Lord of the nations, govern those who govern us, your servant . . . President of the United States, and those who share the public trust in every land." Usually Christians who are Democrats—give or take a few scandals—pray that prayer more easily when a Roosevelt, Truman, Kennedy, Johnson, Carter, or Clinton occupies the White House. Christians who are Republicans find it easier to utter the President's name when an Eisenhower, Nixon, Ford, Reagan, or Bush occupies the oval office. Praying ungrudgingly for Caesar depends a little on who wears Caesar's toga. What should we make of a prayer that asks people to bring one of those sulphurous political names to their lips? At a minimum, such a prayer calls for something other than scorn for political leaders.

Intercessory prayer has a further public significance: it invites Christians to pray for their competitors and enemies. Psychologically, competitors usually preoccupy the petitioner as much as do friends and family. The very existence of competitors threatens; they can become an obsession. Supposed or real, his enemies make every man his own Kremlinologist. He ponders their every move, believes them subtle and malignant; they crowd him; he wishes them dead. Intercessory prayer forces Christians to look at their enemies in a new light, releasing them from the grip of suspicion, hatred, and revenge, and to pray for their well-being. This relocation of his enemies in the public space of intercessory prayer also acknowledges that no world and space exists wholly free of competitors. As Freud rightly taught, it takes only three parties—a man, a woman, and a child—to create the conditions for enmity in the world, and the introduction of a fourth, as scripture tells us, raises Cain. As Martin Luther King Jr. taught, praying for one's enemies need not lead to a quiescent politics; such praying reminds us that one may contend sharply with the unjust enemy yet still leave him some room to turn around. (Martin Luther King Jr. insisted in his "Letter from a Birmingham Jail" that nonviolent resistance should both begin and end with the effort to negotiate, a process which requires concession on both sides.)[8]

Finally, intercessory prayer pulls back into public consciousness those people whom we ordinarily hide in the outer edge of the firelight—the lame, the halt, the blind, the sick, the poor, and the captive. We fix focus on our friends and enemies; we hide the needy from sight. We bury them prematurely. We herd the sick, the deviant, the defective, the aged, and the delinquent into isolated institutions and hire professionals to manage them, a strategy that frees the rest of us to attend to our own interests. Prison inmates become "forgotten men." When we ignore the needy and consign the inmate to oblivion, we shrink and depopulate the public realm. We reduce the number of those who can be seen and heard, can make their wants known, and can participate in public debate. Intercessory prayer for "all sorts and conditions" of men and women requires us to bring them from the margins back to the center of our consciousness to attend to their well-being.[9]

The Prayers of Confession. Their placement in the worship service before intercessory prayer offers a clue as to why we neglect the needy. Neglect does not usually spring from the fact that we are too smug, too complacent, or too engrossed in our own riches to bother with the bereft. If we examine our excuses for neglect, including our reasons for institutionalization, we discover not so much smugness but anxiety, not complacency but a sense of harassment, not riches but a feeling of bankruptcy. The question "What can I do?" often means, in despair, "I have nothing for the real needs of another because I cannot satisfy my own. How could I help him? Better to avoid him. To have to face him would be too depressing. He would remind me of my own emptiness." Not all expediency in our treatment of the distressed derives from gross callousness; usually, we are simply too busy obscuring from view our own poverty. We consign to oblivion the maimed, the disfigured, and the decrepit, because we have already condemned to oblivion a portion of ourselves. To address them in their needs would require us to confess to God our own needs. But we do not want to accept the depths of our own neediness. The needy, hidden away, threaten us because of what we have already desperately hidden away from ourselves. For some such reason, we prefer, even at great expense, to have the needy hidden from sight. And what better way to cover them with shadows and to obscure our own neediness, than to put them in the hands of professionals who know how to make a great show of strength, experience, and competence in handling a given subdivision of the distressed? Thus we convert the exigent into occasions in and through which the community exhibits its precedence and power.

What have these strategies of neglect got to do with the prayers of confession? The French commentator Michel Foucault[10] offers a clue. He observes that medieval society, except for its treatment of lepers (and religious minorities), tended, less than ours, to incarcerate its own members for deviancy. But by the seventeenth and eighteenth centuries, society imprisoned the idle, the poor, the insane, and the criminal without distinction in the former houses of leprosy. Foucault believes that the religious ritual of confession helped shape the medieval attitude toward deviancy. Prayers of confession openly acknowledge human imperfection; they thereby imply some confidence that we can meet evil in the open without its engulfing those who pray. But after the seventeenth century, western society felt increasingly "ashamed in the presence of the inhuman." It assumed that one could handle evil only by banishing it. An age that aspires to total autonomy finds it more difficult to acknowledge in the mainstream of its life the dependent, the defective, and the irrational. They remind us of a negativity so threatening and absolute that the society can deal with them only by hiding from them, by putting them out of sight.

Confession, by inviting a person to acknowledge evil and fault in himself, allows him to see and address the distress of others. Confession makes intercession possible. The faith that shapes the Eucharist and its prayers of confession and intercession assumes that the negative is real but not ultimate. The quarrels and the defections of first-generation disciples, the sins of disciples in our own generation, and the defects and delinquencies of the race at large are grave indeed but not so grave as to engulf us all.

The Prayers of Thanksgiving impel the church toward giving—toward its service function—but differently motivated than philanthropic giving. The ideal of philanthropy (which informs much of the giving of voluntary communities, conscientious professionals, and corporations with a conscience) commends a love of humankind that issues in concrete deeds of service to others. However, the ideal of philanthropy tends to divide the human race in two: relatively self-sufficient benefactors and needy beneficiaries. It presupposes a unilateral or one-way transfer from giver to receiver. This assumption of asymmetry dominates not only private charity, professional *pro bono* work, and corporate philanthropy, but also the conventional self-interpretation of America as philanthropist among the nations and the American church as patron to the churches in the Third World.

This idealist's picture of a social world divided into givers and receivers, while morally superior to a callous neglect of the needy, overlooks the fact that the benefactor receives as well as gives. Scripture and the prayers of thanksgiving provide powerful warrants for giving but always within the setting of a primordial receiving. The Scriptures of Israel urge the Jewish farmer, in harvesting, not to pick his crops too clean. He should leave some for the sojourner, for he was once a sojourner in Egypt. Thus God's own actions, his care for Israel while a stranger in Egypt, prompts and measures Israel's treatment of the stranger in her midst. The imperative to give rests upon the narrative account of a gift already received. Thus the moral/legal element in scripture (the *halacha*) rests upon a narrative base (the *agada*). Similarly, the New Testament reads, "In this is love, not that we loved God but that he loved us. . . . Beloved, since God loved us so much, we also ought to love one another."[11] The imperative derives from the revelatory event of the divine love.

These passages push the believer toward a different notion of love from the philosopher's principle of beneficence. Benevolence is self-derived. The rational principle of beneficence presupposes the structural relationship of *benefactor* to *beneficiary*, of giver to receiver. These sacred narratives reposition the benefactor; they open up a revelatory horizon against which the potential benefactor can discover herself to be a beneficiary. Her petty benefactions merely acknowledge love already received beyond her deserving.

Luther located the political order under the fifth commandment, the duties to one's parents; he therefore put politics under the ethics of gratitude. He thus one-sidedly emphasized the duties of citizens to their rulers, who, in Luther's view, filled the role of fathers to whom children owed grateful obedience. He failed to direct his study of the ethics of gratitude to those who most need to learn it: the power-wielders themselves as ministers, politicians, and other professional doers of good.

The Minister As Servant

This chapter began with the split between inner life and outer forms and institutions. Debates over the service function of the church reflect this split. The kingly office of Christ (remembering that Jesus defined kingship not as domination but as service) authorizes the minister as servant. But the church provides two kinds of service:

internally, it serves its own members; externally, it serves the world. Conservatives in the modern church have chiefly emphasized the minister's internal pastoral service; and liberals and radicals on the left (and sometimes the right), the minister's external role as activist. These differing demands reflect and exacerbate the split between inner life and outer forms that one already finds in the society at large.

But matters in Christendom were not always so. St. Augustine exemplified in his own life and writings the ultimate unity of the two realms. He was at once mystic and bishop, master of the interior life and a leader of the institutional church. His most influential works reflected his personal testimony—*The Confessions*—and his public vision—*The City of God*. In *The Confessions*, he wrote the first Western autobiography; and in *The City of God*, the first comprehensive history of the human race.

In America, the Puritans, the early Roman Catholics, and the Jews recognized both the personal and the communal dimensions of biblical faith. Recently, the black churches, perhaps more than all others, have kept alive both concerns. Their ministers have accepted responsibilities as both the pastors of souls and the leaders of communities. White Protestantism, however, in its various forms—conservative, liberal, and radical—has often suffered a disconcerting separation of the two activities, splitting the personal from the social. The conservative majority traditionally reduces the faith to the experiential, the intimate, and the familial. More recently it has ventured out into the political under the banner of family values. The minority (the social gospelers in Protestantism) has more regularly sought to influence politics under the banner of peace, justice, and human rights.

A traditional conservative parishioner, representing the basic complaints of a group of lay people in her church who were about to ease an activist minister out of office, once grumbled: "Father X, I come to church in order to be consoled!"—clearly implying that he had not dispensed much consolation since he resigned from the staff of an important government agency to study for the priesthood. The distinguished conservative Edmund Burke once put the woman's complaint in more sophisticated terms when he criticized progressive clergymen of his own day in England for busily importing some of the more fashionable ideas of the French Revolution:

> . . . politics and the pulpit are terms that have little agreement.
> No sound ought to be heard in the church but the healing voice

of Christian charity. The cause of civil liberty and civil religion gains as little as that of religion by this confusion of duties. . . . Wholly unacquainted with the world in which they are so fond of meddling—and inexperienced in all its affairs—on which they [clergymen] pronounce with such confidence—they have nothing of politics but the passions they excite. . . . Surely the church is a place where one day's truce ought to be allowed to the dissensions and animosities of mankind.[12]

Social activists, on the other hand, have argued that the church should not deserve any holiday truce with the dissensions and animosities that afflict humankind. They would define the church's ministry as a service to a world riven with conflict. (The activists further subdivide into radicals and reformers: radicals push for comprehensive and systemic action and reformers plead for more discriminate criticism and for more limited interventions.)

This division within the church, which cuts across denominational lines, would not pose a problem if either the conservatives or the radicals could faithfully constitute the church by themselves. But clearly they cannot. The conservative majority cannot form a fully faithful church. The Lord who served the church called the community to serve, not merely to self-service. Without social action, the church mocks its Lord who ministered to others; it perverts his pity into self-pity.

However, the activist minority also faces its spiritual dangers. Quick to condemn the apathy of the majority, it only grudgingly recognizes the pride and arrogance in itself. This restless minority tends to think of itself as a church within a church—the real church—formed of academics who stand aloof from the institutional church and disillusioned professionals and activists who have written it off, especially the local parish.

Early Christians named the minority's spiritual temptation Gnosticism. When Christian elitists fly from the church to do their own thing, they become religious Gnostics who try to prove their religious superiority by abandoning the hippopotamus church, the flesh and blood church of ordinary men and women, for an overspiritualized, disembodied movement. They pretend that they serve the needs of others while exempting themselves from need. The *illuminati* remove themselves from the palpable, the sweaty body of the congregation, and deny their own bodily need. Pastoral service to members reminds activists that no one can escape from need, least of all the disciples of Jesus who needed to receive all things from the Father.

The traditional pastoral care of individuals—whether or not they are members of the congregation—most closely approximates the services offered by other of the helping professions: law, medicine, social work, and nursing. Tensions inevitably develop in all these professions between duties to clients and the obligations to the wider public. In the case of pastoral work, the professional promise of confidentiality—the sanctuary of the confessional—sometimes conflicts with responsibilities to the public and can expose others to real danger. Thus duties to clients, patients, and parishioners might seem at odds with public responsibilities.

However, a democracy can justify offering some shelter even to those at odds with the state and its purposes. The public has a moral and practical interest in extending human services to those whose ignorance, sickness, infirmity, or crimes have marked them as beyond the ordinary circles of public life and utility and who may even oppose or resist the state. If the state weeds out the useless or the hostile, then, at one time or another, we all need fear weeding. (A geneticist once warned that genetic engineering rigorously applied could find four or five reasons for deleting each of us!) The helping professions, including especially the pastoral ministry, perform an important public service in reaching out to the anomic, the stateless, friendless, or resourceless, and offering them help and, perhaps, reintegration. So doing, the public offers hope and it recovers and renews its own perishing life. Without such pastoral care, the grander schemes for reform and revolution often merely exploit the misery of the outsider. A former Benedictine monk, whose religious and political convictions led him to work summers in the civil rights movement, sensed a profound wariness among blacks toward Northern whites in the movement who, they felt, merely used them for the sake of the cause. These blacks expressed to him their appreciation for those ministers who, in the midst of the impersonal urgencies of the political movement, showed some personal and pastoral concern. Pastoral work of this kind renews people at the bedrock on which they can build a life.

In its service beyond pastoral care, the church traditionally relied on two appeals: to corporal works of mercy and to the doctrine of vocation. First, through occasional works of mercy church members responded to fire, famine, flood, sickness, and other misfortunes. Second, through their vocation, Christians could offer a continuing, temporal extension of service to others. Rightly understood and deployed, a vocation supplies the regular means through which Christians serve the common good. We have already adverted to this idea in the thought of the Puritan William Perkins. Rightly conducted, the professions can constitute a lay ministry: lay people can minister to others through their services as doctors, lawyers, engineers, accountants, corporate and union leaders, politicians, journalists, and teachers.

However, both forms of service to the world fall short of fully effective service. Although occasional works of charity offer temporary relief, a thousand points of light will not solve deep structural problems. Further, the slide of vocations into self-serving careers increases the difficulty of solving structural problems through jobs alone (however earnestly professionals may serve others as doctors, lawyers, and librarians). Thus Christian critics argued that service to the world must also include social action in more explicitly political forms. Put another way, one's calling includes not simply occasional works of personal charity and steadfast service to others through one's job, but also through one's duties as a citizen. The church, as well, must accept its institutional duties of citizenship and serve as a public within the public at large.

Thus, the "mainline" churches, especially through their national leaders and clergy, reacted to social service restricted to occasional charity and to one's job. They wanted the church to respond to social crises and structural problems as pressure groups or educational forces in the public arena. But eventually the churches' national leadership operated out of one *ethos*, the laity, by and large, out of another. This divided consciousness divided the church. Even well-founded activist objections to a church that relied exclusively on sentimental works of love helped perpetuate—though unintentionally—a divided consciousness. Without the experience that derives from personal service, the ordinary churchgoer lacks touch with the structural distortions of our time. Increasingly, the churches' leadership tried to solve structural social problems, as laypeople expected their ministers to concentrate on personal pastoral care.

Personal charity falls short of love when we substitute it for humane and just legislation, but legislation and personal works of love need not conflict. Indeed, the prospects for social legislation can improve when the church engages her laypeople in hands-on service that helps create a more favorable *ethos*, atmosphere, or receptivity to such legislation. When horizons narrow to immediate experience, people shrink from the strange—the mentally defective, the prisoner, the aged, the ill, the young, the culturally alien. Service, even of the amateurish kind, helps create experienced men and women whose lives are not merely private, narrow, unimaginative, frightened, and unsympathetic.

How can or should the church best serve as an intermediate institution between citizens and the mega-institutions of our time, particularly those huge bureaucracies that currently offer professional services to those in need? At first glance, it appears that these huge institutions run smoothly on their own self-laid rails; they do not need the interference of so marginal an enterprise as the Christian church. But appearances deceive. As suggested in the chapter on corporate leaders, we may need to sustain a dual social organization. On the one hand, we need the huge bureaucracies, in effect, our own organizational Egyptian pyramids, massive, formal, geometrical, hierarchical—the corporations, the public bureaucracies, and the like—that help mobilize professional talent. But on the other hand, we need smaller-scale, informal, spontaneous communities that counterbalance the majestic impeccabilities of grand scale and design.

In such a dual social structure, the church, along with other volunteer communities, may perform five important social functions: supplemental, critical, protective, alimentary, and experimental. The church needs: (1) to provide supplemental services beyond those that the bureaucracies provide; (2) to criticize the bureaucracies for failing to provide what they ought to provide; (3) to serve as advocate for and shelter those who need an intermediary between themselves and the *colossi*; and (4) to provide the community at large with sufficient knowledge of the plight of the deprived and the forlorn and thus help create an ethos of support for the bureaucracies should they do their job.

Finally, the church—against the day that the institutions and the skyscrapers about us, which look so impassive and permanent, will, in their turn, crack and decay—must experiment to develop alternative patterns of common life that may help shape and sustain the world to come.

This experimental task of the church evokes one of the most promising, but partly neglected, opportunities which the liberation movement offers the church. Hannah Arendt argued in her comparison of three revolutions—the American, the French, and the

Russian—that only the American Revolution succeeded. It alone had already developed in miniature those institutions that could shape and sustain a new society.[13] To succeed at the deeper levels of historical change, the negative task of freedom *from* must anticipate the positive destination of freedom *for*. Exodus needs Mount Sinai. Those famous shipboard Puritans reached some advance agreement as to how they wanted to live in the land ahead. Similarly, liberation theologians today may need to attend as much to the experimental reconstruction of institutions as to the work of prophetic criticism. Otherwise, the movement may end up too much defined by its reaction to the Egypt which it leaves and too little oriented to the specific institutional needs of the land ahead. Liberation theology—like the church at large against which it protests—may suffer from too little rather than too much *praxis*.

The Minister As Prophet

The ministry forms one of the three learned professions, but, more than that, it is a *teaching* profession. The rabbi, priest, and protestant minister cannot do their jobs without effectively teaching their congregations. In fact, "rabbi" means teacher. The Catholic Church defines the magisterial (or teaching) authority of the church as one of its three basic authorities and responsibilities (the other two are sacramental and governing). Some protestant traditions call the minister the "teaching elder," to emphasize the importance of teaching in the church's life. That special emphasis derives from Christ's prophetic office. In his discussion of that office, Calvin emphasizes Christ as Teacher. Salvation includes not only reconciliation with God and the celebration of God's presence (the priestly office), but illumination. "The purpose of this prophetic dignity in Christ is to teach us."[14] Derivatively, the minister should teach, primarily through preaching, but also through counseling, church leadership, and social action.

The minister's teaching helps establish the church as a public body, rather than a mere interest group, within the public at large. If the church merely aggregates wants and interests, then a congregation can proceed with a wholly contractual or transactional understanding of the agreement it reaches with the minister it calls and pays. "Here are our wants in a minister, can you satisfy our wants?" We have already explored the obligation of other professionals to move beyond the client's self-perceived wants to deeper needs. But the ministry, even more than the other helping professions, requires a covenantal or transformational understanding of professional responsibility.

Scripture sharply distinguishes desires from needs. The true prophets of Israel knew only too well that people want a message that skitters in the shallows. Jeremiah accused the false prophets of crying "'peace, peace,' when there is no peace;" they "prophesy falsely, and . . . my people love to have it so."[15] Despite these tastes for saccharine, authentic religious leaders recognize a responsibility to their congregations above and beyond merely gratifying wants. They must offer, not candied words, but a word that will help mend their lives.

However, transformational leadership slips into paternalism unless it teaches rather than commands or manipulates. The professional today who insists on transforming her clients, but who neglects to teach them, inevitably relies on managerial, manipulative, and condescending modes of behavior modification. Teaching respects the client as a rational, self-determining creature. Unfortunately, the teaching component in the minister's responsibilities has been obscured in our time, and this for two reasons: one, specific to the recent history of the ministry; the other, general to all professions. Too many talented divinity school graduates across an extended period from World War II through the 1960s, chose academic careers in preference to the ministry. Often they made their original decision to go to seminary on the strength of college course work in the field and consequently found their models in teachers rather than ministers. Talented students feared oblivion in the parish ministry. Churches at that time seemed rather more absorbed in building campaigns than in enhancing Christian life. Plentiful jobs, for a time, in the colleges allowed young teachers freedom to attend there to religious issues. But the academic discipline of religious studies clung to a rather probationary status in the academy, and, in due course, many young teachers distanced themselves from (or altogether abandoned) the church. They tended to disengage themselves from the church as from a poor relative who slightly embarrassed the upwardly mobile young academic, anxious to do well.

The so-called "mainline" protestant churches suffered the most from this vanishing intellectual leadership in the parish. In the total economy of the church in America, these protestant churches had a special responsibility to teach the Christian faith with clarity and power. Unfortunately, they recruited and retained too few talented young intellectual leaders; and their placement services did not always put the talented and dedicated into strategic positions. Theological instruction in the parish suffered accordingly.

The minister's job as teacher took a back seat for a second reason common to all the nonacademic professions. The modern professions, in general, have defined their practitioners as dispensers of technical services rather than as teachers. They have tended to restrict teaching to the academic professional alone. We assume that most professionals dispense technical services; they do not teach what they know. The modern university has structurally reinforced this segregation of teachers and scholars. It distinguishes graduate schools from professional schools—as though the traditional disciplines in the graduate schools do not prepare people for a *profession* and as though other professional schools are not obliged to prepare their students to *teach* what they know.

All the professions need to begin teaching again, but especially the ministry. The pastor's obligation to teach derives from the priestly, as well as the prophetic, office, particularly as the priestly office embraces the principle of the priesthood of all believers. The notion of the professional as the dispenser of technical services tends to establish a gulf between the dispenser and the receiver, like the gulf between benefactor and beneficiary, but teaching aims to share and therefore to empower those taught, a project that provides the intellectual base for the priesthood of all believers. At the same time, this emphasis on a teaching component in ministry enlarges the minister's role. Other professions, such as medicine, law, engineering, and accounting are, at a purely technical level, more interesting than ministry. The ministry acquires much of its intellectual challenge not through technique but through its teaching function, as ministers draw on an endlessly rich tradition and connect it with the full complexity of their parishioners' lives.

The priest teaches in the course of worship by reading and interpreting scripture. The ancient division of the worship service into the mass of the catechumens and the mass of the faithful accentuated teaching. The so-called learner's mass defined what remains to this day the basic Protestant worship service: prayers and reading and interpreting scripture in homily or sermon. But in the nineteenth century Protestant ministers often fell into the trap of romanticism and interpreted the worship service as a chance to lure the congregation into a religious experience. Thereafter ministers aimed chiefly for emotional impact; they became magicians of mood. No longer content to teach the faith and invite the congregation into the universe which the faith opens up, ministers relied increasingly on techniques to manipulate mood in sermon and song. This reduction of the faith to religious tonality substantively diminished what the church covenanted to offer in its worship: to testify to a Word full of grace and *truth*.

Ministers must also teach in fulfilling the "royal" office of service and this in two spheres. First, they teach intramurally to the church's own membership through pastoral counseling and care. As we have already noted, this teaching resembles the teaching which other counselors, such as doctors, lawyers, and social workers, perform. Second, ministers teach extramurally through the congregation's service to the world in the form of social action.

Social action of the conventional sort may or may not tangibly benefit its recipients, but it usually helps educate those performing the service. Middle-class social action often produces this important reflexive impact on those engaged in the action. The ghetto suffers from economic poverty, but the white, middle class suffers from impoverished experience. The city certainly needs social action to ameliorate the injustice afflicting the ghetto, but social action can also help the middle class break out of its suburban pale. For this reason, social action does not conform technically to the ideal of philanthropy insofar as the philanthropist tends to define himself exclusively as giver. Christian social action travels down a two-way street of giving and receiving. The giver receives more than she gives in giving to others.

In addition to its relatively nonpolitical social service, the church engages in politically oriented lobbying or demonstrations designed to influence public policies. Such activities can offer substantial teaching. However, when the church lobbies without teaching, it plays the game of interest-group politics. It lines up as a pressure group alongside other pressure groups in the society—allying with some and opposing others. Such lobbying demands that we classify the church as one more organized articulation of wants and interests alongside others—the oil kings, the Tobacco Institute, the unions, the AMA, the highway lobby, hairdressers—and value it for whatever money and power and votes and senators the churches may control.

At one level, the church should not hesitate to participate in interest-group politics if it would influence this, rather than some other, world and if its action will help make the world a little more humane and compassionate. At the same time, the church deprives itself of its full capacity to influence the society if it lobbies without educating. As a lobby, the church counts only to the degree that it controls votes and power. But politicians often discount this limited claim to power, knowing that church leaders (who appoint church lobbyists) have often failed to carry their lay congregations along on the policy at issue. Since neither the lobbyist nor the leadership speaks for members or controls their votes, the power of the lobby dwindles.

The church has also engaged in social action through movement-based activity targeting the media. The strategy has sometimes substituted placards and demonstrations for teaching. It exclaims rather than explains, frightening and angering rather than persuading the viewer and the reader. The action provides believers with the exhilaration of action but not always the satisfaction of success. Such movements constitute a kind of *glossolalia* on the right and the left, a speaking in tongues rather than in words that clarify and illumine the fateful choices of the day. A cry of pain gets attention, but it does not, in and of itself, reshape the community for remedy. Moans of pain and indignant ejaculations are idiotic in the literal Greek sense of that term. Unless combined with other modes of speech, they remain essentially opaque and unshareable.

Thus such statements can end up apolitical and antipolitical except in those rarest and briefest of apocalyptic movements when politics has been suspended in a country. Politics by exclamation point fails to open up a vision which all sorts and conditions of men and women can share. It despairs of politics as the art of acting in concert with others for the common good.

Theological conservatives, liberals, and radicals in the church differ profoundly in the content of their politics, but they tend to agree on its form when they rely either on lobbying and demonstrations alone. They pressure for action abstracted from the educational task of the church and the teaching responsibility of the ministry.

That educational task aims at two targets: one internal, the other, external. Internally, the church needs to educate its own members; it needs to acquaint the laity with a vision which connects its worship to social action. Lacking this educated laity, the leadership of the church finds itself in the embarrassing position of speaking for no one when it claims to speak as and for the church on a policy issue.

While the church must educate its laity, it cannot simply postpone action to that ever-receding date when the internal task of education is complete. The tasks of education and service supplement rather than succeed one another. To order them successively would effectively postpone action, and, in effect, it would deny the educational value of action. Liberation theology, to say nothing of the experience of our land grant universities, attests to the intricate connection between *praxis* and reflection. Social action often precedes reflection as its indispensable experiential base, just as surely as the action of worship preceded those creedal formulae of the early church that sought to illumine, interpret, and defend the church's worship.

Further, the church cannot restrict its education to its membership, as though it had no educational obligation to the society at large. By confining education to its members, the church would admit that outside that membership the church can act only as a pressure group—pushing but not persuading, pressing but not educating legislators and administrators in government. It could not act at the level of moral conviction and argument and social mission. When it genuinely attempts to educate other constituencies, the church shows some confidence that it can explain, clarify, and explicate both without and within.

However, the church must not address outsiders condescendingly as though the church wholly and alone transcends self-interest. A society dominated by the ethos of interest-group politics runs the danger of underestimating the degree to which men and women can act and think from moral conviction. Such a society assumes that the country is simply a bag of scratching factions. In its public actions, the church must respect others as having the capacity to behave as publics within the public at large.

Finally, scripture obliges the church to speak with and for those in a society who in their powerlessness cannot speak for themselves. The American Catholic Bishops Pastoral Letter on the Economic Order referred to this obligation as a "preferential option for the poor."[16] This special obligation derives from the scriptural insistence that God will hear the cry of the voiceless. The church must undertake the role of advocate and speak on behalf of those who otherwise have no voice. Of the voiceless there are always plenty. The anthropologist Mary Douglas has schematized the varying groups of the powerless: the repressed in hierarchical societies, the excluded from communitarian societies, and those hobbled at the starting gate in competitive, egalitarian societies. Whatever its prevailing form, a society usually finds a way of creating some who cannot voice their pain; and the church and its ministers must find its way to them.

The Minister As Leader

The three offices of Christ as priest, prophet, and king define the mission of the church and therefore the work of ministry. However, the form that professional leadership ought to take in a church defined by the several actions of worship, teaching, and service needs fleshing out. Just how ought church members understand the role of the minister as leader?

H. Richard Niebuhr and his colleagues in *The Purpose of the Church and Its Ministry*[17] sought a comprehensive metaphor for interpreting the minister's role. They found it in church architecture in the 1950s; namely, the expanding space for the church office that serves as the administrative hub of the enterprise. They chose the term "pastoral director" to underscore the modern minister's duties as they bear on the leadership of an active community. The pastor, in effect, functions as bishop of the congregation, directing the church as the priest of priests, the teacher of teachers, and the counselor to counselors.[18] That term nicely preserves the notion of a lay apostolate. Laypeople and the clergy ideally form a priesthood of all believers, a college of teachers, and a household of servants.

However, just how should one understand this executive responsibility? In the '50s Niebuhr and his colleagues distrusted a perverse understanding of the office of pastoral director as the "big-time operator," the busy, successful minister whose prestige increasingly lets him run the church officiously. (The big-time operator resembles the shepherd in Navajo lore who tells the sheep which weeds to eat.) Externally, the big-time operator enjoys celebrity, symbolizing and representing the church to the outside world and begins to buffer himself (it was overwhelmingly himself then) from parishioners.

However, even if one sought to refurbish today the title of pastoral director, the term probably reflects too closely the rapid and uncontentious expansion of the mainline churches in the '50s, with their already settled notion of which activities the church ought to pursue and which to neglect, and the pastor's role as overseer and manager of that pursuit. The image does not acknowledge the ensuing deep divisions within the church about the substance of those activities—liturgical, pedagogical, pastoral, and social activist. The recent chasm between leaders and congregations in the mainline church argues for the necessity of deliberation in the church's life and the minister's role as leader in helping the community clarify and define its ends.

What analogy or metaphor, then, helps illuminate the minister's leadership role, in preparing the church to set and achieve its proper public goals? Niebuhr's emphasis on the minister as *director* suggests the executive heads of organizations—voluntary associations, corporations, and the government—as an appropriate analogue. To cite the two extremes: the chief executive officer of a corporation and the executive director of a voluntary association offer obvious models. Both of these models mislead.

The Pastor As Chief Executive Officer offers the most powerful conception of leadership: the CEO leads the organization largely (but not exclusively) by command, expecting obedience. Traditional hierarchical societies depended heavily (but not exclusively) on government by fiat. I say not exclusively because, to the degree that the commands enjoyed the reinforcement of myth and ritual, they occurred within an explanatory context that made sense of them. They didn't simply bludgeon people with stark, bare imperatives. Nevertheless, authority moved from the top down often without either the formal or substantive need to persuade: the CEO sought not inward consent and collaboration, but obedience. This mode of leadership largely determines authoritarian governments and autocratically run corporations, where the effort to persuade usually comes as lagniappe, if at all, but does not constitute the *sine qua non* of the enterprise.

This type of leadership won't work in the church for reasons extrinsic and intrinsic to its life. As indicated in the chapter on the politician, government by command and obedience won't work in the setting of modern democracies that at least partly depend upon the consent of the governed. But, intrinsically, this type of governance cannot define churches that subscribe to a Lord who does not merely control externally but who rules the inward motions of the human spirit. Salvation infuses the whole person, including the deliberations of the heart. The notion of the CEO fails not simply for the practical reason that laypeople in democratic countries won't put up with it, but because it foreshortens deliberation and therefore diminishes the reach of the salvation to which the faith testifies.

The Pastor As Executive Director borrows from the weaker model of the professional who works today as paid chief of staff for voluntary communities in the United States. Most voluntary organizations look, not to their executive directors, but to their boards of trustees to guide the organization and exercise legislative, deliberative, or policy-making powers. A board, in turn, appoints a paid executive director or administrator to carry out the board's decisions and conduct its affairs. This model of the executive director largely defines the minister's role in Protestantism today. Whereas the CEO wields too much power and the wrong kind of power, the executive director usually draws on too little power, whether of command or persuasion. Executive directors tend to receive their marching orders from boards that operate above them. As executive director, the pastor becomes a "clerk of the works," the manager of an institution rather than the leader of a community.

The Pastor As Leader of a Republic comes in two political models: presidential and ministerial. The office of the president, in its U.S. political setting, combines several ingredients, one of which we may wholly reject as germane to the ministry—the president as commander-in-chief. The pastor commands no troops and imposes only minimal authority on subordinates. While executive management duties in the larger churches may be considerable, pastors handle relations to professional and even nonprofessional staff more effectively when they treat them as colleagues rather than subordinates. While the president of the nation must accept a very substantial responsibility as head of a hierarchy, the ministry at the parish level bears such responsibilities only marginally.

The power of persuasion offers the president his or her most substantive powers. In that respect, the powers of the presidential office seem more Athenian than Spartan. Sparta rested upon the power of tight-lipped command; Athens, upon the power of the word, the art of persuasion. In the absence of the word, a society relies on the noise of weapons, not on the meaning of words. Historians may make much of the tension and conflict between Jerusalem and Athens, but these two cities agree on the centrality of the word to a truly human cult and culture.

The presidential power of persuasion takes two forms: (1) exemplary/symbolic and (2) deliberative/legislative. The U.S. president thus tends to combine two roles which in the British parliamentary form of government remain quite separate: the king and the prime minister. The king traditionally symbolized the unity of the people, while the prime minister actively led the parliament (the house of words). The American president, however, functions both as king and as political leader. Unfortunately and only too often, the president's skill in performing his royal office has obscured his ineptitude in fulfilling his political office; or, conversely, his awkwardness as symbol has thwarted his political agenda.

These two powers of persuasion also appear in the pastorate. Whether one likes it or not, one cannot dismiss the importance of the pastor as a symbol. The religious, as well as the moral, life is caught as well as taught. The minister partly leads by example and certainly he or she undercuts the persuasiveness of that leadership when the pastor's deeds mock the pastor's words, when the pastor preaches confidence with a furrowed, worried brow, or personal charity with bitterness in the throat, or forgiveness, with a pouty and resentful look. As embarrassing episodes regularly remind the church, the scandalous minister distracts from the true scandal of the cross. Pulpit committees have good cause for concern about their minister as symbol.

And yet a huge danger lurks here. A symbol fails to point to the central figure in Christian faith unless it recognizes its inadequacy as a symbol. Only one person served wholly, fully, perfectly, and all-sufficiently as symbol, and that one rejected the description of himself as good, saying, "Why do you call me good? No one is good but God alone."[19]

Increasingly today the church may need to borrow from the second, ultimately more legislative, aspect of the president's office and recognize the responsibility of the pastor as prime minister. The minister must lead a deliberative community if a divided church is to equip itself for the performance of its public tasks of worship, education, and service. The manse, to be sure, is not 10 Downing Street, but the minister cannot lead as commander-in-chief nor as clerk of the works, nor as the white-haired or fair-haired symbol of piety. The title of prime minister leaves much to be desired, but the reality of the responsibility cannot be dodged. As prime minister—as leading (which is not to say ranking) minister among the ministering and the ministered to—the pastor must help guide the congregation and shape its policies, and, largely by persuasion. A church divided and troubled over its ends requires at least this much of its minister if, as a body, nourished by its worship and informed by its teaching, it equips itself for its own forms of service to the common good.

Notes

1. Edmund Burke, *Reflections on the French Revolution* (Chicago: Henry Regnery Company, Gateway Paperback, 1962), 71–72.

2. Joseph Pieper, *In Tune with the World: A Theory of Festivity* (New York: Harper & Row, 1973), 7.

3. Dietrich von Hildebrand, *Liturgy and Personality* (New York: Longmans, Green, 1943).

4. Luke 22:24–27.

5. In "The Catechism of the Revolutionist," variously attributed to Nechaev and Bakunin, the phrase "the revolutionary is a doomed man" is a repeated litany. "He must be ready to die at any moment." See Max Nomad, *Apostles of Revolution* (Boston: Little, Brown, 1939), 228. The Algerian F.I.N. (in its paper *El Mondjahid*, August 20, 1957) observes, "As soon as the terrorist accepts a mission, death enters his soul. Henceforth he has a rendezvous with death." Quoted in Roland Gaucher, *The Terrorists*, trans. Paula Spurlin (London: Secker & Warburg, 1968), 201.

6. *Time Magazine*, January 29, 1973.

7. Isaiah 40:15, 17.

8. Martin Luther King, *Loving Your Enemies, with Letter from a Birmingham Jail and Declaration of Independence from the War in Vietnam* (New York: A. J. Muste Memorial Institution, 1981).

9. For more on the neglect of the needy, see my book *A Catalogue of Sins* (New York: Holt, Rinehart, & Winston, Inc., 1967), 104–5.

10. Michel Foucault, *Madness and Civilization* (New York: Random House, Vintage Books, 1973), 68.

11. First John 4:10, 11.

12. Burke, *Reflections on the French Revolution*, 23.

13. Hannah Arendt, *On Revolution* (New York: Viking Press, 1965), 34–68.

14. John Calvin, *The Institutions of the Christian Religion* (London: James Clarke & Co., 1953), vol. 1, bk. 2, chap. 15, p. 427.

15. Jeremiah 6:14 and 5:31.

16. U.S. Catholic Bishops, "Economic Justice for All" in *Catholic Social Thought: The Documentary Heritage*, ed. David J. O'Brien and Thomas A. Shannon (Maryknoll, N.Y.: Orbis, 1992), par. 52, 85–95, 591, 599–601.

17. H. Richard Niebuhr with Daniel Day Williams and James M. Gustafson, *The Purpose of the Church and Its Ministry* (New York: Harper & Row, 1956).

18. Ibid., 83.

19. Mark 10:18.

Chapter 8

Professors

Credentialed for What?

John Adams believed that a constitutional republic needs, in addition to its religious institutions, a strong educational system to tame the corrosive power of self-interest in human affairs. Teachers, along with religious leaders and media experts, shape civic consciousness today. University professors also undertake the additional responsibility of preparing all professionals for their credentialing, including teachers themselves. This chapter will compare three different forms of higher education and teachers in each setting—the liberal arts college, the modern university, and the counterculture reaction to the university. It will explore the ways in which they have contributed to the current decline of civic consciousness and yet can help form the citizen. However, we can hardly turn to the academic profession in this final chapter expecting redemption. Academicians do not constitute a Gnostic elite disentangled from the ordinary mass of humanity, poised to redeem careerists or the society that nurtures them. Nevertheless academicians, as well as clergy, constitute an important potential counterpoint to the prevailing cultural forces that shape professionals and citizens alike.

The nineteenth-century liberal arts college in the United States largely flourished in the setting of small-town Protestant culture. American colleges took the colleges of Oxford and Cambridge Universities as the basic templates for liberal arts education in the New World. In America, however, each college sat on its own bottom as an independent institution and supplied its students with its own, rather than university, terminal degrees. Such colleges persisted into the twentieth century, partly on their own terms but more often as vestibules to research-oriented universities and their advanced technical degree programs.

Today's research universities in the United States have shifted from the British to a continental pattern of education. For several reasons,

Americans have looked to the French and German universities for their model. First, as an industrial democracy in the twentieth century, America needed to supply its corporations with large numbers of skilled persons. Professional students fit that social need. Further, America, a continent, built an educational system suited to a continental scale. America, largely a society of strangers rather than a community of friends, understandably opted for an educational system based on the impersonal credentials of a Ph.D. rather than on the informal networking of friends in an insular setting.

The counterculture protest against higher education in the '60s and '70s did not produce an enduring institution comparable to the liberal arts college or the research university. However, the protest period threw light on these more lasting institutions. It also illuminates persistent themes in American culture that affect civic consciousness. Thus the main body of this chapter will describe and compare these three differing visions of higher education on a grid covering the following issues: the educational ideal to which the institution aspires; the view of intelligence it presupposes; the kind of teacher it prizes; the social setting in which the institution offers education; the social destiny for which it prepares its students; the social virtues it tends to foster; and, finally, the understanding of vocation it espouses. The chapter will conclude by exploring the specific professional standards for research, teaching, and service that prevail in the dominant institution, the research university, as these standards shape the public responsibilities of teachers.

The Liberal Arts College

The Ideal. The liberal arts college with its roots in the nineteenth century has tended to define its ideal as the cultivation of the well-rounded person. To that end, it leads its students through a highly structured curriculum. While it requires its students to major in one of the several branches of knowledge, it emphasizes a common educational experience achieved either through distribution requirements or core courses which it expects all students to take. It offers students the goal of self-realization, but we misinterpret this goal if we think of it as wholly narcissistic. In tacitly accepting an idealist philosophy, educators believed that students could realize themselves only by connecting themselves effectively and fruitfully with the goals and purposes of the society at large.

Intelligence and the Teacher. By and large the liberal arts college interpreted (and still interprets) intelligence aesthetically. It acknowledges (and seeks to develop) the human capacity to taste and appreciate a wider range of goods and values than those available to instinctually driven animals. It argues that the study of art, music, math, history, and other conventional subjects in the curriculum broadens horizons. Clearly this emphasis on aesthetic intelligence in the nineteenth century did not escape criticism. In Europe, Soren Kierkegaard challenged morally and religiously the Hegelian philosophy that justified broadening intellectual horizons but often merely postponed moral decision making. A decision, Kierkegaard believed, etymologically signaled and morally required the cutting out of possibilities. Too much of life, he felt, floundered in the possible. Decisiveness requires us to be more than tasters and appreciators of a wide range of goods. In America, early inventors and industrialists also dismissed the importance of aesthetic intelligence. *Homo faber* did not need a college education and its broadening of horizons to succeed. Just how aesthetic intelligence might serve the social purposes of leadership eluded the practically oriented American frontiersmen.

The liberal arts college prized teachers for their wisdom and insight more than specialized expertise. Humanities teachers often served as intelligent amateurs. Independent incomes allowed some of them to teach for love rather than for money. Moreover, they did not need a Ph.D. in order to secure appointments in some of the most prestigious liberal arts colleges. The tradition of independence from formal credentials remained alive in the Eastern women's colleges as late as the 1950s. Students scrupulously called their teachers Mr., Miss, or Mrs., rather than doctor or professor, as a way of indicating that formal credentials and hierarchical rank did not of themselves generate that respect which a teacher might hope for.

British universities, which provided the template for the prestigious American liberal arts college, only recently and defensively began to grant the Ph.D. degree. Private tutorials and conversation at the faculty table and tearoom provided better evidence than formal credentials of talent, culture, and breeding. Those who held this ideal of the intelligent amateur into the 1950s viewed with some alarm the descent of degreed barbarians into modern academia: careerists, freshly armed with Ph.D.s, whose ambition gave them little sense of loyalty to the local institution which temporarily employed them. Of course, the ideal of the intelligent amateur often camouflaged those considerable professional deficiencies associated with the injustices and mediocrities of the old boys network.

Social Setting and Destiny. The nineteenth-century liberal arts college was small, collegially oriented, personal, and highly structured. (More recently, counterculturalists have valued smaller institutions on the grounds that they permit an unstructured, informal education.) The nineteenth-century liberal arts college did not associate smallness with informality. Both the education and student social life were highly structured; nevertheless they allowed for personal contact. The college formed a small community of familiar names functioning usually in the environment of a small town. Both faculty members and students gave their loyalties to the college as their significant social unit. Many of these institutions, of course, emerged under the sponsorship of the Protestant denominations whose chief strength lay in small-town America. Higher education in America, until the second third of the twentieth century, was largely a rural enterprise. Colleges afforded students the chance to escape from the small towns their parents led and to grow up in a social setting that nevertheless resembled the towns of their origin. Their education helped broaden their intellectual horizons and provided them with a partial antidote to the narrowing and restrictive tendencies of life in a small town. The enlargement of their sensibilities helped prepare students for a more spacious leadership role in the towns to which they would return.

One should not, however, so emphasize this social destiny of students as to overlook the importance of the liberal arts college in producing graduates who eventually helped lead America in its transition to a modern industrial state. A young student at Oberlin College developed in his chemistry class the electrolytic process indispensable to the production of aluminum. He eventually helped establish this important sector of American industrial life and thereby symbolized the social importance of the liberal arts college in preparing for the country's next stage of development.

Social Virtues and Vocation. The college largely relied on a consensus on ends and goals that shaped its life. Reflecting this consensus, the president of the college often offered a course in ethics for all graduating seniors. This arrangement may have produced courses badly taught but it also created an important symbol. Ethics did not contract into a merely technical subspecialty in religious or philosophical studies; it served rather to crown the student's education.

Various factors contributed to the possibility of this consensus in the liberal arts college. The college often owed its existence and support to a specific religious tradition. Even as the college distanced itself from its specific religious origins, its faculty members had not burrowed so far into various areas of specialization as to lose their sense of themselves as a *collegium*. Faculty members identified with the college rather than thought of the college as a temporary location from which they pursued their eventual advance in a discipline. Further, although explicitly religious values lost their binding power to unify the college, faculty members informally agreed upon a list of the "greats," the *auctores*, an acquaintance with whom defined the truly educated person. These authors constituted a quasi-religious, sacred canopy under whose sheltering presence Western civilization would presumably continue to flourish.

On the whole the consensus which the liberal arts college presupposed fostered a sense of vocation which embraced more than the graduate's job. The ideal of well-roundedness correlated with a vocation that included additional responsibilities as a spouse, parent, citizen, and participant in voluntary communities. Liberally educated graduates would reflect a *pleroma* of shared values that let them play out a variety of social roles within the setting of the common good. So went the ideal.

The Twentieth-Century Positivist University

The fate of the president's course in ethics illuminates the shift from the nineteenth-century liberal arts college to the twentieth-century positivist university. No longer the crown of an education, ethics vanished into a subspecialty in formal philosophy and even there, strictly speaking, ethicists could not properly deal with normative questions. At best ethicists could report on the history of ethics or analyze the nature of moral discourse. They did not offer serious judgments about professional practice since the positivist university rejected moral reflection and nurture as part of its mission.

Normative questions did not fit into the classroom. Professors could teach facts but not values. The positivist university generated disciplines that deemed it their special vocation and glory to avoid distracting questions of value and utility in their disinterested pursuit of the truth. Values express only subjective, emotive preferences. They do not inhere in things; we read them into things. Spongy and slippery, they do not deserve a place at the lectern. The faculty member cannot judge values without sinking into subjective propaganda and advocacy. In his essay "Science as a Vocation," Max Weber both described and recommended this restriction of the university to purely factual, objective inquiry. Weber, in effect, asks: do you want to be a leader or a teacher? A demagogue or a pedagogue? If you want to be a teacher or a pedagogue, then you must hang up your values on a peg in the cloakroom outside the classroom along with your hat and coat.[1]

This ascetic restriction of the university to purely factual inquiry dominated the American universities during their manic phase of expansion after World War II through the mid-1960s. While this ideal did not altogether eclipse the function and task of the traditionally conceived liberal arts college, it increasingly shaped the ideology behind the various disciplines within such colleges and limited the purposes of the professional schools. The professions moved into the university for their education at approximately the same time that many faculty members began to exclude discussions of value from the university's classrooms.

The commitment of the university faculty to the ideal of objectivity justified itself socially on the grounds that the acquisition of objective knowledge eventually produces a skilled person. Peddled in the marketplace, these skills enable graduates to pay for those goods which aesthetic intelligence enjoys. Ultimately, the objectivist creed of faculty members encouraged careerism in its students. Faculty members believed that questions of value could not surface in the classroom without hardening into propaganda or advocacy. Teachers can transmit factual knowledge, which eventually yields power, but they cannot pose questions about its responsible uses. Ends reflect only subjective preferences. Since ends cannot claim objective public status, graduates can treat their knowledge as a purely private possession, which they can manage as they please without fearing criticism.

Intelligence and the Teacher. The modern university has concentrated on cultivating technical intelligence. While aesthetic intelligence enlarges the student's capacity to enjoy a wider range of goods, technical intelligence hones skills useful in producing goods—largely economic goods. Weber observed that education cannot help decide which ends one ought to choose and serve; it can only supply objective information important in choosing means useful (or inconvenient) in reaching various ends. The university can help develop technical reason—reason in the service of preferences; it cannot sort out the noble from the ignoble, the worthy from the spurious among these preferences. Technical reason can illuminate the paths we travel but not the destinations which we choose. It leaves bare feeling or preference to choose our ends, goals, or values.

The standard of the formally credentialed professional has replaced the liberal arts ideal of the intelligent amateur. The United States made this transition during the 1950s. Young ambitious teachers recognized that rapid promotion required the leverage of offers from outside institutions; and publications attracted those offers. Increasingly, loyalty shifted from the college, where teachers worked, to the organized discipline to which they belonged. Disciplinary leaders at the graduate schools determined job offers, and therefore even job promotions in the institution from which one drew one's salary. While academics read David Reisman's *The Lonely Crowd* and viewed with alarm the dominance of the other-directed person in American society, academic institutions themselves became increasingly other-directed. The reputation and self-esteem of a faculty depended upon the approval of gatekeepers working elsewhere in the several disciplines. Decisions about promotion traditionally depended upon the criteria of research, teaching, and service, but, inevitably, the emphasis on external peer review meant that the primary *desideratum* for the appointment, retention, and promotion of the academic depended upon published research.

The meaning of research itself changed substantially to an industrial model. Researchers manufacture and wholesale; but mere teachers serve as retailers. The teacher imports, packages, and sells what others have produced. Of course, the specialization of knowledge within disciplines has led to extraordinary progress in some fields. Clearly in the sciences, but even in the humanities, thoughtful reflection on the detail sometimes allows a new theory to surface. But, on the whole, specialization in the humanities led to the miniaturizing of knowledge. To demand that graduate students mimic their colleagues in the laboratories and write a thesis on a novel subject only too often forced them out into the desert of the trivia. Further, ambitious young academics, pressured to make tenure within five to six years, could not afford to cultivate a large idea that might not sprout, much less mature, within that time. They had to choose a manageable thesis topic in order to convert it into a book, or at least a series of brief, publishable articles. Apologists justified this period of indentured servitude by claiming that after five to six years, tenure would now give the academic the security to pursue a major idea across a life-time. But meanwhile, training imposed on academics made it more and more difficult to undertake a more ambitious topic. Too much crawling to achieve tenure made it difficult to walk and run once it had been won.

Social Setting and Destiny. The large scale of the modern university results from the extraordinary variety of disciplinary subspecialties that have developed both in its professional schools and in its own version of the liberal arts college. Within that setting, the institution offers a highly structured education, though, apart from basic distri-bution requirements, departments largely control that structure. While professionals think of themselves as colleagues, the institution, as a whole, arranges itself hierarchically. The hierarchical erodes the collegial. Hierarchical distinctions obtain not only between different ranks of faculty members, but, just as important, between faculty and students. The university assumes a greater gulf between faculty mem-bers and students than traditionally separated them in liberal arts col-leges, where the two groups usually came from similar social and cultural backgrounds.

The university has increasingly restricted the scope of its responsi-bility to its educational mission. It has largely shed responsibility for the student's personal and social life, renouncing the role of *in loco parentis*. This renunciation fits into its general orientation to the future rather than the past. While the liberal arts college tended to initiate students into the community and culture of their birth, the university prepared them for the economic and organizational iden-tities which they would assume on graduation. In the language of the German sociologists, the university is *gesellschaftlich* rather than *gemeinschaftlich*. It orients not to origins but to destination, not to past tradition but to future possibility. Less a community than an organi-zation, the institution specializes and fragments and often provides no more than a site, a campus, on which many kinds of educational and research enterprises happen to intersect. Thus it often relies on nonsubstantive activities to provide a kind of surrogate for that intel-lectual unity which it lacks. A new class of specialists, athletes, pro-vides the university with liturgical forms that gather the community together and thereby substitute for the unity it lacks at more substan-tive intellectual and spiritual levels.

The university helps provide students with their own complicated social transition from *Gemeinschaft* to *Gesellschaft*, from status in a community to some kind of future identity in an organization. The latter identity depends partly on the acquisition of formal credentials but also upon the acquisition of a social style that helps one cope with the rigors of anonymity and at least temporary marginality. The social style that the nineteenth-century, largely rural, liberal arts college encouraged relied heavily on the rhetoric and speech of understatement. In small towns, self-advertisement tends only to isolate the advertiser and proves that he does not belong, that he possesses no status. A more anonymous twentieth-century university (and society at large) relies more heavily on verbal hustling. It emphasizes and develops skills in self-display, as one attempts to silhouette oneself against a dark horizon. The application forms, sorority and fraternity selections, job interviews, and the verbal free-for-all of the beer party and the cocktail party require the cultivation of promotional skills.

Social Virtues and Vocation. The university does not claim to possess an extensive set of shared values. Indeed, the university fit itself neatly into an America which increasingly depended upon four mechanisms, rather than a specific set of shared values, to allow the country to function without requiring too much virtue of its citizens. Those mechanisms, noted earlier, include the U.S. Constitution, which allows people of varying interests to pursue their diverse goals within a legal framework of checks and balances that keeps various factions within the society from tearing each other to pieces; the mechanism of the marketplace, which allows people to pursue their own self-interests exclusively, and yet, through marketplace exchanges, to contribute indirectly to the well-being of all; and the mechanism of the large-scale organization, the corporation, which mobilizes purely technical skills and provides economies of scale which increasingly crowd out the ma-and-pa stores and dominate the marketplace. Finally, the country has relied on the university as a mechanism which develops, in young, unformed people, skills salable to those large-scale organizations which increasingly dominate the marketplace within a constitutional framework. Together, these mechanisms allowed a highly pluralistic and interest-group-dominated society to work together despite substantive differences about values among its citizens.

This vision of American social life as processual emphasizes what we have called the secondary, rather than the primary or substantive, virtues. One needs less those virtues that flow from shared goals than those virtues that will contribute to the process of reaching whatever goals people choose. Thus the university tends to encourage and inculcate virtues required for the attainment of skills: sufficient stamina to stick to a program of long, arduous, and sometimes boring professional training and sufficient self-discipline to defer personal gratification for the training's sake. The university and the society at large also foster the secondary virtues of cooperativeness upon which the successful operation of a large-scale organization depends. Finally, while the university, through its regularized grading standards, does not encourage in its students (any more than in its faculty members) unusual, heroic, or extraordinary achievement, it does emphasize reliable performance, precisely those habits so convenient in large-scale organizations whose specialization of functions demands that all workers contribute smoothly and predictably to the operation of the whole.

In this setting the traditional vocation transmogrifies increasingly into a career. One orients less to the common good than to one's own private ends, achieved and monetarily sustained through a career. Students' single-minded devotion to their own careers, however, does not mean that their lives lack public significance. A kind of fit exists between the skills which the young acquire for their own private reasons and those which an industrial and post-industrial society needs to fulfill its public purposes. Further, since a market economy establishes an ontological break in identity and dignity between the employed and the unemployed, the acquisition of a marketable skill gives to the careerist some sense of belonging to a public and thus bestows a limited public significance upon his or her life. Membership ranks first in social goods not only because it supplies the member with a claim on other goods but because it is a good in itself. As indicated earlier, students in the universities tended to drift from their origins. In this respect, they resembled the late-nineteenth-century immigrants who boarded steerage-class ships, leaving Europe for this country, to escape the limitations and misery of origins. Twentieth-century students converged on the universities as the new ships that would carry them out of the city ghettos and working-class neighborhoods. They hoped to acquire a university degree, a passport that would license them to move, with some kind of recognizable public identity, from city to city and from city to suburbs in America.

Still, the fulfillment of public purposes and goals in a careerist society depends excessively upon the degree to which they further private agendas. The virtues of cooperativeness suffice only as long as no fundamental disputes erupt over the ends collaborators pursue. Universities could neglect the issues of public life and goals in the late

'40s and '50s in the afterglow of shared national purpose during the war years, but later, two issues divided society in varying ways: civil rights and the war in Vietnam.

The Counterculture Protest

The third moment in higher education did not reflect or create an institution but pitted itself against the prevailing institutions of its time. Briefly characterized, the counterculture movement sought immediate relationships to people, power, truth, and morals and rejected all mediated relations in these spheres. Its quest for immediate relationships to people made it suspect all large-scale organizations and their hierarchies. It rejected the constraints on people that traditional roles imposed. Its quest for immediate relationships to power led it to affirm participatory democracy, as opposed to representative government. Communes preferred to do business as a committee of the whole rather than to trust delegated authorities, working subcommittees, or deputized representatives to mediate. Such traditional representative devices, the movement believed, dangerously distanced any given gathering of people from the wielders of its power. The quest for an immediate relation to truth led to a profound suspicion of the liberal arts college and the positivist university. The college had depended upon tradition to mediate truth, the university, upon the expert. Finally, the counterculture's conviction that we can immediately and self-evidently relate to morals led it to emphasize the virtue of moral indignation which animated both its militant engagement in politics and its subsequent disapproving withdrawal from working politics.

The Ideal. The protest movement rejected the received ideals of the well-rounded self and the skilled self. Instead, the movement, in its political form, aimed at raising and, in its religious form, at altering, consciousness. Religious enthusiasm ultimately tinged both aims. In effect, the movement associated authentic education with a kind of alchemy. The traditional liberal arts college did not expect or hope to achieve a radical transformation of the self. It simply aimed to help the self fulfill its already established capacities. The positivist university expected to develop individual skills which would transform the external circumstances of life, but not the self's interior life. The goals, however, of raising consciousness and altering consciousness aimed much higher spiritually. In its political version, the movement held that authentic education must lift students above the false con-sciousness which oppressive institutions impose. In its religious ver-sion, the movement resorted to meditative techniques, which help devotees transcend the common sense polarities of I and Thou, sub-ject and object, self and world, human and natural, cosmic and divine. An alteration of consciousness requires moving beyond the surface polarities which engage the superficial self to the deep self, where the self dissolves and merges into the world and the divine. The specific religious inspiration for this ideal came from the East rather than the West and rejected that Western distinction from which so many other basic distinctions and polarities derive: the distinction between the Creator and the creature.

Intelligence and the Teacher. Critics of the political counterculture objected to its hostility to the intellect. But its anti-intellectualism (more posture than program) rejected the classical confidence in wis-dom and despised the positivist reduction of reason to purely techni-cal reason. From the perspective of student radicals, purely technical intelligence served those patently false goals which the society pur-sued and for which the university assiduously prepared its graduates. Further, the evils of the Vietnam War and racial oppression were self-evidently wrong. The immediacy and self-evidence of moral truth made the radicals disdain the convoluted training of technical intelli-gence. Young teachers emphasized the cognitive significance of the feelings and criticized the objectifying tendencies of technical reason, which emulated academically the bombing at a distance which occurred in the war. The religious version of the counterculture movement emphasized not simply the myopia of technical intelli-gence but the inherent limitations of discursive reason. The propen-sity of reason to analyze, define, and circumscribe removed it from that oceanic union to which the religious person in the counter-culture aspired.

The counterculture both dethroned and elevated the teacher. On the one hand, it condemned the positivist ideal of the teacher as spe-cialist. Placards in the French student protest of 1968 put it simply: eliminate the expert. A few teachers complied by handing over the choices of topics in course syllabi to students. On the other hand, the ideals of a raised consciousness or an altered consciousness cast a few teachers in the role of *guru*. This role bestowed upon the teacher a more redemptive significance and power than either the intelligent amateur or the specialized professional displayed.

Social Setting and Destiny. Counterculture students objected to the huge size of the positivist university and celebrated small as beautiful. They pressed either for a relatively private, tutorial, custom-made education within the confines of the larger institution or created a contrapuntal free university—small, unstructured, and relieved of the demeaning burden of a grading system and the other controls upon which a meritocracy depends. This vision of a free college in a small-scale setting differed from the ideal liberal arts college in that the vision also opted for the unstructured. One needs to distinguish, however, between the first and second stages of any reaction against structure. As the free churches long ago discovered in their protest against highly ritualized liturgical and institutional forms, the original charismatic impulses quickly settle into their own set of routines. Further, the protest of young faculty members against a highly bureaucratized university generated its own ironical outcome. Young Turks, suspicious of the academic bureaucrats, proceeded to establish more and more procedures, the immediate purpose of which was to hem in administrators. But these new procedures further elaborated bureaucracy. Thus bureaucracy happily metastasized through the contributions of its sworn enemies.

One also needs to distinguish between the two stages in the counterculture's conception of the student's destiny. In the first stage, student radicals repudiated the very notion of social destiny. The movie *The Graduate* dramatized that repudiation, suggesting that education, if successful, should not lead to that plastic promised land which its middle-class sponsors offered. Haight-Ashbury and other gathering places of the flower children symbolized this repudiation and disturbed the parents who saw it leading the young to a personal cul de sac. The rejection of our military-industrial civilization led the radicals to a romance with the rural, a preference for the organic to the plastic, the self-sufficient to the specialized. But the parents' nightmare persisted: the flower children would become cut-flower children.

In its second stage, of course, the apparently permanent, irreversible repudiation weakened. Absolute rejection, for many, turned into a merely temporary moratorium. Many radicals eventually finished professional degree programs and joined the upwardly mobile in a society over which Ronald Reagan could not have presided so readily had not substantial numbers of their generation returned to conventional careers. The astute social critic Richard Sennett anticipated this development in his early essay *The Uses of Disorder*.[2] There he observed that the apparent turbulence and anomie of the young covers, at deeper levels, a fixing of forms and attitudes. More than one powerful anti-authoritarian of the sixties has turned out not to oppose authority as such, but rather simply to wait, impatient to exercise it himself.

Social Virtues and Vocation. The social virtues that the counterculture fostered resembled those which flourished in the left wing of the Reformation in the sixteenth century. The virtue of moral indignation energized the political militants. The Vietnam war, self-evidently wrong, offered no grounds for either patience or tolerance toward those who supported it. The quest for communal purity motivated the religious version of the cultural protest. In a sense, the assumption of innocence and purity underlay the radical responses of both militancy and withdrawal.

Attention to the virtues alone, however, would miss an equally important way in which the protest movement jarred the liberal arts college, the positivist university, and the entire society. It assaulted prevailing manners. Edmund Burke once observed that the French Revolution's breach with decorum—its challenge to manners— offended the Western world more than its moral and political ideas. The same might be said of the '60s. Manners serve the very useful social function of partially veiling ourselves even as we reveal ourselves to others. Social style acts as a fig leaf that spares us the chill of total exposure. The new culture movement began appropriately with the free speech riots at Berkeley. Students assaulted the nervous system of their elders less by their ideas than by their hair length, their ragtag clothing, unwashed bodies, littered pads, noisy music, and ready resort to the rich loam of four-letter Anglo-Saxon words. Shared manners as much as shared virtues give coherence to a civilization; but the radicals no longer took the manners of the bourgeois West to be decent clothing but rather indecent hypocrisy.

A sense of vocation often develops a specific orientation to time. The liberal arts college oriented chiefly to the past, to transmit a valued tradition, to infuse and shape the present and future. The positivist university looked chiefly to the future and sought those transformations of the world and one's own life which the controlling power of technical intelligence makes possible. The counterculture dove headlong into the present, earning its epithet as the "Now" generation. It rejected the past, certainly the past the positivist university mediated. It also gagged on the future which political leadership offered the nation—winning the war—and the personal fulfillment which the profitable career would place within reach.

We need not rehearse here the rejection of the rejection, in which so many students of the current generation and their elders have enthusiastically participated, as they have returned to the mercantile, aesthetic, and technical ideals now proffered by the college and the university.

The Professional Standards
of Research, Teaching, and Public Service

While we have located the teacher within the aims of the liberal arts college, the university, and the counterculture, we have not yet detailed the specific received standards of teaching, research, and service nor how these standards bear on the public responsibilities of the academic professional, particularly in the pacemaking institution at the beginning of the twenty-first century, the research university.

Conventionally, distinguished researchers discover the truth and teachers share it. In addition, professors offer varying services to the employing institution, to the profession (the discipline), and to external constituencies in the society.

Research, teaching, and service—these three—but the greatest of these is research. Published research produces results that peers and superiors can see and measure. In-house service, such as student advising and committee work, commands the least prestige (a dean at a major university referred to it as donkey work); and teaching is often sucked into the dismissive quicksand category of "service" courses. However, prestige can often accrue for external service in the form of contract work for the government, corporations, or foundations and through consultancies and private practice. Such service generates substantial income and often funds research.[3]

We will not progress very far in understanding the distinctive public service of the academic profession if we think of service as a third activity, marginally added to research and teaching. If the academic life is a profession, then at its deepest level and in its central activities of research and teaching, it must offer a service. We must begin, then, with research and teaching and ask how they serve the community. What is the distinctive service of the academic profession in the total range of professions?

All other helping professions, formally and ideally considered, purport to serve the common good by drawing on theoretical knowledge to address and resolve a client's practical problems without violating the common good. Materially considered, the professions differ in the practical problem they address, the body of knowledge they invoke, and the benefits they deliver. These differences distinguish law, medicine, ministry, and other professions.

The academic profession differs formally from the others in that it attempts to discover and transmit truth; it does not itself directly apply truth to a client's practical problems. The discovery and transmission of the truth constitutes the academy's primary service to the common good. The university cannot defect or flag from this primary task if it would serve the society well and if it expects and deserves the society's support. This definition of its task does not deny that the university has an intellectual interest in the nature of applications. Knowledge, which is its domain, includes the knowledge of applications, especially in professional schools; but, even there, the knowledge of applications so acquired is justified by its contribution to its primary mission: to discover the truth and transmit it. This mission distinguishes the academic from all other professionals, who apply knowledge to the clients' needs.

We misunderstand discovery and transmission if we limit the discovery of knowledge to published research and its transmission to teaching. Transmission takes two forms, of which teaching is but one. The other is published writing. When we separate writing from teaching, we obscure the fact that writing *teaches* to a *wider* audience; it creates a classroom without walls. However, too many academics write to impress leaders in their fields and not to teach a wider audience of inquirers. Much academic writing is filial rather than collegial; academics aim their prose *upward* to gatekeepers rather than *outward* to inquirers and peers and thus vitiate it as teaching.

Unfortunately, our educational system engraves the habit of filial writing very early on the malleable student. Students write papers and exams to impress their professors with what they know rather than to teach colleagues who may know less than they do. The graduate school seminar, in which siblings compete for the attention of the professor, illustrates the point. The seminar paper embodies a private and filial transaction between the student and the professor. Other students listen dully to an often unintelligible paper, waiting resignedly for the seminar session in which they will in their turn perform. Rarely does a student treat the session as a colloquium in which she has responsibility for teaching her colleagues well. Cumulatively, academicians have lost the sense that writing and teaching are but two aspects of sharing discoveries.

We also err—at least in the humanities—when we separate sharply the task of discovering knowledge from the social tasks of teaching and writing. Teaching and writing complete the process of discovery. We understand them better when we hyphenate them: research-writing and research-teaching. When scientists share the results of their research through publication, the work of discovery lies behind them. They seldom make new discoveries in the course of writing up their reports. James D. Watson closes his extended account of the long, exciting, pressured research that led him and his colleague to discover the double helix code with a brief report on the task of writing the results for publication. He wrote up the results with astonishing speed because Watson and Crick were only packaging what they had already discovered; writing did not itself contribute to the work of discovery.[4]

But in the humanities, and often in the social sciences, we cannot separate the content of research from its social form. The interconnection makes teaching and writing more difficult and rewarding enterprises for the humanities than "reporting" on research for the sciences. Writing and teaching are partly heuristic acts which do not merely package but help discover the content of research. The efforts to teach and write continue the process of discovery. They shift an inquiry in unexpected directions and open up a subject in unforeseen ways. Through these social activities, scholars in the humanities not only give to but receive from their audience, as they complete the task of discovery.

Scientists and social scientists distinguish between applied and basic research in justifying their service to society. Applied research claims to offer direct instrumental benefit to society, or rather, to particular constituencies within society. As an instrumental good, applied research cannot escape the possibility of regulation by law or moral censure. The very word "instrumental" suggests that this research must look beyond itself for vindication. If it takes credit for benefits, then it must also accept responsibility for harms wrought in either the course of the research or its application. Applied research must also answer questions of justice or equity, since harms and benefits do not always fall equally on all members of a society.

Basic research in the sciences can also justify itself, though with more difficulty than applied research. Scientists must assert the value of the disinterested pursuit of knowledge that does not promise immediate, specific benefits. Even so, basic research can justify itself in a cognitive culture. If all knowledge pointed to immediate, and thus defined, instrumental good, the future would lose some of its openness. Some thoughtful genetic engineers have cautioned against manipulating the gene pool too closely to promote some traits and eliminate others, on the grounds that, in the long run, the human race needs diversity in the gene pool. By analogy, the human race needs diversity in its research pool, a diversity not filtered too finely to promote only obvious and immediate profit. The society has a stake in pressing the human mind to its limit on fundamental problems, even when no obvious payoff is in the offing.

The financing of research today increases the emphasis on applied research, especially of interest to private investors, such as pharmaceutical houses, giant agribusinesses, and the chemical and electronics industries. While the federal government bankrolled much research since World War II, devices, such as peer review procedures and the recovery of indirect costs on government grants for other discretionary uses, preserved some increase of independence for both the several academic disciplines and for the university. The tight partnering today of universities with corporations in their research projects tends to convert universities into the intellectual arm of private interests. This privatization of inquiry (and the intellectual properties issuing therefrom) threatens to weaken the traditional commitment of a university to the commonwealth of learning.

The commercialization of inquiry also affects the clock by which the university lives in the conduct of its inquiry. Educationally, universities have traditionally lived by the seasons. Time unfolds organically. Students grow in knowledge. They are more like plants that need tending than products to be engineered. Research ideas take seed and mature. But the sponsoring of research and education by partners driven by mechanical time and quarterly bottom lines moves the university in a very different direction, away from that reflective pause which traditionally marked discovery.

As compared with the sciences, scholars in the humanities (and in the humanistic aspects of the social sciences) enjoy few opportunities to demonstrate their social utility. Advocates for research in the natural sciences point to world-transforming products and technologies that issue from the laboratory. Apologists for the social sciences, with John Dewey showing the way, try to emulate them and establish a link between the social sciences and the practical problems citizens face in a democracy. They justify asking support for their various investigations in the wider social laboratory as a public service.

The humanities offer no obvious, comparable, direct payoffs. The humanities do not bake bread. Some scholars in the humanities compensate by foregoing (or disdaining) any attempt to vindicate themselves to a wider audience. They proudly uphold the liberal arts as unfettered by considerations of social utility. They point to the historical link of the humanities with wisdom and an aristocratic culture, and, like some tattered remnants of the aristocracy, have grown accustomed, in academic circles, to genteel and sometimes philosophic poverty.

However, the humanities can justify themselves to society. They contribute to a society in at least three ways: by honing critical intelligence, by cultivating the civic self, and by preparing graduates to be good teachers of what they know. In laying out the importance of these three contributions, we need to return to the liberal arts college and the modern positivist university, with a view both to what they have accomplished and to their unfinished agendas. In returning to that unfinished agenda, we bring back modern professionals—beleaguered rulers—to the source of their power and shaping ideals.

Reconnecting Higher Education and Public Life

It would be misleading to suppose that either the college or the university wholly disconnected itself from preparing students for public life. The nineteenth-century liberal arts ideal of the well-rounded person had a civic as well as a personal justification. Students emerging from colleges expected to provide leadership in small-town America. But, in time, the ideal lost its tie in a changed social order. Graduates left the small town for a large, anonymous, mass society. Thus the merely well-rounded person sank into obscurity unless he or she acquired technical skills useful to a rapidly developing industrial and urban society. The ideal of the broadly educated person lost its tie to civic life. It came to describe merely generally educated persons, who knew something about a lot of things that contributed to their quality of life. It signified a capacity for savoring, but it required at length some marketable skills to finance a privately defined happiness.

The twentieth-century positivist university also served a general public need, even though its students pursued skills that would serve their private happiness. It trained people in the expertise that allowed them to work in the huge bureaucracies of the Ford Motor Company, the Pentagon, IBM, and the hospitals and law firms of the country, whose scale and structure the university increasingly emulated. Further, the positivist university dramatically broadened and diversified the population that could work for a university education and thus offered a much wider range of Americans the chance to acquire a stronger public identity and social and economic mobility.

Neither of these goals of education—the well-rounded and the skilled person—deserves disdain. But the quality-of-life and the careerist arguments, taken together, are today too narcissistic, and self-preoccupied, to provide a sufficient and worthy aim of education. The counterculture produced a kind of institutional spasm that reflexively acknowledged the deficiency of those aims. Yet its reaction against a too narrow understanding of the intelligence often led to anti-intellectualism instead of the recovery of substantive reason. And its reaction against a politics gone awry in its commitments and goals too often led to the protests and withdrawals of the monadic self instead of the recovery of the civic self.

Higher education can fully contribute to public life and happiness only if our institutions of higher learning and the humanities within them recover three ancient purposes of a liberal education. They can recover these purposes because all three purposes have had their continuing, though muted, influence in the university, even during its burgeoning positivist years.

The university needs first to recover its vocation to cultivate critical intelligence. The word "critical" has its roots in the Greek verb meaning to judge or decide. Thus, the task of criticism in the intellectual life has included judging worth and value in politics, art, economics, religion, philosophy, and morals. Operational intelligence tells one how to get from here to there; critical intelligence questions whether the there is worth getting to. It asks what recently and thuddingly has been called the question of values. Critical intellect must undertake normative as well as descriptive inquiry. This is precisely the activity of the intellect called for in professional life but deemed by many professionals in the academy to be merely subjective and emotive, and, therefore, an inappropriate intrusion in the classroom.

The professional schools especially need to employ critical intelligence, that is, to reflect on ends, goals, and values. Behind many of the quandaries in medicine—whether to pull the plug or not, whether to tell the truth or not—loom critical questions about the basic goal of medicine. What defines the end of medicine? an unconditional fight against death? the relief of suffering? or the pursuit of health? What basic goals should shape the legal system? Does the law find its ultimate justification in the values of truth and justice or in the some-times opposing value of order? On these questions turn the justifica-tion and the potential reform of the adversary system. What defines the goal of the corporation? Milton Friedman's maximizing profit? Or a somewhat more socially complicated notion of economic per-formance at a profit? What defines the common good for the politi-cal leader? The overlapping interests of a coalition of interest groups? Or something more?

To the degree that the university ignores these questions, it threatens the professions with moral impoverishment, as they turn out techni-cians incapable of, or hostile to, critical thinking, and it also dimin-ishes the university itself by stunting its intellectual life. The university is precisely the site where critical inquiry should pose alternative goals for the society at large and the professions in particular. We concede too little to the range of the human mind and grant too little to the capacity of the university to organize itself for civil and fruitful discourse, if we assume that the only alternative to objective inquiry is subjective advocacy. Critical inquiry is not only licit but required in the institution devoted to cultivating the whole human mind.

The need for critical inquiry shows up especially today in the rela-tions of the university to the media—that alternative teaching authority in the modern world. So far the universities have responded to the media instrumentally—either by exploiting the additional capabilities afforded them by the computer and the Internet or by developing huge academic programs in advertising and public rela-tions designed to turn out skilled graduates for jobs in those sectors of the economy. The universities have not as fully developed courses in film criticism and media studies that might help break the lifelong hold and thrall of the media on the minds of young people and on the politics of the nation. (Lacking the public forum of the European film club, Americans usually watch their movies in solitary devotion before a screen in a darkened theater or in the privacy of their homes before TV, with little discussion and criticism to follow.) Few forums exist to convert media watching from the privately mesmerizing and stupefying into a public occasion with critical intelligence on the alert. The university will not fully recover its teaching authority unless it helps students pass from being private consumers into public participants in disputation and debate.

The university has traditionally undertaken this ancient, related, and continuing responsibility to cultivate the civic self. The university must claim its heritage, dating back to the Greeks, that accepted as part of its most comprehensive purpose the cultivation of citizens skilled in the art of acting in common with others for the common good.

In the United States we have democratized education, but, at the same time, to our own disadvantage as a people, we have also privatized it and justified it for what it can do in enlarging merely private opportunities. This accomplishment is salutary, but extraordinarily fragile. Private opportunity, in the long run, flourishes only through healthy institutions, and healthy institutions depend upon citizens who acknowledge some sense of public identity and responsibility. When the social covenant weakens and the professional thinks of himself as an opportunist alone, uninvested with a public trust, then our institutions suffer, and people get hurt when their institutions are hurting. Both by its ancient traditions and by the terms implied by its modern social support, the university cannot deny its public responsibilities and the civic destiny of its trained professionals.

A strategy of tacking onto the university curriculum courses in civics and ethics or courses that strain for relevance would trivialize this responsibility. Cultivating the citizen requires a more fundamental change in the university, a change that connects it throughout with critical inquiry. Ultimately, nurturing the civic self and encouraging critical inquiry overlap and reinforce one another if value questions are not merely matters of private, subjective preference. To engage in critical inquiry teases the mind out of the bottle of private preference and opens it out toward a community of inquirers. It makes a person publicly accountable and responsible for his judgments and decisions and assumes these judgments to be interpretable in civil discourse. The classroom is a public place; the library, a commonwealth of learning; critical inquiry among peers, a kind of parliament of the human mind. Such inquiry is indispensable to a professional life that has more than technical services to offer for personal gain.

The well-being of a democratic society and its citizens depends upon the vitality of this kind of reasoning in its common life—in its politics, its work life, and personal morals. It requires taking positions and discovering that rejected alternatives do not go away. They pop up in the arguments of one's spouse, in the criticisms of colleagues, and in the views of the political party not one's own. The university can hardly be removed from all this: It is exactly the place where the value conflicts of the age ought to surface and be subjected to reasoned discourse and debate.

At the same time, this justification for humanistic inquiry complicates somewhat the more common rationale for the liberal arts discussed in the paragraphs on the nineteenth-century college. Traditionally, apologists were wont to justify Western literature and culture for its adhesive value. One assumed that the cultural tradition of the West, unitarily conceived, filled the role that functionalists among sociologists used to assign to religion: to provide the glue that binds a civilization together. The interpretation I have proposed concedes the value of appropriating a received tradition; but it acknowledges the importance of contest and dialogue with other traditions rather than prizes an umbilically received unity. For example, a college or university, formed originally by the Christian tradition, has powerful warrants within Christianity itself for opening the intellectual life of the university to a full range of traditions. The university must provide one of those open spaces in a civilization where the deep cultural conflicts within it can surface. The Latin root for the word "campus" means literally an open field, a flat place—the traditional site for rival armies to encamp and do battle. Just as the legal system permits us to substitute a contest in the courts for the brawl of the streets, in order that justice be done, so the campus permits us to marshal arguments, rather than troops, in order that our common life in truth be cherished. The metaphor is about right. The university is a campus more than a canopy.

Whether canopy or campus, the liberal arts serve the society best when their contributions are not restricted to direct services to public want. This holds true for the humanities both as they allow us to participate in tradition and as they engage us in substantive criticism. As bearers and interpreters of the received traditions, the humanities inform and enrich the ethos in which men and women grow and by which their minds are nourished. But the nourishing soil is more than the living plant. By the same token, the critical work of the humanities does not reduce to a particular ideology or translate into a single program of social action; the humanities open up horizons in which to address problems rather than provide a few tactics with which to retire them. The humanities belong to the pneumatics of freedom rather than to the statics of a particular program. The professional schools—tied as they are to turning out professionals for the world as it is—need the liberalizing air of the arts and humanities as they go about their work.[5]

Finally, the university must turn out graduates who can teach. For several decades, the teaching vocation seemed to be drying up. Students (and the best students) flocked to the so-called non-academic professions. These professions increasingly defined themselves as dispensers of technical services, in which case, it appeared, the academy needed to concern itself less and less with the teaching ability of its graduates. (Professors reacted to this development with self-pity. They could no longer produce large numbers of teachers for the public schools, colleges, and universities. They bemoaned their lot, since turning out Ph.D.s had offered the functional equivalent of immortality in academic life. Teachers seemed to fall into the position of mules and Shakers who, for differing reasons, could not reproduce their own kind.

The task of the liberal arts looks somewhat different, however, if modern professionals and business leaders must teach in order to perform their tasks well. At first glance, this line of argument does not appear to be too promising. Professionals, generally, estimate the ability or interest of their patients or clients in learning as low to nonexistent. Corporation executives prefer to run their organizations by command and obedience rather than persuasion. The quarrel on this issue in medicine goes back to Hippocrates. The "rough empirics" in classical Greece (who knew treatments but not the scientific reasons for their success) used to ridicule the more scientifically oriented physicians who sought to teach their patients. The empirics argued: patients don't want to become doctors, they want to be cured! Since then, the increasing complexity of medical knowledge has tended to increase professional skepticism about the therapeutic value of teaching patients.[6]

Yet the physician must teach if she would enlist her patients actively in maintaining their own health. To the degree that the physician accepts her patient as partner or collaborator in the pursuit of health, she must use shared truth as an important ingredient in that partnership. Preventive medicine, rehabilitative medicine, chronic and even terminal care often require effective teaching of the patient and the patient's family. Other professionals must also teach. The nurse and the social worker who would perform well must teach their patients and clients. Lawyers must draw up contracts and litigate in the courtroom—technical services that resemble acute care medicine. But, in drawing up those contracts and litigating, in counseling and negotiating, they often need to teach their clients— activities that resemble preventive and rehabilitative medicine. The title rabbi means teacher. Some Protestant denominations define the minister as the teaching elder. Roman Catholicism identifies teaching as one of the three basic authorities of the Church. Politicians, public administrators, and corporate executives must also teach if they would lead their subordinates, at least partly, by persuasion.

One does not want to exaggerate here. Leadership depends partly on command, not entirely upon persuasion. But our leaders of huge hierarchical organizations will function better if they learn something about persuasion, if they follow the political development of Athens and not simply the military development of Sparta. The Athenian art of persuasion helps create the *polis*, the public domain, not only in politics, but in the work place, and in the professional exchange. (A liberal education is hardly the *sine qua non* of the art of persuasion. The prophets of Israel make it amply clear that one does not need a higher education to be skilled in the "word." But a modern society does not live by inspiration alone. Education can help.)

If professionals and leaders must teach to wield their powers effectively and responsibly, then one needs to rethink the liberal arts component in both undergraduate and professional education so as to cultivate the fundamental qualities of the teacher—a capacity for critical inquiry, a direct grasp of one's subject, a desire to share it, verbal facility, and sensitivity to one's audience. Theoretically, at least, requiring a liberal arts background for professionals and locating professional education in the university should produce professionals more pedagogically skilled than the "rough empirics" of whom Plato complained. Unfortunately, however, academicians have assumed that only some of their graduates become teachers; the rest do not. Therefore, they have treated teaching as a segregated profession. Teaching constitutes, of course, a special profession, but, at the same time, a liberal arts education ought to aim at producing good teachers whether students go into teaching or not. Nonacademic professionals and leaders must teach, even as they dispense expert services. How else will they practice their art fitly and contribute to public life and happiness?

The three aims of education interconnect. The young person who makes his first stammering moves out of the sphere of private likes and dislikes into the arena of critical discourse and judgment has begun to develop a civic self. He enters into that public domain—however tentatively and modestly—that eluded Mishima's stutterer. At the same time, professionals who learn how to teach what they know, leaders who persuade and do not simply command, help to enlarge and empower and sustain that public domain. In the course of relieving private distress, they contribute to public happiness.

Notes

1. See especially Max Weber, "Science as a Vocation," in *From Max Weber: Essays in Sociology*, trans. and ed. H. H. Gerth and C. Wright Mills (New York: Oxford University Press, Galaxy Book, 1958), 146–56.
2. Richard Sennett, *The Uses of Disorder: Personal Identity and City Life* (New York: Knopf, 1970).
3. Service to external constituencies generates a series of problems. Outside contracts begin to skew the areas in which faculty members do research, as money sweet-talks. Heavy moonlighting can cut into faculty time devoted to preparation for teaching. (The claim that faculty engaged in outside work are also the best teachers fails to respond to the complaint. Professors should be compared not with less talented colleagues but with themselves—with what they might be if they were not on the jet so often.) Outside service can also threaten collegiality within the university. Faculty members in business, engineering, law, and medicine enjoy levels of compensation, inside and outside, that tend to mark them off as working for a different institution.
4. James D. Watson, *The Double Helix: A Personal Account of the Discovery of the Structure of DNA* (New York: Athenaeum, 1968).
5. Robert B. Reich, the Secretary of Labor in the Clinton administration and office holder in the Ford and Carter administrations, bemoans the weakening sense of civic responsibility in the upper twenty percent of Americans who hold jobs as "symbolic analysts" in the new economy. These job holders currently engage in what Reich calls "the secession of the successful" (*The Work of Nations*, chap. 24) But his two chapters on the education of symbolic analysts concentrate exclusively on the development of operational intelligence: the four basic skills of "abstraction, system thinking, experimentation, and collaboration" (chaps. 18 and 19). Reich fails to show how an education oriented exclusively to the honing of operational skills will encourage leaders to shoulder the duties of citizenship. Educationally, he offers no substantive reasons why members of the overclass should not withdraw behind the walls of their privileged schools and communities. While he bemoans their failure to become citizens, he does not make educational provision for their assuming the responsibilities of powerful citizens. They need the cultivation of critical intelligence for that.
6. For an extended discussion of the physician as teacher, see William F. May, *The Physician's Covenant* (Philadelphia: Westminster Press, 1983), chap. 5.

Afterword

On the whole, this book has concentrated on questions of character and virtue rather than developed a set of structural reforms for the professions. It asks what it means to profess—to witness faithfully to a profession—irrespective of circumstance. Nevertheless, the book could not neglect issues of structural reform.

Addressing the professions with a view to character and virtue that neglects structural reform will eventually fail to support adequately those virtues. Achieving excellence in performance requires institutional protections and accommodations. In medicine, for example, young residents will hardly absorb the moral ideal of respecting their patients as persons if the practice of short rotations abruptly and frequently disconnects them from their incipient ties with particular patients. Residents will also fail to develop their skills in teaching patients as long as the system tightly rations their time at the bedside on morning rounds. Guild calls for engineers, accountants, and others to blow whistles on unethical practices in corporations will produce few persons willing to identify and expose such practices, unless corporations include institutional protections for whistleblowers (or unless, in the absence of corporate protections, guilds and unions back professionals and workers who blow whistles). Journalists will not likely perform their tasks of prophetic criticism unwaveringly without some institutional protection of their independence, not only from the government but from the conglomerates that increasingly own the newspapers. Most church leaders prize ecclesiastical independence from the government, which the separation of church and state assures, but often fail to notice their substantial dependence (and deference toward) the social class that pays their salaries. Calls for politicians who lead their constituencies justly will not be fully heard without reforms in the financing of political campaigns. In the absence of such reforms, political leaders deteriorate into fund-raisers,

271

gratifiers of the whims and appetites of major contributors, and expert equivocators, with sound bites and wisecracks at the ready, rather than leaders by persuasion. To cultivate fully fledged professionals, a society needs to tend to the institutions that shape them, that equip them, and that pay them for their work. Among the professional virtues, public-spiritedness supplies one of the taproots for such structural reform.

However, structural reforms that neglect interior transformations of character and virtue will only too often succeed in rebottling old rotgut. The shift from a fee-for-service to a prepayment system in medicine, unaccompanied by the virtue of fidelity, simply shifts patient abuse from overtreatment to undertreatment. Rules of discovery, originally instituted in the law to facilitate the quest for the truth and reach equitable judgments will, in the hands of meanly adversarial lawyers, simply impose costly delays on trials and exhaust the resources of the opposition. The structural development of the academic tenure system in the United States since the 1940s has not of itself produced intellectually courageous professors. While protected by the system from the interference of outsiders, timid young faculty members have only too readily indentured themselves to dominating insiders. Structural reforms of themselves do not relieve each generation of the task of facing its own set of temptations and aspiring to excellence in personal and professional virtue.

In this book, I have concentrated on questions of professional character and virtue more than on proposals and strategies for reform, but not with the intention of dismissing the latter as illegitimate or unimportant. Programmatic and structural issues figure in each chapter. The first chapter argues that the very nature of health care and legal protection as fundamental goods—not optional commodities— necessitates a distribution system that does not depend entirely upon the dice of the marketplace or upon the whims of personal charity. Chapter 2 highlights the need for structural reforms that temper the adversary system; it does not simply call for more individual restraint on the part of advocates. Without changes in the law governing professional conduct, an individual lawyer's restraint can play into the hands of ruthless lawyers seeking advantage for their predatory clients. Chapter 3 argues that ethically responsible corporations need a structure of laws governing the care of the environment. Otherwise their individual efforts to act responsibly may place them at a suicidal disadvantage in the marketplace. Chapter 4 sketches a portrait of transformative leadership, but it also recognizes that governments, professional guilds, unions, and other, often unwanted, monitors, critics, and regulators have their responsibilities to fulfill in disciplining corporate behavior. Chapters 6 to 8 note that journalists, religious congregations, and universities cannot broadly and effectively fulfill their roles as mentors and critics without structures and traditions in place that foster their independence.

Still, the book deals basically with the question of professional character and virtue: with the intellectual, moral, and organizational characteristics of professional identity and the specific virtues required to make good on those characteristics. The chapters sought to highlight the issues professionals face in sustaining that identity, whatever the structural adversities they face. In this sense, the book belongs primarily to the tradition of an ethics of witness.

The Greek term for witness, *martyr*, reminds one of a price paid. Virtues do not come free. Virtues spring from strengths of character that grow in adversity, including some of those adversities and awkwardnesses which practicing the virtues itself generates. What would it mean for professionals to insist on the fantasy of a vocation without price or to expect the advance installation of all reforms and protections before they lived out their identity? Such professionals would, in the first instance, overlook their instrumental job of instigating and sustaining reform, of guarding against predators, and of providing professional services in the absence of reforms. In the second instant, they would overlook the inner logic of professing. The argument for witnessing, for living out one's professional identity irrespective of circumstances, springs, not simply from its instrumental, but its intrinsic, value. Professionals witness out of inner necessity. Professing is simply what professionals must do to be fully themselves.

I have not hesitated in this book to identify the adversities—and temptations—professionals face in paying the IOUs they issue when they assume their public identity and responsibility. Contemporary doctors, lawyers, engineers, business leaders, politicians, journalists, academics, rabbi, priests, and ministers, and other assorted power-wielders grumble about these adversities. However, these adversities pale in comparison with the tribulations of the professional who heads the list of beleaguered rulers—Abraham Lincoln. Lincoln did not have much of a fan club. The secessionists despised him; the abolitionists badgered him; leading cabinet members contemned him; and his generals balked at his commands. Nor did he enjoy inner serenity. Depression plagued him; and he suffered inwardly from the tragic conflict between the two great public goods he sought to serve—the abolition of slavery and the preservation of the Union. Yet we dare not demean him with our pity. In acting for the common good, he led and professed out of inner necessity; he did what he had to do to be fully himself; and, in that, he embodied an austere public happiness. By comparison, the burdens of latter-day rulers seem light; and the inner necessity of acting on behalf of the common good, if they would be fully themselves, persists.

Acknowledgments

Debts expand geometrically in academic life, and the eventual book simply acknowledges; it does not repay indebtedness. An early grant from the Guggenheim Foundation let me begin work on the topic under the title *Beleaguered Rulers: The Public Obligation of the Professional*. The title has held, but the structure changed from the original proposal, as I began to work on each of the eight professions covered in this volume. Participation in an early Hastings Center project on The Teaching of Ethics in Higher Education convinced me that specialized inquiry into a particular profession might benefit from work on family resemblances across the species. A generous gift from Cary M. Maguire, a trustee of Southern Methodist University, enabled me to serve as founding director of the Cary M. Maguire Center for Ethics and Public Responsibility, 1995–1998. Reflections on the professions in the setting of American culture set the agenda for many of the Maguire Center's conferences and contributed to the maturation of this volume. At the conclusion of my three-year term at the Center, a grant from William Stubing, president of the Greenwall Foundation, provided me with indispensable research support across a sabbatical leave, 1999–2000.

I have four abiding professional debts. Cary M. Maguire established the chair I have held at SMU since 1985. His personal interest in my work has graciously accompanied his support of the chair. A. Lewis Soens cast a disciplined editorial eye on this manuscript; he continues to instruct me on the promise and the demands of the English language. David H. Smith of the Poynter Center, Indiana University, a colleague and friend beyond deserving, read a late draft and offered detailed comments in the midst of his own heavy duties. Oleg Makariev, a graduate student at SMU, served as my research assistant on the project and has made many excellent substantive suggestions.

His intelligence as a conversation partner has helped remind me why I am in the academic profession.

A host of colleagues at SMU and elsewhere have invited the development, or read and criticized portions, of the manuscript: Charles E. Curran, William J. Bridge, Thomas W. Mayo, and Richard O. Mason at SMU; Robert Veatch at the Kennedy Institute of Ethics; Daniel Callahan of the Hastings Center; Allen Verhey of Calvin College; Neil W. Hamilton of the Mitchell College of Law, St. Paul; William B. Hilgers, Chair of the Board of Trustees, the Texas Center for Legal Ethics and Professionalism; Michael J. Rabins of the School of Engineering, Texas A & M; Courtney Campbell of Oregon State University; John A. Hague of Stetson University; William Lee Miller of the University of Virginia; and Jeffrey Maletta of Kirkpatrick and Lockhart. G. Nick Street and Richard Brown, former editors at Westminster John Knox Press, offered me timely encouragement and helpful criticisms.

The National *Phi Beta Kappa* Society invited me to be one of its Visiting Lecturers at eight campuses, 1999–2000. The appointment allowed me to share portions of six chapters in public forum. As a visiting professor at Yale University, fall semester, 2000, I was privileged to conduct a series of biweekly faculty seminars devoted to reading and discussing chapters from the manuscript. Carol Pollard of the Institution for Social and Policy Studies and Thomas Duffy of the Yale University School of Medicine graciously arranged these occasions. As all authors only too painfully know, the imperfections of the book remain mine.

Occasionally, a museum will exhibit the preliminary sketches a painter has made of details in a scene that will eventually appear in the final canvas. Anyone engaged in painting or writing knows the transformations that parts must undergo as they eventually contribute to the whole. Early sketches of details in this book include the following:

The Humanities and the Civic Self (Bloomington, Ind.: Poynter Center, January 1979).
"On Slaying the Dragon: The American Nature Myth," in *Katalagete* (*Journal of the Committee of Southern Churchmen*), Part I (Winter 1981), 29–35; Part II (Summer 1982), 29–38.
"Moral Leadership in the Corporate Setting" Clifton, N.J.: Humana Press, 1983).
"Notes on the Ethics of Doctors and Lawyers," *Moral Responsibility and the Professions*, ed. Bernard Baumrin and Benjamin Freedman (New York: Haven Publications, 1983), 93–125.

"Professional Ethics, the University and the Journalist," plenary address delivered at the 1985 Annual Meeting of the Association for Education in Journalism and Mass Communication; published in the *Journal of Mass Media Ethics*, vol. 1, no. 2 (Logan, Utah: Utah State University: Spring/Summer 1986), 20–31.

"The Virtues of the Business Leader," *Proceedings of the Second National Consultation on Corporate Ethics*, The Center for Ethics and Corporate Policy, ed. David A. Krueger (Chicago: May 13–15, 1987), 75–91.

"Adversarialism in America and the Professions," *Community in America: The Challenge of Habits of the Heart*, Robert Bellah, et al. (Berkeley: University of California Press, summer 1988).

"Public Happiness and Higher Education," *Caring for the Commonwealth: Education for Religious and Public Life*, ed. Parker J. Palmer, Barbara G. Wheeler, and James W. Fowler (Macon, Georgia: Mercer University Press, 1990), 227–47.

"Images that Shape the Public Obligations of the Minister," published in *Clergy Ethics in a Changing Society: Mapping the Terrain*, ed. James P. Wind, Russell Burck, Paul F. Camenisch, and Dennis P. McCann (Louisville, Ky.: Westminster John Knox Press, 1991), 54–83.

"The Beleaguered Ruler: The Public Obligation of the Professional," *Kennedy Institute Journal of Ethics*, vol. 2, no. 1, March 1992, 26–41.

"Money and the Professions: Medicine," *Focus on Surgical Education*, Winter 1995, vol. 3, no. 1, 23–28.

Testing the Medical Covenant: Active Euthanasia and Health Care Reform (Grand Rapids: William. B. Eerdmans, September 1996), 51–83.

"Money and the Professions: Medicine and Law," *William Mitchell Law Review*, vol. 25, Number 1 (1999), 75–102.

"The Religious Underpinnings of the Marketplace," delivered at the *Third International Symposium on Catholic Social Thought and Management Education* in Goa, India, January 2000.

I dedicate this book to my sons, Ted May and David May, whom I hugely love and admire.

William F. May
Cary M. Maguire Professor of Ethics
Southern Methodist University

Index